The 421st

Brave Men

This story which I tell you depicts the bravery bold,
Of men who flew the battles beneath the moon so cold.
They drenched their souls in whiskey and to their Gods they curse,
They gave no damn for any man, live on four twenty-first.

Their guns were heard at Nadzab, they fought a bloody war,
They left their mark up in the skies while flying from Saidor.
On Wakde and Owi their names are loudly sung,
Their fame while based at Leyte, climbed another rung.

There was no greater effort, so give the men their due,
Just lift a glass of wine for those who died at Peleliu.
Their guns got hot on Luzon, and Ie Shima saw,
Some nights hard cut with honor, and courage in the raw.

Although the war is over, there still is plane and man,
Who searched the skies for danger in old, God Damned Japan.
Don't frown upon their craving, don't anger at their thirst,
Just step up boys and have a drink with the old four twenty-first.

Unknown

The Night Fighter's Lament

Oh, I have a story to tell you,
A story of bold men and brave.
Who have fought and some have died for their country,
With a brightly burning plane for their grave.

On an island we called Ie Shima,
With the broad blue Pacific all around.
We set up our tents and our shelters,
And we dug holes for our safety in the ground.

At night when day fighters were sleeping,
The nocturnal raids were begun.
And the heavens were sore split asunder,
By the roar of our P sixty-ones.

On a cold moonless night back in August,
The order was read with a sigh.
And a happy-go-lucky young pilot,
Took his plane and crew to die.

They went with a smile unknowing,
'twas only a routine patrol.
Too bad that their duty included,
Their answering God's final roll.

Pineapple gave them their vector,
Surveillance up to Japan and back.
They say the last words they transmitted,
Were "We wish we were lying in our sacks."

One hour stretched into seven,
It was no time to jest and grin.
They knew as they waited and listened,
That another night fighter augured in.

There was no one to see and report it,
No help from a searching submarine.
Just three names written off the roster,
And three faces no longer to be seen.

So lift up your glasses my buddies,
In honor of those who fought their fight.
The sleep you enjoyed out of danger,
Was because of the boys who flew at night.

Unknown

The 421st
Night Fighter Squadron in World War II

Jeff Kolln

Schiffer Military History
Atglen, PA

Acknowledgments

A special Thanks to the members of the 421st past, present, and future. Thanks also to David McLaren, Wayne Mutza, Garry Pape, Col. William Behnke, Carl Bjorum (and Mom), DOC Howard Blanchard, Gerald Bliss, Carl Bong, Robert Buchanan, Harold Burdue, Curtis Burgess, John Chew, Bryan Cox, John Cutshall, Raymond Daniels, Larry Davis, Bob Dehaven, Lee DeHaven, Don Flaherty, Herbert Godstein, Bill Gorman, Arthur Hagan, Frank Hamilton, Wes Harding, Col. David Hopwood, Ralph Hulsey, Col. Richard Kiick, Fred Kohl, Col. Laurence Lackey, Afraim Lopez, Dave McDonald, Virgil Moe, Tom Malone, Ray Mazalan, Richard Mulligan, John Myers, Nicholas Natiello, Lawrence Neville, John Olley, Lloyd Partridge, Robert Pew, Col. Walter Pharr, Douglas Ponsford, Col. William Odell, Carl Remington, Col. Elston Roady, Henry Simacek, Robert Sims, Warren Stevens, Bill Sykes, Col. Gordon Timmons, Col. Dave Weisman, and David L. Youker. Honorable mention goes to Ellie and Rosie Kolln, Thereasa Kolln Darrington (and the rest of the Kolln family, Tigger, Mark "E" Bub, Kenny Hendricks, Jerry Miller and the guys and gals of Capital HS Cross Country, the Austins, James Vannousdle, Alison, and all my other friends that have given all their support, friendship, and love. Thanks also to A-1 Photo and Tom and the guys at Kitz Camera for working so hard on my photos. And finally, thanks to the 421st Fighter Squadron at Hill AFB, Utah, for their support.

Dedication

To my grandmother, Edith Kolln, who gave my life wings,
and to my wife Debbie, who keeps me flying.

Book Design by Ian Robertson.

Library of Congress Catalog Number: 2001087185

Printed in China.
ISBN: 0-7643-1306-1

We are interested in hearing from authors with book ideas on related topics.

Published by Schiffer Publishing Ltd.
4880 Lower Valley Road
Atglen, PA 19310
Phone: (610) 593-1777
FAX: (610) 593-2002
E-mail: Schifferbk@aol.com.
Visit our web site at: www.schifferbooks.com
Please write for a free catalog.
This book may be purchased from the publisher.
Please include $3.95 postage.
Try your bookstore first.

In Europe, Schiffer books are distributed by:
Bushwood Books
6 Marksbury Avenue
Kew Gardens
Surrey TW9 4JF
England
Phone: 44 (0) 20 8392-8585
FAX: 44 (0) 20 8392-9876
E-mail: Bushwd@aol.com.
Free postage in the UK. Europe: air mail at cost.
Try your bookstore first.

Contents

Squadron Photo (pp. 6-7)
1st Row (L to R)
Henderson, Farr, Reece, Krueger, Beard, Mulligan, Flickner, Roady, Berg, Woodring, Jones D., Wolf, Allain, Mott, Hartsock, Malone, Glynn, Carr, Zimmer, Bradley, Bennett, Pharr, Townsend, Govoni, Robbins, Crawford, Bjorum, Pahlka, Hulsey, Corts, Gill, Clodfelter, Eynon, Blanchard, Wilson, Jones J., Buchanan, Olley, Farnum, Gressett, Stout, Paulo, Babb, Bradford, Andre, and Meeks.

2nd Row (L to R)
Tesh, Battershell, Lopez, Males, Dornoff, Podibinski, Bryan, King, LePage, Fehrman, Cown, O'Neil, Dove, Brown L., Mercer, Hollandsworth, Uribe, Ciesialski, Foster, Martinez, Loran, Goldstein, Skoug, Yorns, Belcher, Starr, Hernandez, Pellicone, Scoles, Hoffman, Geigen, Hankins, Romonchak, Grasso, Radisich, Jarvis, Oxley, Pattison, Patrija, Gillian, Hoko, Bittenbender, Greenberg, Allen, Burdue, Renker, Heeb, Popovich, Brown J., and Cox.

3rd Row (L to R)
Meeks, Lange, Olmstad, Heldt, Mende, Dietel, Gold, Bechtold, Stancik, Picard, Lesovsky, Bush, Meadors, Wheaton, Nelson, Crawford, Dooley, Anderson, Cashion, Poyner, Johnson, Vermillion, Silverstein, Yando, Domke, Vander, Ploeg, Foster, Wolfrom, Dew, Williams, Munn, Brannon, Knight, Pokorski, Umfreville, Polter, Pokorski, Russo, Keener, Kniss, Grayson, Ponsford, Hudson, Petric, and Levesque.

4th Row (L to R)
Gorman, Ernst, Young, Shepard, Zylonis, Bosworth, McCarley, Coleman, Dearing, Dolan, Barrick, Harper, Zane, Dobrovolsky, Rees, Stein, Humphreys, Hall, Barth, Haproff, Garrison, Smith H., Sikersky, Gay, McGuire, White, Davis, Mrotzok, Sabella, Foster, Powers, Demyanchik, Wiig, Smolowitz, Braun, Samudio, Welder, Lee, Finchum, Buchanan, Schleichor, Zimmerman, Grossman, Karwowski, and Lutgens.

5th Row (L to R)
Byland, Harding, Barker, Voland, Knapp, Albrecht, Archibald, Bagwell, Danko, Nabasny, Meeks, Lockman, Hagen, Della, Springer, Moss, Hixenbaugh, Ellwanger, Blodis, Harden, Brown J.D., Farmer, Brown J.O., Baucom, Cude, Green, Hayes, Halleran, Rishal, Smallwood, Lugara, Ballard, Atwell, Schwedler, Montgomery, Bryan, Bloomgren, Shaver, Bloyd, Bouchard, Costillo, Stevens, Powell, Bossman, Snyder, Neville, Ferrari, and Rogers.

Foreword

During the course of World War II, some significant events began quietly. Such was the case with the organization of the 421st Night Fighter Squadron in May 1943 at Orlando Army Air Force Base. No bands played and no flags were flying. Its beginning was hardly noticed by other personnel on the base. The few men who came together on that first day, May 8, 1943, formed the nucleus of what was to later become a unique and effective fighting force in the Pacific.

The 421st, along with 16 other night fighter squadrons, came into existence because of a decision by the Air Force to duplicate an air arm that had been so successful in Great Britain earlier in World War II. When the U.S. started the program in 1942, their plan was to turn out one night fighter squadron a month. So it was, in fact, a "crash" program, though no one wanted to use that term in describing it.

Our beginning was at the Signal Hill area of Orlando Army Air Base. As the days went by more and more men were transferred in, sometimes one or two, sometimes ten or twelve. We were all new to the organization and new to each other. My initial concern about the quality of training of those assigned to the squadron gave way to the realization that we were being sent top-men in all departments. It was as if someone higher up the line was seeing to it that only the best were being sent to the 421st.

1st Sgt. Herbert Goldstein typified this point. He was the first enlisted man assigned to the 421st. He immediately assumed his responsibilities and soon became indispensable to the squadron. Further more, he stayed with the 421st from the beginning to the end, through the whole Pacific Campaign.

After completing its training in late September 1943 and surviving the "potato salad attack," the 421st moved to Kissimmee, Florida, just south of Orlando.

We were there for a month's period of intense training and final clearance for overseas assignment. Part of this training was an exercise worked out by M/Sgt. Goldstein, involving dropping paper "bombs" of flour on some unsuspecting troops. While this was unsettling at the time, it proved beneficial when we were later subjected to bombing in New Guinea. In early November all personnel boarded a train for the week-long trip to Camp Stoneman in California to begin our overseas trip to the combat area.

We left California in early December 1943 aboard a converted freighter, called the "Sea Pike," and sailed out under the magnificent Golden Gate Bridge headed west. The seas were rough, and there was concern that the cooks were too seasick to prepare the first meal. But when the time came to eat, no men were there, either—everyone was sick!

We arrived in the harbor of Townsville, Australia, three weeks after leaving San Francisco and were there through Christmas Day 1943. Since we could not go ashore we were soon happy to weigh anchor, head on up the tip of New Guinea, and unload at Milne Bay, January 4, 1944.

At that point, all personnel were trained and eager to get into the action, but no aircraft were available. After several weeks, headquarters assigned some old P-70 and P-38 aircraft, and we moved our base to Nadzab. Finally, by mid-summer 1944 the new night fighter began arriving for the 421st. It was built by Northrop and designated the P-61, or "Black Widow." It was the first plane designed for night fighting and utilized a crew of three. With this new plane, so air worthy and heavily armed, the 421st was fully equipped to carry out its dual mission; defensively, by protecting our own bases against enemy raids at night, and offensively, by attacking enemy bases at night.

The effectiveness of the 421st was given official recognition by General Kenny, who credited the 421st P-61s for bringing a halt to damaging night raids by the Japanese. The 421st was one of only 17 night fighter squadrons on the leading edge of technology. Night fighter crews had to posses certain attributes of stability and be highly motivated. Night fighter proficiency required constant practice and special flying techniques. Because of its effectiveness, the 421st received numerous citations, including the Presidential Unit Citation with seven stars.

All those associated with the 421st can take pride in knowing that it fulfilled its mission with honor and effectiveness. We are grateful to Jeff Kolln for taking on the task of putting this history of the 421st together. It has not been done before and has required many hours of persistent effort. It will be valuable to those who are especially interested in the art and tactics of night fighting, and it will be treasured by all those members of the 421st, their families and friends, as it highlights a decisive episode in their lives.

Walter S. Pharr
Colonel USAF (Ret.)

Captain Walter S. Pharr, Commander of the 421st Night Fighter Squadron May 1, 1943, to May 13, 1944. *Pharr*

1

The Birth of the Night Fighter Program

Unlike the Royal Air Force or the Luftwaffe at the outset of World War II, the United States Army Air Corps had made little or no preparations for the new theatre of war that would now take place in the night's sky. Traditionally, the Army Air Corps had been geared to, as well expected to be used to provide coverage over all American ground operations, and everything else was considered secondary. Burdened with this particular train of thought in the higher echelons of U.S. leadership, it was no wonder that the development toward establishing a night fighting system as an essential fighting force within the Army Air Corps was painfully slow. Consequently, the construction of any kind of formal night fighting training programs would lag far behind the need at the time. However, the Air Corps, even with its limited resources, was in the best position to undertake the task at hand.

The Night Fighting program came to the Air Corps with the establishment of the new Air Defense Command. In March 1942 a project under the code name "Trigger" had been set in motion. The U.S. system would be designed along the same lines as the RAF, who had established their own successful system of night operations in their struggle against the Luftwaffe. To put this into operation, an Air Defense Operational Training Unit under the Interceptor Command School was brought about and headquartered in Orlando, Florida. This organization would have its own group of American officers in charge, with a number of RAF personnel (advisors) with expertise in night operations on hand and assisting in the development of an American radar system. Personnel to man this new project were drawn from a number of organizations within the Army. Colonel Willis R. Taylor, who had designed the training structure, assumed command of the Interceptor School. Colonel Taylor's plan included a Night Fighter Division under the Fighter Department. The Night Fighter training section set up the groundwork for the instruction of future pilots and radar observers that would fly with the squadrons. This would allow the new crew members to become acquainted with the equipment and procedures they would use in combat. At this time, too, pilots and their operators were trained together as a team, which later proved invaluable in actual combat conditions. Gunners were assigned to the team at a later time.

On October 27, 1943, the Army Air Forces School of Applied Tactics was activated. Colonel Taylor was the interim Commander, but Brigadier General Hume Peabody was later assigned to that post. On July 15, 1943, the Night Fighter Division became the 481st Night Fighter Operational Training Group. At this time the 481st NFOTG would have the 348th, 349th, and 420th Night Fighter Training Squadrons set up as the foundation of the group. The leadership of the 481st NFOTG would fall under the command of Lt. Colonel Winston W. Kratz. Kratz had been the assistant operations officer for VIII Fighter Command and had also served as Eighth Air Force headquarters liaison officer. In this position he was exposed to RAF night fighter operations and gained valuable experience, which in turn could be used in the establishment of the American system. Some would later call Lt. Col. Kratz the "father" of the AAF night fighter program.

This photo was taken at a meeting of some of the key night fighter personnel at Orlando, Florida, in July 1943. Left to right in the group are: Lt. Col. Winston W. Kratz (Head of Night Fighter Operations); Captain Carroll Smith (C/O of the 418th NFS and future USAAF Ace); F/L Carol Kutelvasher (Royal Air Force Night Fighter Ace); Captain Oris Johnson (C/O of the 422nd NFS); and Captain Walter S. Pharr (C/O of the 421st NFS). ***Pharr***

Lt. Carl Bjorum standing in the cockpit of P-70A #39-794 at Kissimmee, Florida, in July 1943. ***421st NFS***

The structure of the training program under the 481st NFOTG would be divided into three phases under each of the squadrons. The 348th Night Fighter Training Squadron at Orlando, who would provide the basic training consisting of flying and ground school, would accomplish the first phase of night fighter training. The pilots picked for the program were selected for having keen night vision and superior instrument flying ability. Army Air Force units were also searched for specially qualified pilots with twin engine time. They would receive their training in the form of lectures, classes, synthetic operations, and actual operation in night controlled intercepts. Upon the completion of the first phase of the night fighter course, it was at this time that a Radar Observer, or "R/O," was teamed with a pilot by mutual agreement. From then on the night fighter pilot and R/O took all future training as a team. Radar observers were called radio observers during the war years. The word radar itself was considered secret and was never to be mentioned or printed in any form.

The 349th Night Fighter Training Squadron at Kissimmee, Florida, accomplished the second phase of the night fighter training. The squadron's curriculum was designed to provide realistic combat conditions for the pilot and Radar Observer. The course, as a combination air-ground school lasted seven weeks for the teams. The training that they would receive here would cover things such as interception techniques, aircraft recognition, aircraft performance, air defense systems, radio, parachute instruction, and combat training.

The 420th Night Fighter Training Squadron at Dunnellon, Florida, accomplished the third and final phase of training. This was to be the Operational Training Unit (OTU) that would simulate actual field conditions in all respects and provide the most realistic training possible. Upon completion of the course, the night fighter teams were deemed ready for combat, and with their squadrons would prepare for overseas movement.

Most of the pilots assigned to the night fighter squadrons all went through similar training. Lt. Carl Bjorum of the 421st Night Fighter Squadron explains his training and preparation for night combat:

The Night Fighter program was conducted at the outset in the State of Florida, and I went through this particular program upon graduation from Flying School at Williams AFB, Arizona.

This was actually called Williams Field at the time. I graduated with Class 44-D (44 being the year and D standing for the fourth month of the year) on the date of April 12, 1943. Williams was a twin-engine school, and we flew AT-9, AT-17, and some T-6 aircraft. I was fortunate to have 12 hours in the P-322. The P-322 was an export version of the P-38, and the problem with it was that it had no blower or supercharger on the engines, so you could not get any altitude in it to speak of. As far as the P-322 itself, there were a couple of reasons for it having no superchargers.

First was the availability of the supercharger units. Foreign nations such as England were made low priority and the last in line to get superchargers. The superchargers were also used on the B-17, B-24, and the American version of the P-38, and it took everything for General Electric just to keep up with the U.S. demand. These superchargers would take an average engine and make it, as some pilots would say, "super-powered." Another problem was, of course, the maintenance of these units. This technically complex piece of equipment took a lot of training and work to maintain. The Americans simply did not have the time or resources to train the British or anyone else to take care of it. The British had initially ordered about 300 P-38s, which were without superchargers and the propellers rotated the same way. American versions rotated the opposite way of each other. The British ended up only accepting three.

At the time of graduation I had 224 hours and 15 minutes flying time. The Night Fighter training program in 1943 was conducted at three bases in Florida; Orlando, Kissimmee, and Dunnellon Army airfields were all used. The first phase was at Orlando, where we checked out in the A-20. This was the initiation into the Night Fighter business. We had some classroom instruction on night navigation, night vision, and so on. This was also the main instrument training phase of the program. I flew 21 hours of under the hood training in the BT-13, AT-11, and UC-78, plus 23 hours in the link-trainer. Under the hood training consists of two people in an aircraft. One was the safety observer, while the second had a hood over him and could not see anything but the instruments. This method is still used today. Also, of the 72 hours of total time in Orlando, 15 hours was at night in the A-20. This was in May and June 1943.

In July we moved to Kissimmee Army Air Field, Florida. This was about 20 miles south of Orlando. Here we checked out in the P-70 and were joined up with our Radar Observers. This was a team that would stay together for almost 2 years. Our gunners were not assigned until we began to fly the P-61. The main differences between the A-20 and the P-70 was the airborne intercept radar, the 20mm gun bay attached under the bomb bay, and a rudimentary set of controls at the Radar Observer's position. This consisted of a control stick that was stowed near his seat and could be stuck in the floor to control the airplane in straight and level flight in case something happened to the pilot. There were no rudder pedals and throttles. It was hard enough for a Radar Observer to fly straight and level during the daytime, but I was unmerciful in making my Radar Observer, Lieutenant Robert C. Williams, do it at night. The P-70s that we had overseas had two .50 caliber machine-guns at the Radar Observer's position. One to shoot up and one to shoot down.

At Kissimmee I flew 66 hours in the P-70, of which 25 hours was at night. I also had another 4 hours in the link-trainer. During this phase we ran practice intercepts, one after the other, until Williams became quite well tired out. This paid off, however, because in actual combat we had two good chances for intercepting a Japanese aircraft, and in both cases we were successful.

In September we moved to Dunnellon Army Air Field, Florida. This was about 75 miles northwest of Orlando, and this was the final phase of the program. Most of the flying here was done at night, although we did have two daytime air-to-ground gunnery missions, which were a lot of fun. At the time and even now there is no method that I know of to conduct nighttime air-to-air practice gunnery. We had several night cross-country missions, along with hours of practice intercepts. I can see by my records that on one night I flew 6.5 hours on two sorties. In September I flew 62.5 hours in the P-70, in which 50.5 was at night. In summery for me this night fighter program consisted of a total of 212 hours of flying time, 88 hours of which were at night, 25 hours under the hood time, and 27 hours of link training time. In other words, 41% of the flying time was at night and 12% was hood time, so 53% was either hood or night. I would not be surprised if the Night Fighter aircrews were not some of the best and most highly trained Air Corps crews to go overseas during World War II, except for the night air-to-air gunnery, that is.

In October 1943 Williams and I were assigned to the 421st Night Fighter Squadron. There was no further flying training conducted before going overseas. I left for overseas with a total flying time of 452 hours. The next time I flew was in January 1944 from a base in Australia in a P-38.

Lt. Carl Bjorum photographed in late 1944. ***Bjorum***

In reflection, after the training program we had gone through we had very little trepidation about blasting off in the murky black night from any runway in the world. By the way, sometimes it was a dirt runway and sometimes very sparse lighting.

2

Origins of the 421st Night Fighter Squadron

The 421st Night Fighter Squadron was born on May 1, 1943, at the U.S. Army Air Forces School of Applied Tactics Orlando, Florida. Officially the squadron was organized under the authority of General Order 67, HQ, AAFSAT, Orlando, Florida. Major (then Captain) Walter S. Pharr assumed command. Squadron Order #1 for the 421st NFS was published on May 8, 1943, recording the assumption of command by Captain Pharr, under the authority of Special Order #96, paragraph 25, HQ, Air Defense Department, AAFSAT, of the same date.

Walter Springs Pharr, of Charlotte, NC, was 25 years of age when he took over the 421st TFS. 2nd Lt. Pharr had trained as a pilot at Brooks Field, Texas, in the spring of 1941 and from there joined the 22nd Observation Squadron at DeRidder, Louisiana. During this time Pharr served with Lt. Gordon Timmons, who would go on to command the 415th Night Fighter Squadron and by some interesting twist in history would also be the last commander of the 421st NFS in 1947. Pharr and Timmons both volunteered for training as night fighter pilots, and both were, of course, accepted, and they made their way to Orlando, Florida. Pharr was promoted to 1st Lt. on March 15, 1942. In October 1942 Pharr transferred to the 348th Night Fighter Training Squadron to begin his training in the P-70 Night Fighter. He later became an Instrument Instructor in the squadron and achieved the rank of Captain. In January 1943 he transferred again to the 349th Night Fighter Squadron, where he served as the Operations Officer. During this time at Orlando a number of Night Fighter Squadrons had been activated. The 414th, 415th, 416th, and 417th were all established, and new squadrons were in the works. Colonel Winston Kratz, Commander of the Night Fighter program, endorsed the young Pharr to lead one of the new squadrons. The 421st NFS needed a Commander, and it was felt by Col. Kratz, and others, that Pharr was the man. The squadron was soon assigned an area at Signal Hill, Florida, and a couple buildings. It was now up to Pharr to bring the new squadron together.

The original members of the 421st Night Fighter Squadron in parade formation at Kissimmee, Florida, in November 1943. Captain Walter Pharr is front row and center. To his right is Lt. Charles Townsend, and to his left is Lt. Robert E. Buchanan. ***421st NFS***

The 421st Night Fighter Squadron began as most newly activated units did, with little or nothing to work with. When Captain Pharr took command he did not even have a desk to call his own. Within a short time personnel and material began to arrive at the new squadron. One of the first officers to report in to Pharr was 2nd Lt. Howard Blanchard, who would later be the squadron's Communications Officer. He had joined the squadron with the hope of getting an overseas assignment, since the 421st NFS was slated to go.

The building Blanchard reported to was a wooden barracks building, which was for the most part empty except for a few enlisted men and Captain Pharr sitting at the end of the corridor with an orange crate for a makeshift desk. Captain Pharr welcomed Blanchard and gave him all of the squadron officer's duties, such as Supply, Mess, Transportation, etc., pending the arrival of assigned squadron personnel. So, in the beginning Blanchard had only a stack of papers to tell him how to organize a squadron. Personnel showed up on the orders, but the reality was a whole different matter for Blanchard:

> I don't know for sure, but I believe 2nd Lt. John Olley and 2nd Lt. Robert Buchanan were assigned on paper about a day or two earlier, but they never actually reported in until later. On my orders, in another paragraph 2nd Lt. Olley was relieved

The 421st NFS in formation. Captain Walter Pharr is in front on left. In the first row left to right are: Lt. Charles Townsend (Executive Officer); Lt. Kenneth E. Bennett (Flight Surgeon); Lt. Bud Farnum (Intelligence); Lt. Robert Buchanan (Intelligence); Lt. Elston Roady (Radar Officer); Lt. Preston Wilson (Ordinance Officer); Lt. Howard Blanchard (Communications Officer); Lt. John Jones (Armaments Officer); Lt. Edward Flickner (Weather Officer); and Lt. John Olley (Engineering Officer). In the second row left to right are: M/Sgt. Herbert Goldstein (1st Sgt.); T/Sgt. Jake Loran (HQ); Corporal Richard Barker (HQ); Corporal Billy Battershell (HQ); and Corporal Lloyd Davey (HQ). ***421st NFS***

> from assignment with the 421st the same day I was assigned. It was a bunch of paperwork shuffling men around in those days.

Captain Pharr also handed Blanchard a large book called the T.O.&E. (Table of Organization & Equipment) and stated that getting the items listed in the book was his primary duty. The book listed every item the squadron was supposed to have, including aircraft, bedding, and flight jackets for the aircrews, guns, parachutes, tents, mess kits, etc. Captain Pharr also added an incentive. If Blanchard could do the job within six months he would be promoted to 1st Lt. The 421st NFS passed an Operational Readiness inspection in September 1943, and was sent on to Kissimmee Field, Florida, for combat training shortly thereafter. Blanchard was promoted to 1st Lieutenant in October 1943.

As the Communications Officer, Lt. Blanchard had his own agenda to take care of. This entailed the management, training, and operation of the personnel of the Communication Section. This section was responsible for the operation and maintenance of the airborne electronics systems, camp lighting, teletypes, telephones, and in a few instances control tower operation. Blanchard was also the squadron's Cryptographic Officer. This meant decoding all messages sent to the squadron. All combat orders, or "FRAG" Orders, were in code.

One of the next members to join the squadron was 1st Lt. Robert E. Buchanan, who was assigned as the squadron's Intelligence Officer. As the unit was not operating aircraft in the early stages of its organization, Lt. Buchanan undertook the duties of personal Adjutant, and for several months rendered valuable service in this capacity. His early work in the selection and distribution of personnel contributed materially in establishing a firm foundation for training and making the squadron an efficient organization.

M/Sgt. Herbert Goldstein reported to the unit on May 14, 1943, to undertake the duties of the First Sergeant. Goldstein was given much of the administrative and organizational duties to help Captain Pharr turn the 421st NFS from a collection of individuals into an effective fighter unit. Within the next two weeks after M/Sgt. Goldstein's arrival in the squadron, additional officers and enlisted men began to swell the ranks. All of these new individuals would be assigned key positions within the 421st NFS.

Sergeant Richard L. Shepard reported in on May 15, and assumed the duties of the unit's first clerk. He would later go on to be the squadron's chief non-commissioned Intelligence Officer. 1st Lt. John Olley would report on May 26th, closely followed by the Armament Officer, 2nd Lt. John Jones. The Adjutant, Captain Joseph F. Govoni, and Executive Officer Charles M. Townsend also reported in and began their duties. Townsend brought with him a background of twelve years in the regular Army and seven years in Foreign Service.

Over the next few months personnel strength gradually increased, and necessary changes were effected as the squadron approached T.O. (Technical Order) strength. It had been the policy of

Lt. Col. Howard Blanchard photographed after the war. ***Blanchard***

M/Sgt. Herbert Goldstein working with the squadron's radio. ***Stevens***

Lt. Robert E. Buchanan was assigned as the squadron's Intelligence Officer. ***Stevens***

Captain Pharr that a man must be a good soldier before he can be a good specialist. To this end no effort was spared to give the squadron a thorough foundation in courtesy, drill, discipline, and military subjects. A concentrated program was started on August 25th for the entire squadron, which would also cover subjects such as first aid, use of arms, motor marches, gas discipline, and camouflage. This four-week program ended on September 20th. Overall, emphasis was given to the training of the squadron as a military organization, and the spirit of soldiering was fostered over and beyond all other duties. When aircraft became available the aircraft maintenance personnel began work on the planes that they were given, which at this time consisted of seven Douglas P-70 Night Fighters supplied by the 481st Night Fighter Operational Training Group based in Orlando. The various other sections concentrated on their own technical specialties.

On October 1st the squadron received its first pilots and R/Os. The word radar was itself secret and never mentioned in orders. Twelve flight crews reported in from their training, the most recent of which had been at Dunnellon Army Air Base. Lieutenants Paul R. Zimmer (who had flown with the RAF), Dorrie F. Jones, and William D. Robbins were appointed flight leaders of A, B, and C Flights, respectively. Captain William T. Bradley came in as the

Parades and drill at Kissimmee were commonplace. Since the 421st NFS would not get aircraft for some time, military basics were the order of the day. ***421st NFS***

Kissimmee was the final staging area before going overseas. It was fall, and the squadron lived in these tents in a very damp area of the world. Cold weather set in, and the men nearly froze at night. They had canvas cots and two blankets, and were faced with the decision to put them on the top or bottom. Newspapers were finally used on the bottom with the blankets on top. *Stevens*

Captain Pharr and his wife sit down for dinner at the party at the Carolina Moon, located near Kissimmee, Florida, on October 2, 1943. *421st NFS*

Operations Officer, with Flight Officer Carl H. Bjorum as his assistant. Lt. Alton Woodring, Jr., also reported in as chief R/O. This brought flying personnel up to full strength. Orders were soon received to move the squadron to Kissimmee Army Air base, Kissimmee, Florida, for a few month's training under field conditions. Kissimmee was destined to be the main base for training of future night fighter squadrons for years to come.

In August 1941 the City of Kissimmee acquired a dilapidated airport west of town and received a government grant in the amount of $233.000 for making much-needed improvements. On January 30, 1942, the airport was closed to all air traffic so that the field could be made ready for use by the United States Army Air Corps. The runways, taxi strips, barracks, and other buildings were built during the ensuing months of that year. On January 1st, 1943, the headlines in the local "Kissimmee Gazette" read: "ARMY TO TAKE OVER AIRBASE THIS WEEKEND." The 349th Night Fighter Squadron would be the first squadron to use the base, with the 421st NFS following some time later to occupy another part of the field starting in October 1943.

The move to Kissimmee was accomplished on October 4th, 1943. Starting early in the morning, the squadron equipment and personnel were moved in a single day to the prepared camp at the new location, and by 7:30 that night the squadron was settled into their tents, ready for a new day and new phase of advanced operational training. With the assignment of pilots and R/Os the training emphasis changed from ground duties to the prime assignment of the unit; night fighting and interdiction. The squadron had their seven P-70 aircraft, as well as the men to use them. Flying training commenced without incident, with particular attention given to gunnery, high altitude flying, and, of course, night operations. Operations were hampered at times due to the worn out condition of the aircraft. Flying was pushed to the limits at Kissimmee without any flying accidents, nor damage to aircraft through pilot error. In the meantime, instruction for the ground personnel continued with-

Lt. Joe Govoni leads the food line at a squadron party. Captain and Mrs. Walter Pharr follows close behind. M/Sgt. Goldstein and Hank Greenberg can be seen in the background serving the dinner. *Stevens*

Doctor Bennett and his wife also joined the squadron at the Carolina Moon. *421st NFS*

out let up. The men were given instruction in scouting and patrolling, infantry tactics, and the principals of aerodrome security, as well as a steady review of basic military subjects.

As far as the training at that time, Lt. John Olley would later say:

> As far as "tactical training" at Kissimmee we were issued gas masks and the training directive stipulated that every man had to take a hike. I think it was four to six miles with the masks on.
>
> Each officer was responsible for his section. I was very conscientious about doing it right and I had a hell of a time keeping my own mask on while running up and down the line of marchers to spot cheaters who had cocked their masks to one side to make a gap so they wouldn't be restricted by having to breathe through the filter.
>
> I don't know whose idea it was, but they also thought that during the gas mask hike to simulate a strafing attack on the men on the ground. The first man to hear the approach of an aircraft was suppose to yell "Air Raid!" and the other men were supposed to echo the warning to be sure everybody heard it. We were warned that we were going to be strafed; but as time went on, with the heat, the hike, and the inconvenience of wearing the mask, we lost our awareness. With orange groves on each side and the aircraft approaching us from downwind, we didn't react till it was upon us. If it were real, we surely would have been killed. We did not react until it was over us and gone. For a little more reality Pharr had taken M/Sgt. Goldstein along for a joy ride in a P-70 on one of those flights. Goldstein dropped several two-pound paper bags of flour right on the road. More fun, but serious.
>
> One thing that comes to mind at this time is that we were issued with our overseas gear at Kissimmee what was called a "pup" tent. Since we were in tactical training, I decided to set my tent up behind the barracks to show the men what we might be doing in the field. Night came, and I crawled in. I had just gotten to sleep when the tent fell in on me. At the same time I heard a bunch of footsteps running away and delighted giggling. They were probably getting back at me for the strenuous calisthenics I was leading them through each day.

During their time at Kissimmee the 421st NFS held a number of informal get-togethers for squadron members to get more acquainted. The first party on June 6th, however, was marked by a mishap that almost brought the social season to an abrupt close. This later became known in squadron annuals as "The Great Potato Salad Attack," and it proved to be an enemy much stronger than the men of the 421st NFS.

The decision was made to use the facilities at Sanlando Springs, just a few miles north of Orlando. Ladies, including WACS (Women's Air Corps), were invited, and a cold luncheon buffet was planned. The piece de resistance of this repast was a potato salad that had been at Signal Hill. However, unbeknownst to the 421st NFS members, the warm afternoon was working its spell on the huge supply of salad prepared much earlier. Because of the nice weather the men took advantage with a cooling dip in the springs and other activities. By this time everyone had worked up a hearty appetite, and when the food was laid out everyone ate his or her full share.

"Report to the Nation" broadcast that took place on July 10, 1943. From left to right are: Lt. Bud Farnum; Captain Walter Pharr; Don Pryor (CBS Announcer); Lt. Robert Buchanan; and General Hume Peabody. ***421st NFS***

A bit later in the afternoon one man began to complain of a stomachache. This complaint began to slowly spread throughout the partygoers. Soon the park grounds were littered with men and women doubled over with ptomaine poisoning. It did not take long before all available transportation was called into emergency use, and there was an endless line of ambulances going back and forth to the Orlando Base Hospital, which was filled to capacity. New wards were opened; extra doctors were called in from every medical unit in the area. The end result of the "attack" was nearly the entire squadron and its guests ended up as potato salad casualties. Captain Pharr would later say; "Many men felt that they were going to earn the Purple Heart before even getting overseas."

There were a few "lucky" individuals who managed to escape the potato salad all together. One was Sergeant Larry Neville. He and a few squadron mates had been restricted to the barracks for the weekend because they had not cleaned up their assigned areas. While most of the squadron had gone to town for the picnic, as punishment they were told to stay behind. When the squadron had left for Sanlando Springs, Neville and his friends made use of the base PX, which was located directly behind the barracks. They managed to get some beer, and some WACS were sent for so they could have their own party. About the time their party got on a roll Lt. Buchanan, who had been at the park with the squadron, began to feel sorry for the guys and went back out to the base to bring them to join the fun. He was met at the barracks by a better party than the one he had left. The whole group ended up together, and Lt. Buchanan had a good laugh because he thought he had been "punishing" these guys.

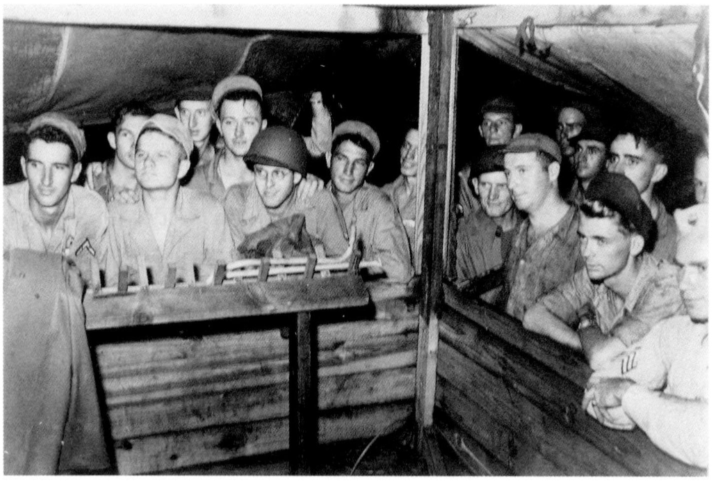

421st NFS members get a ringside seat at the "Report to the Nation" broadcast as it takes place. ***421st NFS***

Fortunately, there was no serious aftermath. After a night in the hospital everyone recovered and returned to their duties. In the days following the incident it was noted that potato salad was not a very popular item on the squadron's menu.

Other parties with less disastrous results were soon to follow. There was a spaghetti party held at the "Carolina Moon" that was a great success. Upon assignments of the flight crews an Officer's party was also held at Makinson Island, just off Kissimmee in Lake Topehikia. It was a good evening despite the drenching received by several members on the launch trip to and from the island. There was also a dunking in a wheelbarrow full of ice water that was experienced by all, including the Commander.

The squadron also took part in numerous local activities, at both Orlando and at Kissimmee. One such role the squadron was involved in was the weekly Army Air Forces School of Applied Tactics radio programs, where the writing and broadcasting talents of Lieutenants Buchanan and Farnum proved valuable. On July 10th, in a coast-to-coast broadcast on the "Report to the Nations" program hosted by CBS, General Hume Peabody, Commandant of AAFSAT, introduced the program and Lt. Bud Farnum, Captain Pharr, Don Pryor (CBS announcer), Lt. Buchanan, and General Peabody aired a skit. This gave the general public an idea of the activities and operations of the night fighters.

Participation in other local events included tennis, baseball, and other sport activities in the area. On August 18th, the squadron trooped down in formation to donate blood to the Orange General Hospital. The squadron received considerable publicity, and besides being featured in the local papers, the unit rarely missed the opportunity to appear in the weekly "AFSATONIAN."

Several events were being set in motion to bring the 421st NFS to the war. The first was the squadron's POM (Prior to Overseas Movement) Inspection on October 14th, to determine if the squadron was "Combat ready." Captain Pharr was worried about the inspection, but he knew the squadron was ready:

> Several days before the end of our training at Kissimmee an Inspection Team of fourteen men marched into camp and began a thorough review of our operations. An expert checked each department of the squadron. After a few days we were relieved to get the word from the top that we were "Combat Ready."

A period of intense activity was brought on by the POM Inspection. Lt. Colonel Charles Fairlamb, the head POM Inspector, with his thirteen assistants recommended that no further inspections were necessary and declared the unit was ready for overseas movement. There was a second inspection that was held by the Inspector General's Department, which followed on October 21st and was also passed by the squadron with favorable commendations. The port call was received from the San Francisco Port of Embarkation on October 30th, and the squadron went to work packing and preparing equipment and themselves for overseas movement.

3

The Long Ride West

On November 3rd, Special Order #6, HQ Army Air Forces Tactical Center (redesignation from Army Air Forces School of Applied Tactics) ordered the squadron to proceed on November 8th to the San Francisco Port of Embarkation to be shipped overseas.

With everything in readiness, the unit en-trained on November 7th for the transcontinental trip to Camp Stoneman, California. The trip to the West Coast was made without incident, and the squadron arrived at the squadron area at 10:00 PM on November 13th. Quarters were assigned in Section "I," and a physical inspection of personnel was held. This examination resulted in the temporary loss of one man, who was sent to the hospital and later rejoined the unit overseas. A number of other men were transferred out of the squadron due to the over manned roster. One man removed from the roster was Corporal Williams, who was serving in Lt. Blanchard's Communication Section. Corporal Williams had served in World War I and appealed to Lt. Blanchard to get him overseas with the rest of the unit. Lt. Blanchard talked to Captain Pharr, and Corporal Williams was allowed to stay, even though some felt that he was a little old.

The Camp Stoneman training program occupied both the officers and enlisted for the next three weeks. The squadron was put through obstacle courses, debarkation docks, hikes, and training films, as well as having the opportunity once again to review their tactical ground training. The alert issued on December 3rd, however, brought these activities to an end, and preparations commenced for embarkation the following day. At 12:30 PM on December 4th the squadron, with full equipment in tow, departed Camp Stoneman for the two mile march to the docks. They boarded the tender boat to the strains of the "Air Force Song" and others being played by the Camp Stoneman band. The tender ferried the squadron across the bay to Oakland, where at 8:30 PM the squadron boarded the U.S.A.T. (United States Army Transport) *SEA PIKE.* This particular ship was 492 feet long and some 7,949 gross tons. The transport remained tied up at the dock overnight, and at 10:00 AM, December 8th, steamed out under the Golden Gate Bridge, destined for the Southwest Pacific. The sea voyage took approximately thirty days and would be something the 421st NFS personnel would always remember. Personal accounts of the men who lived through this reveal just how much and to what limits people could go. The trip, of course, was viewed a little bit differently by all, but in the end all personnel made it through okay.

For Captain Pharr the trip was long, but not very uncomfortable:

> The trip on the *Sea Pike* crossing the Pacific was a trip to be endured. Passing under the Golden Gate Bridge going west, we knew we were heading for the war with the Japanese, but the place was still unknown.

U.S.A.T. *Sea Pike*. The transport that would deliver the 421st NFS to the war. *421st NFS*

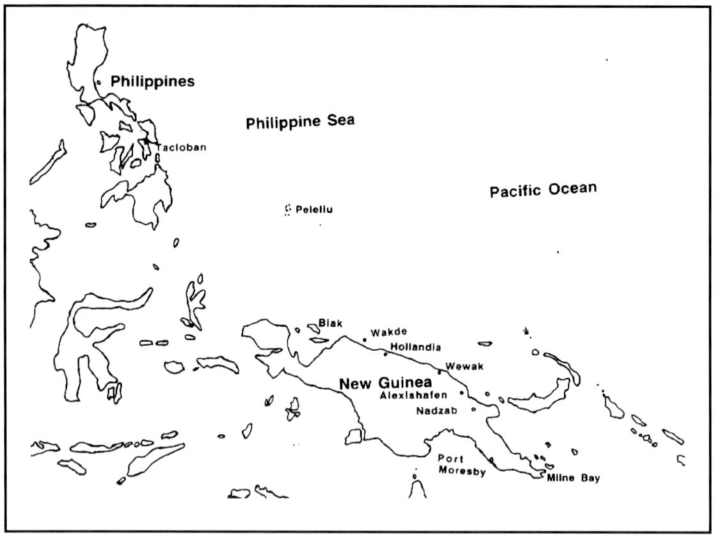

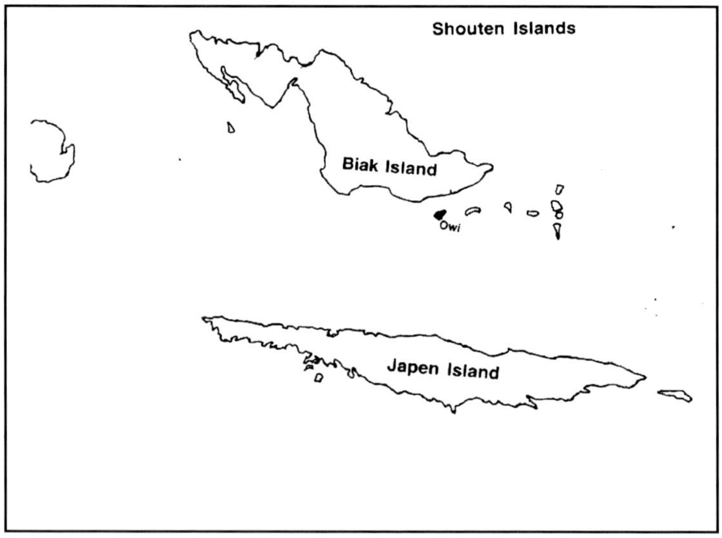

The *Sea Pike* was a converted freighter, and the personnel of the 421st NFS constituted a good part of the passengers. It was up to the 421st NFS cooks to operate the ship's facilities, and it took some days for the new cooks to turn out the usual food. Some men survived day after day on bread, peanut butter, and jelly alone.

To combat boredom, some of us started learning how to play poker and discovered a new way to beat the system for a few games. When we crossed the Equator most of the officers were doused with a hose and had their chests shaved.

In the close confines of a boat for three weeks, rumors are plentiful and new every day. Rumors about the war were most prevalent, especially about Japanese submarines.

For Bill Gorman there was a different reality:

About two days out, we ran into a real bad storm and it caused all types of problems. Three thousand guys getting sick and throwing up at once is bad. I personally did not throw up because I was too sick to do so. I went into the latrine and saw a guy passed out on the floor. Vomit was about two inches thick on the floor, and as the ship would roll he and everything else would slide across the floor. We were all given assignments on board, and mine was the sea-air watch. I was supposed to be looking for enemy aircraft and submarines. I was to be on duty for four hours and off four, and my place of duty was in the gun tub in the front of the ship. I got up there and the fresh air was overwhelming, and I stayed in that tub for two days without coming down because I could not take the stench below the decks anymore. I knew that I could take no more of this, so I asked one of the sailors how long it would be before we got to where we were going? He said he could not tell us where we were going, but the last trip took six weeks to get there.

Upon crossing the Equator a "Pollywogs at the Equator" ceremony was held. Most of the officers and a few others were doused with a hose, and their chests were neatly shaved. *421st NFS*

Sgt. Jake Loran also had a different view of things:

Fortunately, I was assigned to the first deck under the main deck. There were a couple decks under that. Bunks made of canvas and pipes were neatly implanted into the ship structure, row on row, hundreds of rows on each deck, maybe thousands. The bunks were about eight deep on top of each other from floor to ceiling, so the top guys had lots of climbing to get in and out of bed. Space between the bunks was limited; about 20 to 24 inches to the next upper or lower bunk. How or what we used for blankets or other sleeping material, I do not recall, but I know the air got pretty foul and rotten. Your duffel bags had been stored in holds elsewhere on the ship, so you carried only your very personal items and necessary stuff. Those you either took into your assigned bunk with you or strapped them onto the iron pipe on your bunk, together with your steel helmet that you carried or wore every place that you went. The previous day and night had been a nightmare, and we slept very little. We were not used to hard bunks, and the eternal racket, as well as the foul air with so many humans jammed together. The uneasiness of the cramped quarters prevailed.

After a couple days at sea away from the land breakers, the seas calmed and we slowly got better. We were exhausted from being seasick and not having any nourishment. A lot of helmets hanging on our bunks were now full of you know what. The stench was terrific, but, more and more we staggered up, one by one, and we took two or three days with plenty of water, disinfectant, and yes, blood, sweat, and tears, to get the ship in some kind of sanitary order. Soon it got to be pretty nice. Laying on the decks every day with nothing to do but enjoy the warm sea breeze and plenty of sunshine. And it did get a little boring at times. Once in a while the Chaplain or Recreational Officer would line up some kind of talent from amongst us, some music and singing, or even boxing matches on the decks. Lots of these were miss-matches, and some poor guy who thought he was a fighter got his block knocked off.

And, hooray, I was finally able to see an island, but we sailed right passed it. It was about five miles away on the horizon, and that is the only spot of land we saw until we arrived at Australia a day or two before Christmas 1943. Generally, there was very little to do on this journey, except lay around and smoke cigarettes, talk about loved ones back home, and attempt to comprehend our final destination and what action we would encounter with the Japanese in this war. The eternal question was, where are we going?

There were eternal emergency drills. Since we were a single ship and not a convoy, we changed course often, zigzagging as a precaution in case we crossed an area of Japanese or German submarines, which were noted for patrolling such areas of the Pacific. We did not know if the ship contained any submarine detection devices, but the ship was armed with six tubs on each side with twenty-millimeter guns and Navy crews, in addition to a five-inch cannon manned by a Navy crew. One of the Navy crewmembers told me they could hold their own with any submarine that surfaced. When the five-inch gun was fired in practice it was surprising to have a cloud of dust erupt on that deck area. I could never comprehend where the dust came from in the middle of the ocean.

One of the guys by name of Vincent DeLagardelle had a little knowledge of bread baking. When he answered the request over the ship's loudspeaker for anyone with bakery experience, he was assigned to the night shift as head baker to help bake bread for the always hungry hordes of humans on the ship. Being a friend, he made me his assistant, and I was thankful, as it was boring to lie around and do nothing. Our shift started at 10:00 PM, and we were done by 6:00 AM. It was hard work, and I was mostly the clean-up guy, but I did help cutting dough and removing bread from the ovens. I never counted, but we must have baked hundreds of loaves each night. We had so many troops on board that our kitchen facilities were inadequate to feed three meals per day, so there were only two meals per day, but they were substantial, with mutton each day, lots of bread, always a starch item, canned vegetables of some kind, and always either a fresh orange or apple. As it was, breakfast started at 6:00 and ended about 10:00, and then there was a lot of clean up to do. Then we would prepare the evening meal beginning at 4:00 in the afternoon.

There is an old saying that "what you don't know won't hurt you." Anyway, one morning as the large steam vats were cooking oatmeal, powdered eggs, and other goodies, DeLagardelle and I were just getting off our bread baking shift when we noted one of the kitchen helpers apparently sick and

M/Sgt. Herbert Goldstein's certificate for crossing the Equator. ***Goldstein***

falling on the floor. Somehow, he had bumped his head against the side of a steam vat full of scrambled eggs that was being readied for serving. In bumping the vat, he also vomited, with some of it going into this vat of dozens and dozens of eggs, milk, and spices. One of the cooks came running over to the Mess Officer in charge, and together they viewed the vat full of eggs with a bit of vomit already blended into the eggs. They must have considered the chaos and long delay, with hundreds of hungry GIs waiting in line, dumping the eggs and starting over again, which may take hours. The Mess Officer finally whispered something to the cook and walked off. In turn, the cook got his large wooden spatula and began stirring the eggs for serving to the hungry soldiers. In situations like this, one must do what is necessary, and I understand the eggs were served and eaten to the very last spoonful and no one suffered and died. However, I was a little cautious for some time when eating scrambled eggs.

Lt. Howard Blanchard tried to make the best of the situation:

If you had a stomach for it there was a galley with rice and powdered milk for breakfast, the few times I went to breakfast. In the evening (we were fed twice a day), it was a ladle of mutton on the same rice you did not eat in the morning. I mean "mutton." The smell of it cooking in the galley was overpowering. I still do not eat lamb. You wonder how I made it without going to the galley often? I lucked out. I had a friend, Technical Sergeant Vincent DeLagardelle, who was about thirty. He was a man who left a home in South Dakota when he was about fourteen and hitchhiked to California to help his family out by leaving them, making one less for his mother to care for. I think they had about nine children. He learned to cook and take care of himself. He also had built up a fortune and owned Arrow Cab Company in Alameda, which later had grown to about two hundred cabs. When they asked for cooks for the galley, he got in. At his rank he did not have to, but he knew that if he worked in the galley he would find the good food. In the evening he would find me, usually up on the bow where I watched the flying fish and the bow waves sparkle with phosphorescence, and he would bring me up sandwiches and even hot apple turnovers. He baked them himself after everyone had left the galley. He did not lose any weight going overseas, and I only lost about ten pounds.

Finally, Lt. Elston Roady remembered his trip on the *Sea Pike*:

We officers were housed on deck with twenty-four to a "stateroom," and a very, very frugal two meals a day. The rations were almost at starvation level. I went below deck to see the men and can attest to the very unsanitary and stinking conditions there.

I was made Police and Prison Officer below deck. That meant I had to take a crew of enlisted men and clean the ship below deck. You would not believe the conditions. Feces, vomit, and slime in the Heads and all over the decks. We were all seasick, as we hit a very bad storm as soon as we passed the Golden Gate Bridge. For three days hardly anyone left their bunks. A few had crawled out of their bunks and crept into the Head near the bunks, and it was really pitiful. I could see them from my bunk rolling helplessly across the deck in the slop and vomit from the toilet bowls. Up against the toilet, and when the ship rolled the other way, they would roll across the deck to under the hand basin with the slop.

They called my name and several others to report to the Captain's Office for detail assignments during this time, and I had to go, sick as I was. I was taken below decks by some Navy man to the Heads and told that we had to clean them thoroughly. I never asked an enlisted man to do something that I would not do, so on my knees with a razor blade I went through and began scraping the green slime in the toilet bowls away, and the seven or eight men I had all joined me. Boy, we were sick! But within a week we had the below decks looking pretty good. We began to get our "sea legs," and the rest of the trip was not too bad except for the lack of food. Lieutenant Buchanan was the lucky one, since he was the above deck Police and Prison Officer.

The ship made its way down the West Coast and then took a zigzag course across the South Pacific. When the ship crossed the Equator a ceremony was held, and many of the officers and a number of others had their chests shaved and doused with a hose. All those involved were also to receive a certificate commemorating the event. When the ship docked in Townsville Harbor, Australia, on Christmas Day 1943, there was almost a small riot right there. Understandably, the members of the 421st NFS wanted nothing more in the world at that moment than to go ashore. They could have somewhat of a good Christmas and at least get something to eat. The men started banging their GI coffee cups on the ship's railing and yelling, "we want food!" Captain Bigbie, the Military Transport Service Army representative, came out onto the bridge, and using a bull horn told the men that he was going to give them some oranges he had been saving, and they were going to bake some cakes as a special treat for Christmas. He also told them that they were standing by to pick up some Navy ships for protection while crossing the Coral Sea. He could not allow anyone on shore at that time, as they would be leaving shortly. It was said many times afterward that the men were unarmed at the time. Order was finally restored, but things were touchy. At that time 2,500 Army troops were also loaded on board the ship.

An interesting side note to this is that Doctor Bennet, the squadron Flight Surgeon, having taken over from Doctor Rowlands while the unit was in Orlando, filed a complaint with the OSI about the lack of food on the thirty plus day trip to New Guinea. Captain Douglas D. Bigbie, who was the Army captain in charge, explained that because the ship had brought wounded back to the United States and had a rapid turn around, he was unable to load sufficient supplies and the ship was filthy as the wounded were unable to clean. Doctor Bennett himself lost forty pounds on the way over, and most of the men were all in bad condition when they finally made it to Townsville. When the ship made the final destination at Milne Bay, New Guinea, many of the men had to be carried off the ship. It was discovered by the OSI that Captain Bigbie, the Army man with the MTS in charge of the ship, had made a deal with the food supplier in Oakland. In exchange for $20,000 the supplier would provide about $10,000 worth of goods. They planned to then split the remaining $10,000 between them. The Captain was eventually stripped of his rank, forfeited all privileges, and was sent to Ft. Leavenworth for seven years of hard labor. This was all reported to the squadron by the OSI.

4

First Stop, Milne Bay

The squadron left Townsville, Australia, and headed for the new destination of Milne Bay, New Guinea. Many of the squadron members remembered pulling into the bay, looking at the thatched huts dotting the shoreline, and thinking how pretty the scenery was. On January 3rd, 1944, the men landed at Milne Bay. The squadron disembarked at 11:00 on the 4th. Some men, like Curtis Burgess, had to stay aboard an extra two frustrating days to unload equipment, having spent over a month on the ship already. Quarters were assigned at the staging area at Ahloma, and men and equipment were loaded up and taken by truck to the temporary campsite. Jake Loran noted:

> We were only there for a very short time and assigned a space in a sloping area that appeared to be well worn by other campers. We ended up sleeping on the open ground for a couple days.

Howard Blanchard also remembered some interesting things when the squadron first arrived:

> My Commander, Major Pharr, took me to Port Moresby to report in to Headquarters. We left the staging area early in the morning, and I remember little about the trip, except that about noontime we came upon a thatched hut beside the jungle road. I could not believe my eyes. The hut had tables with red and white checkered tablecloths, and we were served tea by a tall Micronesian, with a ring in his nose, and who wore little except a small apron made out of the same materials as the tablecloths. Another thing I remember about the trip is that when we arrived at the airstrip—I believe it was called "Seven Mile Strip"—I saw John Wayne stretched out against a bamboo railing at the Operations tent. I assume he was waiting for a ride to Australia. He was impressive in size, looked like a giant to me. He was dozing, and there was no one around him, which is hard to believe now that I look back. However, it was not too odd, because the whole place seemed to be deserted. I had expected a bustling place, but there was a strange emptiness.
>
> We had some difficulty finding someone to report in to. Finally, we found a Lt. Colonel Breschetto. He was sitting in a dilapidated chair smoking a cigar with his feet up on a makeshift desk, in a squad tent, which at the time served as Headquarters. His uniform was sweat-stained, and this was understandable, considering it must have been at least 120 degrees inside the tent. Major Pharr, who was very military, saluted and stated that he was the Commanding Officer of the 421st Night Fighter Squadron. The Colonel did not return the salute, nor did he take his feet off the desk, but he did look rather disgusted. "The 421st who?" he said. He next asked if we had brought any aircraft. Then Major Pharr said that we were told that we would get our aircraft in the theatre when we arrived. Colonel Breschetto made a few uncomplimentary remarks about the Pentagon, and suggested that we were in the wrong area of operations. Perhaps we should be in the Burma Theatre. When he asked what kind of communications gear we had, I told him that we were equipped with VHF systems. Out came another expletive or two about the great minds that run the military, and a statement that the 5th Air Force was still using old VHF equipment. I do not think that Major Pharr really recovered from the shock of this meeting.

The facilities at Milne Bay consisted of tents, a mess hall, and very little else. The squadron was greeted with a red alert on their

The squadron campsite at Milne Bay, New Guinea. M/Sgt. Goldstein is seen talking to a couple of the squadron's personnel. ***421st NFS***

Squadron mess hall at Milne Bay. *421st NFS*

Taken at payday on February 2, 1944, at Milne Bay. From left to right are: McCarley; Grider; Moore; Rife; Govoni; Barber; Loran; Sommerville; and Tarr. *421st NFS*

first night in camp. As it turned out, this was the first alert the area had experienced in months. The next few days personnel were occupied in getting settled, assembling and arranging equipment, and checking new items, which had been delivered at the San Francisco Port of Embarkation. The squadron had to provide their own power and telephone lines, stringing miles of their own WS-110 Field Wire through the trees to the nearest Army Command Post. An emergency field lighting system had to be set up with most of the wire placed along the side of the runway. The problem with this plan was the Army Corps of Engineers then showed up to work on the strip. Maneuvering their caterpillar tractors around on the field resulted in constant cuts in the lighting wires and phone lines, all of which had to be repaired to keep the squadron in operation.

Even though the 421st NFS was new to the Southwest Pacific, their presence in the area would soon be known to even the Japanese, as Bill Gorman noted:

> I remember we were greeted by Tokyo Rose on the radio. She asked what the 421st Night Fighter Squadron was going to do over there since we had no planes. She was right, we had no planes.

Another view of the Milne Bay mess hall. *421st NFS*

After getting the squadron settled Major Pharr reported to higher Headquarters (5th Fighter Command) at Port Moresby and was assured that the squadron would be moved to the combat area in a few weeks. The main problem faced by the 421st NFS even before reaching a combat area was the lack of any aircraft. The aircraft projected for the 421st NFS, the Northrop P-61, was not scheduled to arrive until sometime in April or May. Major Pharr then requested that some substitute aircraft be found until the squadron could be supplied with the P-61. After all, the flying personnel had been idle since the unit had departed Florida back in December.

Milne Bay was a temporary station for the 421st, but some enlisted personnel, such as Bill Gorman, found other things to do:

> There was not much for us to do in Milne Bay. The war had passed by, and we were gathering our equipment and supplies, which would be needed later on. One day several of us went back into the mountains a little ways and built a rock damn across a mountain stream. It was real nice, and we were swimming and bathing in the backwater. We did not know it that day, but a thunderstorm was going on up in the mountains behind us, and all of a sudden a wall of water swept down on us and we rapidly climbed to safety up the side of a hill. Our truck that we had used to get there was completely covered with water, dirt, and rock. As the water finally went down, all we could see of our truck was the windshield sticking up out of the rocks. Our first casualty of war had just happened.

In the meantime, most of the enlisted personnel were supplying a base detail to the local 15th Replacement Battalion, while the remainder of the squadron made considerable improvements at the Ahloma camp. At 1:00 on January 27th , 1944, orders were received for the 421st NFS to take their next step through the Pacific. The squadron would move from Milne Bay and go to Nadzab, New Guinea.

5

Welcome to the Jungle! Nadzab

Captain Charles M. Townsend was slated to lead the advance party of four officers and sixty enlisted men to Nadzab. Between the time of receiving the movement orders at 1:00 on January 27th and the next day, the advance party loaded the bare essentials (including two jeeps) and equipment onto seven Douglas C-47 transport aircraft. At 10:00 in the morning the advance party was airlifted to Nadzab, New Guinea, on the southeastern coast.

Arriving at Nadzab at 12:30 PM, the first order of business was to select a building site. By mid-afternoon the layout was sketched out, and the advance party went to work. Lt. Robert Buchanan took over the duties of chief road builder; Lt. William B. Robbins handled the mess and supply; and F/O Stuart A. Thorton became the foreman on the squadron's labor gang. Lt. Blanchard oversaw the setting up of the communication system. In short order communications were established between the squadron and 5th Fighter Command. Elsewhere, troops were stringing the wire for electricity to what would be the squadron's Headquarters and other essential facilities.

From the very beginning the advanced party was beset with problems of insufficient transportation, lack of materials and machinery, and the absence of many essential items that would be required for the construction of the camp. There was no way the squadron could get an "official" assignment of a single piece of heavy equipment to do any construction. These problems were soon managed, however, by setting up "creative" agreements and contracts with neighboring units, Australian Forces camps, and some passers-by for the use of bulldozers, scrapers, and graders. Most of the appropriate equipment was put into service for irregular periods of time that ranged in length from an hour to several days. The work on the camp, however, proceeded quickly and on pace. By the end of the second day of the advance party's arrival, tents had been set up to house the entire squadron. The immediate area had been cleared, new roads were cut, and their small strip of New Guinea jungle took on aspects of a livable campsite.

Another major problem that faced the 421st NFS was the need for potable water. At the campsite there were no good sources of water nearby. Water for drinking, cooking, and washing had to be hauled in by continual trips of a 250 gallon water trailer. After days of hard sweaty work, aside from thirst, the men were handicapped for bathing and cleaning. On many occasions the men went without drinking water for periods of hours, which in the jungle environment could quickly become a dangerous problem if they did not

Squadron camp at Nadzab, New Guinea. ***Goldstein***

Nadzab recreation hall. ***Goldstein***

One of the many well digging crews around Nadzab. ***421st NFS***

monitor dehydration, including the loss of body salt. To alleviate this problem work began on seven different well-digging projects around the area. One well resulted in a shaft eight feet square, by some forty feet deep.

At this particular site a group of twenty men began digging early in the morning and ended up spending the entire day on the project. Work on this site eventually stretched into days of labor, evidently a lot more work than they bargained for. At the outset of the project the men found the ground was hard with no danger of a cave-in, so after a while they dug the shaft deeper and wider. At that time they found themselves in a hole measuring five feet wide by twelve feet deep, which then made it necessary to install a pulley system with a very long and heavy rope to haul out the dirt by bucket. Most of the men present said the hole ultimately went down to about forty feet. Crews were organized to take turns due to high heat and humidity down in the hole. Teams of two were pulling up the buckets one at a time. Due to the conditions, a system of rotating fresh crews both in and out of the hole was implemented. People at the bottom claimed that they were down so far that they could look up and actually see stars. Even at this level there was not so much as a drop of water, not even damp sand or gravel. Someone then decided to blast the hole with dynamite to see if that would bring up water. A small hole was dug into the bottom of the shaft, into which went a bundle of dynamite. The crews were cleared out and the dynamite was set off. The explosion filled the hole with very thick dust and caustic gas, preventing resumption of work for a couple of hours. When it was deemed safe two men were lowered to check out the condition of the hole, and began shoveling out any loose dirt. There was, however, a problem, a big problem as it turned out. When the two men reached the bottom of the hole they found thick smoke, no water anywhere, and they were quickly overcome by the fumes. Another man was lowered to put the sick men into the buckets and haul them out. They had a hell of a time, because as soon as they got a fresh man down the shaft to lift one of the others out, they would pass out and the situation kept repeating itself. The process took over ten exchanges to get everyone out safely.

That pretty much dashed all hope of digging their own well. They soon returned to relying on the Quartermaster Corps to tank-deliver the drinking water to the squadron. All the work on the dry well did not go for not. They decided to build a very large outhouse right over the top of the hole. A ten-seater was soon constructed at the site of the former well. The building allowed five seats on each side and a door and chute on one end for the garbage from the mess hall. This was one of the most utilized facilities built while the squadron was at New Guinea. A nice roof was eventually added, and everyone from commander to private could sit there in comfort during his daily ritual.

Within the next week or so there were great strides in the completion of the new camp. The mess hall was erected over a concrete floor, a dispensary was built, and a framed Headquarters building went up. Eventually work was started on buildings to house supply, communications, armament, and a hospital. Each section in the squadron built their own facility.

By February 3rd the main body of the 421st NFS had arrived by air at the new base. A small detachment remained back at Milne Bay to take care of some heavy equipment that was still there. The remainder of the equipment and men would arrive by ship a short time later.

On February 21st, the 421st NFS pilots left for Townsville, Australia, to help ferry fourteen P-38s to New Guinea. This was the first of several of these missions during the next few weeks. All these aircraft were destined for Day Fighter units flying out of Nadzab. It would be some time before the 421st NFS would eventually get their own new aircraft to fly. The pilots being sent were led by Walter Pharr, who would fly lead throughout the ferry mission:

> In February 1944 we were asked to go to Townsville, Australia, to pick up fourteen new P-38s and deliver them to the Day Fighter group at Nadzab. We were flown from Nadzab to Townsville in a C-47. Plans were made to return the second day, and so we had some time for familiarization flights. Now, Townsville seldom has rain all year, and their movie theatres were completely open air. It was an inviting target for low level sightseeing in a P-38. The moviegoers had not counted on see-

The squadron mess hall at Nadzab. ***Goldstein***

ing P-38s flying just above their heads at 250 mph. After a while of this sport we got urgent calls from the control tower ordering us to land. I reported to the Operations Officer feeling rather guilty. But when he saw my Major's insignia he immediately calmed down and was almost apologetic. I wanted to tell him he was just doing his job.

In the morning we headed out together in loose formation for Port Moresby, New Guinea. Our heading was almost due north, flying over the beautiful Coral Sea. It was exciting to be flying a new sleek aircraft, the engine humming along nicely. The air was smooth, and it was hard to realize that we were in a war zone.

After checking our fuel at Port Moresby we lined up for take-off. I looked back over my shoulder and saw thirteen new P-38s ready to go, 26 propellers ticking over in unison. We then took off to fly over the Owen Stanley Mountain Range (13,000 ft.), landing at Lae on the eastern coast. A short time later we flew on to Nadzab, delivering the planes to the Day Fighter Group.

The only problem we had was that before the flight we were cautioned that the P-38's brakes sometimes had to be pumped, or they may not work. Lt. Roland Forrester, while landing had this happen. His P-38 went off the end of the runway, but luckily was not damaged. The higher Headquarters were not really happy, but we did not hear anything more about it.

As I recall, we used almost all our pilots to do this ferry operation. I believe Bill Bradley was the only one that did not accompany us. Bill, being second in command, remained at Squadron Headquarters.

Shortly thereafter the squadron received their first aircraft, two Lockheed P-38F "Lightnings" on loan basis from 5th Fighter Command. Flying out of Gila Gila, the pilots logged all the available flying time possible, primarily familiarizing themselves with the P-38's flying characteristics. The aircraft were old and required considerable work by 421st NFS ground crews to keep them in a safe flying condition.

The squadron medical tent and headquarters. ***Goldstein***

The recreation hall. ***Goldstein***

Lt. John Olley recalls:

Somebody—maybe Pharr—got the 5th Fighter Command to transfer two P-38s so the pilots could hone their skills in a new atmosphere. I do not know whose pilots delivered the aircraft to us. I did not even know that they were delivered until I got a rush call from someone to go out to the hardstand near the strip. There sat a P-38 in the mud just off the hardstand. A bunch of maintenance crews and pilots were there. Some people walked over to me with a scowl on their faces. I could see they were thinking: "Is this what you are giving us to maintain and fly?"

What happened is that Sergeant Walter Gold had been elected, directed, or won a coin toss to make the first engine run-up. The Line Chief, Sergeant Mulligan, was there checking over the situation. Apparently, nobody thought to chock the wheels and the brakes were not firmly set. Gold was the focus of all the attention. The engines turned over and the plane started to move. I imagine there was a lot of advice yelled and general confusion for Gold. He did not apply the brakes, nor chop the throttles, so the plane rolled off the hardstand. The P-38 was not supposed to be towed backwards, especially with the landing gear stuck in the mud. But there were no cranes around, so the Line Chief took it upon himself to use a cletrack to haul it out. The ships they gave us soon proved to be dogs.

With the squadron settled into their new camp, the men were anxious to get going with flying operations and get into the war. The primary obstacle, again, was still the lack of combat aircraft to get the aircrews some flight time. On February 16th two more P-38F Lightnings were added to the aircraft they had eventually received at Milne Bay. A fifth P-38 arrived on February 19th. As with the previous P-38s received, these aircraft all required considerable maintenance work to get them in the air. The pilots finally were scheduled to fly some practice flights to get some much-needed flying.

It was on February 29th that the 421st NFS would fly their first combat mission, flown by three P-38s piloted by 1st Lt. Paul Zimmer, 1st Lt. Dorrie E. Jones, and 2nd Lt. William B. Robbins.

The main street of the Nadzab camp. ***Stevens***

They launched at 05:40 AM from a secondary field at Finschafen, located thirty miles up the coast from Lae. Their mission was to fly top-cover for a U.S. Army assault at Los Negros, in the Admiralty Islands. From the start of the mission unfavorable weather conditions and mechanical difficulties plagued them. Shortly after take-off, Lt. Robbins had to abort the mission due to a number of malfunctions and returned to base, leaving the other two P-38s to continue on. Lt. Zimmer soon experienced even worse luck when his landing gear would not completely retract, his left propeller speed regulator failed, and he could not release his drop tanks. Then, his luck went from bad to worse when his right engine failed all together, and at 1,500 feet his left engine was lost. Zimmer without much thought had to bail out of the stricken fighter. His P-38 crashed and burned two miles inland near the Sanga River. Lt. Zimmer sprained his ankle when his silk chute ride came to an abrupt end some fifty miles from Finschafen. He later reported that he had hobbled onto a nearby road, which he limped along wearing out his brand new English flying boots before a jeep picked him up and took him back to Finschafen. Lt. Jones, the one remaining P-38, was successful in reaching the objective, however, the overcast allowed him only an occasional glimpse of the terrain below. Thus came to an end the very first combat mission of the 421st NFS.

During this time a small, but highly unusual incident occurred within the 421st NFS itself. For lack of anything better, some former members now refer to it as "The Nadzab Incident." This has been referred to by some as a riot, but most likely did not qualify as such. Given it being wartime, the actions could very well have been looked upon as such. According to witnesses at the time the enlisted men in the squadron had reached a point where some tempers were short, and it was felt that their feeling about the officers should be aired-out in public. At one point a "proclamation" with enlisted demands was typed up by one upset 421st NFS member and was posted in the middle of the camp. The "proclamation" read as follows:

To Those Concerned and Interested:

1. The earliest, least costly victory, the completion of our distasteful tasks, rests heavily on the military factors called morale and teamwork. Overseas cause and effect of these factors is closely associated with the feelings between officers and enlisted men, the conditions under which both parties are forced to live, and the degree and time of military accomplishments.
2. The feeling and loyalty of enlisted men toward their officers, which constitutes a fundamental strength of any military organization, is governed by qualities that can be grouped under terms, RESPECT and FAIR PLAY. An officer must earn a reputation for the American sense of these two qualities in order to insure the maximum efficiency of personnel.
3. The qualities of RESPECT can also be divided into two traits of the individual officer. First, an officer must posses those manly characteristics of courage, strength, integrity, and gentlemanliness. The qualities promote the respect of subordinates toward a superior officer for the ability and sincerity with which he pursues his duties and responsibilities. Respect will naturally install loyalty and following from the subordinates.
4. The quality of FAIR PLAY involves just that: the principals of sportsmanship and democracy taught to all of us at home. They are not the least important principles upon which we are determined to fight and win this war. Fair play between officers and enlisted men is not as necessary as respect for the discipline and loyalty of the men in all military organizations. In professional armies it is many time absent: but in our new, unchaste, Army personnel, not yet accustomed to regimentation, there must necessarily be present that quality of fair play to which we are all accustomed.
5. All of the preceding words may seem pointless in the present instance, but they are a necessary background of military fundamentals, which we need to understand properly the dissatisfaction and unrest spreading throughout this squadron. There is not too much idealism or impractical hypothesis in these determinations. Their manifestation must surely be necessary to insure the proper cooperation, the proper teamwork between officers and enlisted men, among all men fighting together. Officers are chosen, trained, and appointed to lead the battle in the most efficient cooperative manner. Their part is not to restrict and inhibit those men they supervise. Neither should their attitudes be one of contempt and heavy arrogance. It is their

P-38 sitting on ramp at Nadzab. ***Harding***

duty to exemplify a superior soldier and make decisions resultant from superior training and ability.
6. Violations of these fundamentals are the things, which provoke the present friction between officers and enlisted men. Some of the specific incidents of violations are probably small in themselves, but each and by all they are indicative of personal and professional characteristics, which discourage the confidence and loyalty of the enlisted men. Instances may be listed as follows:
a. Officers must have their latrine first, to the complete elimination of the enlisted men's necessity and sanitation.
b. Officer tents are erected in advantageous positions.
c. Officers have special washstands constructed by the enlisted men at the expense of work hours required more urgently elsewhere.
d. Officers grab the showers first to the loss of the enlisted men.
e. Officers misuse their superior rank in petty discriminations against enlisted men.
f. Officers exemplify of soldiers in general appearance, self-discipline, and control.
g. Officers use squadron tools and equipment for personal use to the expense of squadron activity.
h. Officers take a jeep to themselves to do with what they please.
i. Officers direct the construction and promotion of superfluous juvenile fixtures around the area to the sacrifice of more necessary facilities.
j. Officers display selfish ambitions, which are extremely undesirous and completely contrary and hypocritical to earlier promises and declarations.
k. Officers display disrespect and negligence of their responsibilities, sometimes endangering the security of other men.

The 421st NFS used Finschafen's field to fly their P-38s, while still maintaining their main camp at Nadzab. ***Burdue***

l. Officers generally order enlisted men about as personal servants and valets, including carrying baggage.
m. Officers argue between themselves over petty personal quarrels before the eyes of enlisted men present.
n. Officers' attempts to have enlisted men, gunners, and cook's helpers wait on them in tent and at table.
o. Officers have uttered threats to shoot enlisted men found within the area of the officer's tent.
p. Flying personnel are completely unsuited and untrained for administrative jobs, and they should not be appointed to do such tasks. This is a fundamental difficulty in this particular squadron. Flying officers should be limited to the jobs pre-

421st NFS P-38 in flight over New Guinea. ***Stevens***

pared for. They will have plenty to do when the time comes, and in the interim there is sufficient material to occupy their time.

7. Other factors of moral and teamwork must be considered also, those living conditions and military accomplishments. In addition, enlisted men have their mistakes and unsatisfactory traits, which must be improved. These are not the point of the present issue, however, nor are these specifications directed maliciously at any individual, but rather represent the thoughts of one enlisted man as a constructive understanding of the situation.

This all came to a head at a squadron meeting held in the middle of the camp. For the most part the meeting started out in an orderly fashion, with Sgt. Richard Mulligan acting as an arbitrator. Each

Major Bong shown with one of the most famous aircraft of the war, his P-38J "Marge." This aircraft is actually a copy of the original that had been lost in New Guinea months before. This one was painted in honor of Bong during a visit back to the States. ***Davis***

Major Richard Bong, America's top Ace in the cockpit of his P-38 March 1944. ***Bong***

man was allowed to speak his mind on the matter. Notably, a number of officers were in attendance, including Captain Townsend. According to most accounts, verbal expression got out of hand when a number of people started to shout and heckle what was being said and the throwing of a few threats. As a result of this, nothing ever came about, nor was any administrative action taken against the enlisted. There was some mention that the author of the proclamation did have his military career hurt by this, but there was never any documentation found to substantiate this.

Two 421st NFS enlisted members remember this time well:

> There was always a firm line where you went to eat and your duties. The Officers had "Officer's Country." They had their own Officer's Club. This separation of living quarters and other things changed when people began to shoot at us. Everyone moved in together at that point. I think tempers got out of hand between everybody. One night I was out walking and I was stopped by one of our officers. I guess he felt that I was a good troop and I did my job and kept my mouth shut. He was obviously trying to find out what was going on with the enlisted. I told him that most felt that the officers needed to pull their weight more. They needed to jack-up their pants and get in with us. The interesting thing is that there were a number of enlisted men in the tents near us listening to the whole thing, and this did not help. We eventually got together and spoke up on our feelings. There was a lot of displeasure at the time, but nothing really came out of it.

One enlisted member also witnessed some bad feelings, leading to action taking place in the squadron:

> One lieutenant we had was very military. At Nadzab when we first arrived we had no aircraft. He felt that he had to keep the enlisted personnel busy, or they might do something bad with their idle time. Anyway, he made the men empty all the kegs of rusty nails into gun cleaning trays and scrub them off with wire brushes. Rust built up fast there, considering you

Lt. Tom Malone taken at Nadzab, March 1944. ***Malone***

have around 136 inches of rain a year and high humidity. One of our senior enlisted men was so upset with the lieutenant that he picked him up by the shirt and told him that he would kill him if he ever saw him in the States after the war.

There were also a couple of other noteworthy events happening within the squadron that showed some of the unrest that was prevalent. One very warped incident occurred when one of the Headquarters Section corporals relieved himself on Major Pharr's desk blotter one morning. When Major Pharr came into the tent to work, there "it" was. He yelled out, "Who did this?" The corporal stood up and stood at attention and said, "I did, Sir!" he was returned to the States with a Section Eight.

A more frightful—and more perilous—event occurred when another young corporal pulled a gun out in Lt. Roady's tent and started pointing it at him, all the while shouting, "There are Japs everywhere! I'm going to kill Japs!" His shouting alerted nearby enlisted men, two of whom jumped him, knocking the weapon to the ground, and then they pinned him to the ground. The event was over in a short time. Many of his fellow squadron mates declared he became a pretty good guy, and after time this episode was later dismissed.

One of the final chapters in this string of incidents was the loss of corporal Billy Battershell, who apparently had a breakdown one night. Squadron personnel found the corporal on the beach trying to swim back to the States. Life in the squadron seemed, after this, to return to normal. Squadron routine took over once again, and the war itself came back to center stage.

On March 13th, the 421st NFS finally began to fly genuine combat missions out of Nadzab. These first flights consisted mainly of daily weather reconnaissance missions for the 5th Fighter Command. Two P-38s of A Flight that were in good operating condition would launch on early morning weather reconnaissance missions up to Tadji. Upon completion of their mission they returned to Nadzab to report the weather conditions to Headquarters. With this information in hand Headquarters would green-light scheduled attack missions for later in the morning.

Joining the 421st NFS on these first missions was the Army's premier Ace in the Southwest Pacific, Major Richard Bong. At this time Major Bong had a total of twenty-five victories to his credit. By the end of the war his aerial tally would rise to forty. Bong was sent to the 421st NFS to give the pilots a few operational combat tips and to fly a few missions with them. All of the pilots were anxious to set down with him and find out why he was so successful. Most of the 421st NFS pilots would later recall that he was a soft-spoken man, not given to any kind of boasting about his feats in the air. He was a non-smoker and a non-drinker, who described success by telling the pilots to simply fly right up on the tail of the Japanese plane and fire with all the guns. He seemed to be very easy going on the ground, but became very aggressive in the air. Lt. Dorrie Jones flew the first missions with Major Bong on March 13th, 14th, and 15th.

Major Pharr flew missions with Major Bong on March 16th and 17th. He recalled that first time up with Bong:

> My first combat mission was flying Dick Bong's wing in P-38s. It was an early morning take-off, well before any light.

A P-70A of the 421st NFS preparing for a mission. ***421st NFS***

A few moments after Dick got into his cockpit, he was taxiing out in a big cloud of dust. I remember I was pushing just to keep up with him. Then, to make matters worse, when we got into the air we could not find each other. We circled the field for several minutes in the pitch black, talking on the radio and hoping we would run into each other.

Finally, we made visual contact, and I pulled in by his right wing and below. As we flew toward the Japanese lines, it gradually became lighter. I was nervous about what I might do if we ran into Japanese fighters. Back in the States, we had no formal training in day fighting and very little time in the P-38. Dick would have cause to be concerned about his wingman that day. But I do not think he gave it much thought. He had, after all, gotten 25 kills without much help.

After a while, I noticed that Dick was pulling away from me. I started advancing the throttle and was still falling back. Finally, I had to give it full throttle to keep up. Then, at about 2 o'clock below us and 30 miles ahead, I saw a twin engine bomber too far away to identify. So that was where Dick was heading! I was greatly relieved in a few minutes to see that it was one of our own B-25s. Later we returned to base without incident.

Dick would sometimes make his own personal plane available to the other pilots. I decided that if I were ever flying it and ran into a Jap fighter, I would immediately turn the side with all the flags toward the enemy. He would probably head for home or be too nervous to shoot straight.

One mention should be made about Major Bong and the fate of his famous P-38J. Major Bong declined the common scantily clad female figures that many of the pilots were using for the nose art on their aircraft. Instead, he enlarged a photo of his girlfriend, Marge Vattendahl, and had it placed on his plane, simply called "Marge." On March 23rd, Lt. Tom Malone of the 421st NFS would fly "Marge" for the last time. Lt. Malone was on a weather mission when the loss occurred. In fact, Malone had flown the plane the day before on a similar mission, which turned out to be uneventful. He had commented to the other pilots that most of the people on the field would all line up and look at you when you went out in that plane. He figured that most of them thought Major Bong was going out to find a few more Jap planes to add to his score. On the first mission in Bong's plane he was flying with Lt. Forrester as wingman. During the flight they spotted a Japanese fighter over Wewak. They were at 2,000 feet, and the Japanese fighter was down on the deck heading north. Malone went after the fighter, but could not catch him. Both 421st NFS pilots returned home without incident.

The following day, March 24th, Lt. Malone earned the distinction of losing the beautifully illustrated "Marge." He later wrote of this tragic loss:

> This was to be a two ship mission, and initially Major Bong was scheduled to fly. However, for some reason this was canceled, and I flew with Lt. Roland Forrester, who was also of the 421st. Lt. Forrester and I took off at 0700 for Wewak. Immediately after take-off we encountered heavy overcast and a lot of turbulence. We headed up the valley and climbed to around 30,000 feet, never breaking out of the overcast. After about 50 minutes I started having trouble with the automatic cooler shutters in the left engine. Radio reception and transmission became poor, and I lost contact with Forrester. I was given a base cancellation order and told to return to base. It was not long before the radio failed completely and the left engine started cutting out. The electrical system soon failed, and the engine quit all together. The prop, of course, would not feather with the electric gone, and I was losing altitude. The aircraft went into a spin or tight spiral, and I had difficulty maintaining altitude down to 11,000 feet. I knew the mountains in the area were at 12,000. I made one good attempt to recover the ship, but failed. I knew that I had to bail out. I pulled the emergency hatch release and started out, but the slipstream forced me right back into the cockpit. I then raised my legs on the edge of the seat and pushed into the slipstream. I came out like a cork on a champagne bottle. For an instant I saw the tail section pass over my face. I reached down, and there was the ripcord, which seemed to slide out. The chute snapped open quickly, almost blacking me out. My gun came off about this time, also. I also remember that I encountered snow in the clouds for a short period, then I broke out of the overcast and looked around to see where I was. There was a river below me, and I landed on the east bank, landing on my back. This gave me quite a jolt. I buried my chute as soon as I could. With my jungle kit and dinghy I walked back to the river. I thought that I was just north of Saidor. Inflating my dinghy, I tried to go down the river, but the current was so swift the dinghy capsized. I felt like I was almost beat to death on the boulders, so I ended up walking down the edge of the river. I had lost most of my first aid equipment, and I had been walking down the river for about nine hours when I came to an outpost. I found a Jap flag on a stick and a red cloth arrow pointing up the river. I began to think that I was in enemy territory, so I stopped to rest for only fifteen minutes. I did not see a living person on the whole trip down. About that time my hips were sore and I could hardly walk. When I came out of the high grass on the riverbank near an outpost, a soldier al-

Another 421st NFS P-70 being made ready for the night. ***421st FS***

Sgt. Joe Cox on left with Sgt. Hayes on a squadron P-70. ***421st NFS***

T/Sgt. Jake Loran. ***Loran***

most shot me. He said the only reason he did not was because of my flying jacket and yellow water bag. When I climbed into his foxhole with him he told me the Japs were on the other side of the river. The only reason that I had not gone down that side was because the water was deeper on that side. He also told me that I had walked directly in front of a Jap machine gun. He guessed that the only reason they did not shoot was that they did not want to give away their position. The soldiers there gave me hot coffee and cigarettes. They were glad to have me in their camp, as they did not have a pilot visiting them every day. They sent a message to Saidor that I had arrived. The next day I went down the river on a barge to the Regimental headquarters, about six miles in back of the front lines. The medic there gave me a rub down, and I ate a wonderful roast pork dinner. They fixed me up with a nice hammock hung between two trees, and I slept till 10 AM the next morning. I was transported by barge to Saidor airstrip, where I was picked up by one of our airplanes and taken home. At first Bong was mad as hell about the loss of his plane. Bong said, "That was the best P-38 in the 5th Air Force." I agreed with him, just saying, "Yes, I guess it was!" After things had cooled Bong had a discussion with me. He indicated that he had also had some problems with the plane.

A few days later soldiers of the 32nd Infantry Division found the wreckage of "Marge" at the Bau Plantation, not far from the Yalau Plantation into which Malone had walked. Instinctively, Malone had probably set the aircraft into a stable gliding altitude by retarding the right engine during his effort to bail out. Beginning at about 11,000 feet high, "Marge" descended smoothly until she impacted the ground about fourteen miles away from where Malone bailed out. To this day wreckage of Bong's P-38 can still be found in an overgrown coconut grove where it crashed.

Preparations were being made to return the aircrews to the mission for which they had been trained, night interdiction work. The squadron managed to acquire a few Douglas P-70 aircraft to use in their nightly missions. On February 13th the first P-70 was transferred in from the 418th Night Fighter Squadron, stationed at Dobadura. Another P-70 arrived on February 16th, three more were transferred in on March 10th, and again all transfers came from the 418th NFS. One more P-70 would arrive from Brisbane, Australia, on March 11th. All of these aircraft required extensive maintenance work before they were expected to be ready for operations at Saidor by the end of March.

There was a desire by all of the aircrews that while awaiting the assignment of more aircraft, full advantage could be taken of those on hand. A program of night harassing raids and patrols was soon underway. The squadron, rich in chief resources of personnel ability, just needed the tools to do the job. By this time the Allies had pushed the Japanese so far up the coast of New Guinea that Nadzab was actually well to the rear of the combat zone.

The ever-present non-flying enemy of the 421st NFS, as well as any other squadron then and now, was an inadequate spare parts supply. Aircraft related supplies at Nadzab were essentially non-existent. The P-70s had arrived stripped down, including most of the radio equipment. To correct the serious operational deficiency a number of "raids" were carried out against the Service Depot. Aircraft which had been seriously damaged by enemy fire, or had crashed on the strip, were towed, or otherwise moved to this area, which was enclosed with barbed wire fence and patrolled by troops. T/Sgt. Vincent DelaGardelle, Lt. Blanchard, and others would sneak through the deep Kunai grass, staying downwind on their approach to the depot. Rumor has it that the native guards could smell another man from over a hundred feet away. The bottom strands of barbed wire would be cut so the men could crawl into the nearest aircraft, mostly B-25s and B-24s. Wherever suitable radio gear was located it would be quietly removed and relocated as fast as they could cautiously go without sounding an alarm. It was slim pickens, so to speak, but it helped. A good point among all the bad was that there was by now fewer units at Nadzab, reducing the amount of parts taken from the Depot and other areas. Before long all of the 421st NFS aircraft were equipped so they could at least call the tower. Once the planes had radios installed related problems arose. Radios and most other communication equipment were filled with vacuum tubes, which were extremely fragile and had an extremely high failure rate. The search for replacement tubes was a constant priority within the squadron.

Whenever the 421st NFS called the Base Supply sergeant for replacement vacuum tubes or other parts, the first thing to be asked by Supply is "What unit is this?" When the 421st NFS was mentioned the Sergeant usually hung up the phone. A counter system was worked out here, as well. One man would go in to engage the Supply Sergeant with talk while an accomplice would go to the back of the tent. By the time they returned to the squadron area the helper would be jingling with the spare glass vacuum tubes as Lt. Roady remembers:

Lt. Alexander Kuzmack. ***Bjorum***

Lt. Dave Corts by squadron P-70. ***421st NFS***

Private James Meeks on the left with Sgt. Vincent DelaGardelle. ***Blanchard***

Like many guys we had a difficult time obtaining needed (necessary) electronic items: vacuum tubes, resistors, condensers, generators, variable condensers, and so on. My men had to resort to "requisitioning" from what supply depot was available, plus cannibalizing un-airworthy aircraft for needed parts for not only Blanchard's communication needs, but also our own airborne radar needs. Those fine enlisted men did what was necessary to keep the airborne radar functioning effectively. It was the correct decision to defeat Hitler and Company, but we got the short shaft as far as supplies, not only of electronic equipment, but everything else. In theSouthwest Pacific Theatre, especially the 5th Air Force, those who administered the supply depots seemed to me to have the attitude that every piece of equipment under their control was their personal property, and damned if they were going to let anything go until major forces were brought to bear on them. We night fighters were always considered as illegitimate children of the "real" Air Force, i.e. day fighters, bombers, air rescue, transport, medical evacuation, and so on. We had no Night Fighter Group to assist us. There was plenty of skepticism from on high as to whether or not night fighting in their air was worth it. Alas, we had the best-trained pilots, gunners, radar observers, and ground officer staff, but the overall perception seemed to be that we were sort of bastard offspring of the "real" Air Force, so to acquire things we needed to keep flying was even tougher.

Another case where the temptation of acquiring spare parts turned into an adventure began when Lt. Blanchard was flying into Nadzab one day. He spotted a crashed Douglas A-20 "Havoc" laying half out of the Markham River. Apparently, the plane had either run out of fuel, or had engine problems on final approach, and the pilot had tried to land on a little island in the middle of the river. As it turned out the island was not long enough, and the aircraft came to a halt with the plane fuselage resting in the river at the end of this island. They could still see the tire marks along the length of the island. The top of the canopy was above the water line. The precious radio gear, which was located on a shelf behind the pilot seat, was clearly visible. The thought of a complete SCR-27 radio set free for the taking was very appealing.

Back at Nadzab, Lt. Blanchard talked to T/Sgt. DelaGardelle about the A-20 in the river. They set out down the road between Lae and Nadzab to a point nearest the crash. They then began to chop a path through the jungle with their machetes. After about an hour of fruitless chopping they called it quits. They estimated that they had only made it about forty feet into the jungle with hundreds of feet yet to go. After careful consideration they then came up with a new plan that might work better. Since they were both good swimmers, why not take the easy route down the river? The Markham River runs through Nadzab to the Gulf of Lae. Their plan was to float down the river to the crash sight. Once there they could salvage as much equipment as possible, then continue on down the river to the Gulf of Lae, a forty mile trip. At the Gulf they could hitch a ride aboard a military truck hauling bombs back to Nadzab, at that time known as "The Red Ball Express." The plan sounded very simple. In reality, it was thought out in haste with no thought given to what dangers the river might hold. There was no thought given to the dangers the Natives might pose, which at this time still included headhunters that lived deep in the jungle. Nor did they take into account the crocodiles, which made their homes on the banks of the river. They decided that they would use a life raft and an air mattress to make the trip.

Early the next morning, T/Sgt. DelaGardelle showed up at the river edge with a small life raft with oars and Blanchard arrived with his air mattress. Without sharing their plans with anyone else they pushed out into the river. No one in the squadron saw them leave. At first all was calm and serene, and the morning was relatively cool. About 9:00 AM they rounded a bend in the river and saw a group of native women washing things out in the river. They heard a scream and saw all the women run back into the jungle. They half expected spears and arrows to be coming at them in no time. However, nothing happened as they slowly drifted on by this washing area.

About an hour later they rounded another bend and headed into a long straight stretch of relatively smooth water. Since

Sgt. Bill Gorman in the R/O's position of a P-70. ***421st NFS***

Blanchard had only his hands to navigate with he stayed close to shore. DelaGardelle had the oars, so he stayed out toward the middle of the river. The river began to widen out, and the bottom gradually came up until they were bumping along on the gravelly bottom next to shore. Blanchard was watching DelaGardelle out in front, and even from a little distance he saw the sergeant's eyes go wide. DelaGardelle turned toward Blanchard and pointed at the shore. Blanchard's eyes also bulged when he saw the ten to fifteen crocodiles sunning themselves on the sandy stretch at the river's edge. They figured that since it was about noontime the crocodiles must have been asleep. Both men kept pushing on the river bottom to get some space away from shore. The crocodiles must have been sound sleepers, or they very well could have become lunch.

Soon thereafter they spotted the island and the rudder of the A-20. The wings and elevators were just under the surface. What caught them off guard was the speed of the current near the plane and island. When they hit the swell created by the submerged wing Blanchard was slammed into the vertical stabilizer. By now both men had been knocked from their rafts by the turbulent current and had to swim to the island for much needed rest.

After a bit they decided to try it again, knowing now what to expect. They forded the river on the shallowest side, walked up along the edge of the river, and shoved out on the current again with their rafts. This time they managed to grab hold of the vertical stabilizer and stand up on the tail section. The radio gear was on the deck behind the pilot's seat; all they had to do was get up to the canopy, open it, and all the radio gear would be theirs. Unfortunately, the current again proved to be stronger than the two men, preventing them from reaching the cockpit area. At this point Blanchard and DelaGardelle had both been beaten up enough by the raging current to convince them to call it a day. Both men climbed aboard their makeshift transportation and headed on down the river. Darkness was not far away, and they had some miles to go down river to reach the safety of Lae.

As they approached the delta at the mouth of the river the sun was low on the horizon. At this point the river branched out into many shallow channels, along which Kunai grass growing on the banks made it impossible to see. Keeping to the northern-most channel, they crept along until the water was shallow enough for them to stand. Gathering their belongings, they waded ashore towards what they hoped would be a dock at the port. They came upon an Australian soldier who took them along to his camp nearby. The "Aussie" was assigned to an anti-aircraft battery protecting the Port of Lae. He did mention to them that he would not have gone down that river for a thousand pounds. The Aussies all gathered around, asking all kinds of questions and generally taking in the sight of the two muddy "Yanks." After sharing some time with their Aussie hosts they began to think about getting back to their home. They were told to follow the path out of the Aussie camp area until they reached the Lae to Nadzab road. The trip along the darkened path lasted about an hour before they reached the road. With a ship in port unloading bombs and equipment, Blanchard knew that trucks would be on the road heading for Nadzab. Sure enough, after only a few minutes a GI truck came barreling down the road. They stuck out their thumbs, but the only effect they got was the driver stepping on the gas. Four trucks later they decided to force one of the trucks to pick them up by standing in the road to make one of them stop. In truth, the drivers were scared to death of the trip to Nadzab, due to the fact that there were still Japanese troops in the area. Finally, a driver stopped only a few feet in front of them. Though he did not quite believe their story about how they got there, they really did not care. Both men were upset that they did not get the equipment out of the plane.

They would not be the last to suffer being upset at this particular failed mission. Several others likewise attempted to get to the plane. Lt. John Jones, the Armament Officer, took a crew the hard way, trying to cut through the jungle to the river's edge. They finally made it to the river and built a raft to make their way across the river. About that time someone saw a crocodile, and the raft began to break up in the scramble to get back to shore.

Still one more attempt was made by Larry Neville leading a group trying to get to the plane by rubber boat. Their attempt also failed, so the A-20 remained where it landed. To this day no one ever found out how the plane got there, with the exception of the actual pilot. No one in the 421st NFS ever retrieved the radio equipment, and to all concerned it remained there.

One last note on the supply situation came from T/Sgt. Jake Loran:

> We got involved in a lot of things. For instance, to get lumber, which was a valuable item, we would get a 2 1/2 ton truck from the motor pool and drive about thirty miles over a rickety road to the Port of Lae, on the coast of New Guinea. There at night we would load up or steal a load of large timbers belonging to the Quartermaster's Corps. They had a lot of material of all kinds stored on the beaches where merchant ships

were unloading our war materials, so we swiped a load of hard to get lumber, and we had to be careful the guards would not catch us. This was not being done by the book, but that was how you got a lot of food and supplies for your own outfit. Many times it was dog eat dog. There were no grocery stores or hardware stores around the corner, so you had to do what was necessary.

Loran also remembered that there was a war going on, and that there was a certain grim reality to remind you that the whole thing was life, bordering on death, and the latter could get you at any time.

> Nadzab airbase was huge, with many large and medium bombers operating from it. Many pilots and crewmen were just kids, usually eighteen to about twenty-five years of age. They were new and just from the States, and were rushed through pilot training. As a consequence, there were bound to be a lot of mistakes. We saw a lot of bombers—like B-24s—crash on landing, badly shot up, or on take-off with a full load of fuel and ammunition, killing all on board. The crashes would usually be on the ends of the runway, in the jungle, or tree and bush-like areas. A crash, fire, and explosion would clean out about a city block, with debris, including human parts, everywhere. The Graves Registration people would, as a rule, promptly attempt to collect whatever could be found for burial. One time I was at a crash site, and in a bush nearby I found a left arm from shoulder to the fingers with a high school ring on a finger reading "Pocatello High."

The month of April involved the 421st NFS expanding their operational activities. With the current events in the southwest Pacific, Nadzab was falling farther behind the combat lines all the time. The 421st NFS maintained operations at Nadzab and began to stage some operations out of Saidor, located on the northeastern coast of New Guinea. Thus started a policy of rotating flights of aircraft to Saidor until a larger complement of aircraft should warrant moving a greater percentage of personnel.

On the 5th of April, Major Pharr and Captain Bill Bradley, the Operations Officer, led a detachment consisting of "A" Flight to Saidor. All six P-70 aircraft, aircrews, and maintenance personnel were sent. "A" Flight was made up of the following flight teams: 2nd Lt. Paul R. Zimmer (Pilot) and Lawrence R. Carr (R/O); 2nd Lt. Thomas E. Malone (Pilot) and F/O Thomas J. Glynn (R/O); 2nd Lt. Frank G. Mott (Pilot) and F/O William H. Hartsock (R/O); and 2nd Lt. Albert W. Lockard (Pilot) and F/O Stuart A. Thorton (R/O). Their mission was to fly patrols, and also to bomb and strafe bridges, barges, and road traffic. Major Pharr later returned to Nadzab to look after the main squadron's operations there.

During the morning of April 8th, the 421st NFS suffered their first casualty of the war. Lt. Alexander Kuzmack was killed during a P-38 landing accident at Nadzab. Lt. Carl Bjorum was one of the witnesses:

> Lt. Alexander Kuzmack was out in one of the squadron's P-38s getting in some flight time when he lost his right engine. He lined up the strip, and he was coming in on final approach to make a single-engine landing. During final approach he had his landing gear and flaps down. Just about then a B-24 bomber taxied out in front of him, and he elected to go around for a second try. His airspeed got too low, and he went out about 100 yards beyond the runway. He then gave his good engine full power, and without sufficient airspeed the P-38 would flip on you. Kuzmack's aircraft flipped, and he lost all directional control. He may have been better off reducing power and making a belly landing, but he should not have tried making another pass. His aircraft actually went vertical at about 300 feet, and he crashed his plane straight down into the jungle. In the trees where he hit, he actually only cut down one tree—none of the others were touched.

The loss effected the whole squadron, but they had to pull together and do the job they were trained for.

The detachment at Saidor commenced flying combat missions against Japanese targets in the area. From the time of their arrival "A" Flight took advantage of the full moon period, instituting a series of night bombing and harassing raids, and flew patrols on occasions that the weather permitted. Enemy activity was negligible, and only one attempted interception took place. Lt. Forrester was airborne during a Japanese attack and was vectored on an enemy bomber. However, the range to the bomber was too far, and after a short pursuit he was ordered to return.

Another view of the Seder dinner. ***Goldstein***

There were numerous successful bombing and strafing attacks launched by the 421st NFS that resulted in damage to enemy installations. On April 15th Lt. Forrester was airborne with Lt. Malone on an early morning strafing mission up to Bunabun Harbor. They each dropped a 250-lb. bomb in an effort to knock out a bridge that appeared to have a lot of traffic. Malone's bomb did not go off, and no damage from Forrester's bomb was noted. Flying down the coast to the village of Mandang, Lt. Malone made a strafing pass on two barges that were near the shore, while Forrester made a run on a large building. Again no damage was noted, but the Japanese troops began to fire back with their machine guns and both pilots exited the area. Neither aircraft suffered any hits.

On April 20th Malone flew two missions to Malas Point and Sarang Harbor. Over the target he dropped a total of twelve 250 lb. bombs on bridges at both targets, causing some damage, but not completely destroying either bridge. On the same mission Malone strafed a number of machine gun positions along the coast at Palas Point, and again the Japanese returned fire. On April 22nd Malone and Forrester were again teamed up on a morning mission south of Hansa Bay. They caught two barges making for the beach in the harbor. Malone dove on them, strafed, and dropped four 250-lb. bombs on the beach just in front of the barges. Forrester followed with three more passes, bombing and strafing the barges and causing both to catch on fire. Between the two pilots they expended over 2,000 rounds of ammunition and about a ton of bombs. On the way home they strafed a couple of villages with the forty or fifty rounds that they had left.

Malone and Forrester were of course not alone in the air. Major Pharr was also doing his part to deliver the message to the Japanese that the 421st NFS was there to make an impact in the war. On April 17th he demolished a bridge just north of Palas Point with a salvo of four 250-lb. bombs:

> I took off one morning fully loaded and headed for the Japanese occupied area. It was a matter of looking for a target of opportunity, with no real idea of what that might be. Pretty soon a target appeared; a small bridge. I circled around to see if there were any guns defending the site and to get a better idea of the size of the bridge. Then I decided to make a high speed pass and drop all four bombs in salvo. This was done, and as I pulled up and looked back over my shoulder, to my surprise the bridge had completely disappeared. In making the dive at the bridge, I had decided to get as close to the target as possible. I was so intent and determined that I went too low. Only by pulling back on the wheel with all my strength did I manage to miss some tall palm trees near the bridge.

Of course, not all the missions contributed directly to the 421st NFS war effort. A case in point is Lt. Al Lockhard and his attacks on small boats. On April 18th, with nothing significant to attack, Lockhard bore down on a lone man in a rowboat, who had just evacuated a barge, with all guns blazing. When Lockhard turned for another pass, neither the Japanese nor his rowboat were to be seen. For some time the squadron scoreboard carried a small notation, "Lockhard, one rowboat, confirmed." Carl Bjorum got to talk to Lockhard after his "famous" mission:

> I was sitting in on Al Lockhard's debrief after this mission. He mentioned one Jap in a rowboat trying to get from one island to another. He said the rowboat was half out of the water, because the Jap was rowing so fast. I said to him, "Al, you didn't?" Al said, "Yes, BJ, I did! There was nothing left but splinters." That was after he made his firing pass.

On another mission Al Lockhard went after another rowboat with even more firepower. The gunner on the bottom of the P-70 was watching the attack first hand. The 421st NFS rigged their P-70s with two spare 50. Caliber guns. One was mounted in the R/O's compartment firing up, and the other was in a tub in the bottom of the fuselage pointing down and back.

In the final mission report, it was noted that Lt. Lockhard and crew went on a mission to strafe and bomb targets up the coast near Saidor. About 100 miles up the coast Lockhard spotted a Japanese barge and started his attack run on the target. Coming in on the deck he passed over a small island, and rowing toward it was a Japanese soldier in a rowboat. Lockhard flew directly over him as he headed for the barge. The mountains in that area are very steep and plunge from 14,000 feet right down to the ocean. To strafe and bomb a target in those conditions was not an easy thing to do. Lockhard dropped one of his two wing bombs at the target, while the crew strafed with their machine guns. They were not sure if they hit anything, but they did scare up a large number of birds, many of whom were found in the engine nacelles after the mission. They continued on and left the target area, flying back over the water and still at about 500 feet. The soldier in his boat was rowing like mad to make it to the little island. Seeing this, Lockhard found a use for his final bomb and attempted to hit the rowboat. Lockhard dropped the bomb too soon and at too low an altitude. The bomb splashed into the water and skipped. It then sailed right over the boat and was following the P-70. The bomb ended up blowing up almost right under the plane. Lockhard asked the crew over the intercom if he had got the boat, but thanks to a time delay set in the bomb's fusing, it most likely saved the Japanese soldier's life and almost got Lockhard and crew.

Meanwhile, back at Nadzab, weather reconnaissance flights were resumed by the squadron on April 8th and continued until they were totally abolished on April 25th. For a short period of

Lt. Elston Roady in his tent at Nadzab. ***Roady***

time, between the 21st and 25th, the squadron was flying two weather flights a day. "C" Flight, who accomplished most of these missions, consisted of the following teams: 2nd Lt. William B. Robbins (Pilot) and F/O Edgar Crawford (R/O); 2nd Lt. David J. Pahlka (Pilot) and F/O Ralph V. Hulsey (R/O); and 2nd Lt. William H. Gill (Pilot) and F/O Robert R. Clodfelter (R/O).

Regardless of the location, these men of the 421st NFS, who were a long way from the States and home, were able to work out a lot of things that were a bit "unheard" of in the jungles of New Guinea. One example of this was when M/Sgt. Herbert Goldstein was asked about organizing a Jewish "Seder" for the Passover celebration:

> Sometime prior to the Passover season, the Jewish Chaplain approached my desk in our makeshift Headquarters tent and asked me to help him solve a problem regarding having a Passover "Seder." A ceremonial dinner held on the first or first two nights of Passover, is a Jewish festival that commemorates the Exodus of the Israelites from Egypt. In Christian observations it is referred to as the Last Supper, which Christ attended. I told him that it was not going to be an easy task, especially since we were in the jungle, and my outfit, the 421st, had only about ten Jewish soldiers. We were in the 5th Air Force, and it was spread all over the area and its islands, as well. It seemed next to impossible to even contemplate having one. The Chaplain had just arrived from the States and was not familiar with the New Guinea war zone. He said he needed someone who could assume the responsibility of getting a Seder started, as he had promised the men that he would, so he asked me for help. I happened to have come from a pioneer Jewish family from Chicago's West Side. I promised the Chaplain that I would do my best to get it done.
>
> The Chaplain assumed the duty of trying to get the wine, Matzoth (unleavened bread eaten by the Israelites), and whatever else he could get from the Army Service of Supplies. He found out that there was very little around to properly run a Seder. The last one the Chaplain did was at Camp Kilmer, New Jersey, during the past year, where about 400 people turned up. It was hard to figure out how many men we could round up so that we would have enough food for all of them. Finally, we estimated that at the most we would have around 500. As you will see later, we were in fact surprised by the attendance. Little did we know that half the men that came were not even of Jewish faith.
>
> A place had to be found for it, and fortunately there was a nearby hospital that had a large mess area, which we could enlarge by adding a few extra tents and tables to seat the men that we anticipated coming. The Commanding Officer, Major Harris Fischbein of San Francisco, gave us the okay to use his mess hall.
>
> Getting and preparing the food was not going to be an easy task. I solved the problem, for fortunately the 421st had cooks from New York who even knew how to make Army Bully Beef taste good. They were Stein, Greenberg, and a few others that volunteered. We also had a man named William Lee, who formally worked in New York's China Town and was an excellent baker. The task of setting up the mess halls and serving food was left to Sgt. Ruby Kaplan, also of New York. He in turn found a number of men to help him out. The night before the dinner things got underway.
>
> The day finally arrived, and fortunately there were no air raids. The cooks and their helpers began to prepare the food. Fresh vegetables were secured from the gardens of the local natives through the help of Captain Michael Ford of the Australian Army. The Jewish community in Townsville, Australia, promised their help also. They contributed Matzoth and wine, and also a lot of baked delicacies. An Air Force supply plane that was picking up war supplies flew these in. They were a great help, and we were grateful to all for their generosity.
>
> The Seder was scheduled to begin at 7:00, but the men began to arrive as early as 6:00. By start time there was not enough seating for all the men, and many had to stand or sit on the ground. Some came by plane directly from missions, some by jeep, trucks, and many on foot through the jungle paths. The mess hall was truly crowded; about a thousand men had been assembled for the Seder.
>
> S/Sgt. Robert Blumstein, of the Bronx in New York, was our Cantor (one who chants prayer). We understood that he came from a family of Cantors, so we were lucky to have him. He was an aerial gunner, and that day he had participated in his 40th mission. He had a strong vibrant voice, and it resounded through the mess hall and brought the men into proper spirit and frame of mind for the Seder. An awe spread over the men, for that was the same Kiddish (blessing of the wine) that many had heard from their own homes in years gone by. They had assembled in the jungles of New Guinea to observe the Passover. They were reminded that their ancestors had also observed the Passover through the ages. Tears were shed from many an eye, as thoughts turned to loved ones back home. Barney Faust of the Australian Army asked the four questions. Four questions are asked at the beginning of the Seder, asking why the Seder is being held. The meal began and was served sparingly, as there was not enough to go around. But we made sure that

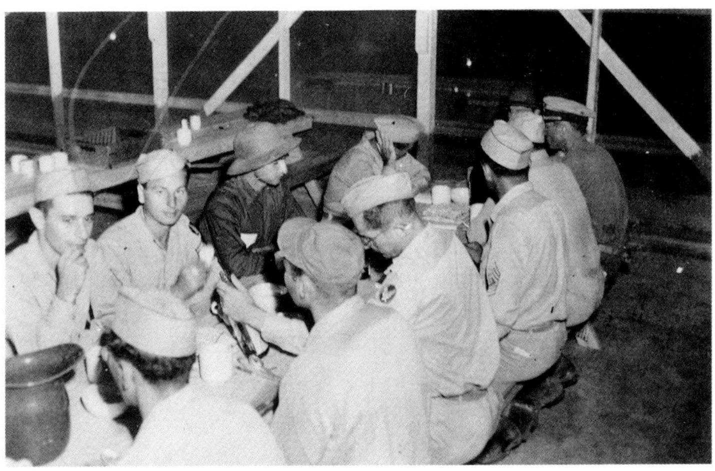

Personnel sitting down to the Seder dinner at the hospital mess hall. *Goldstein*

all got a taste of Matzoth, Kugal, and some wine. Fortunately, there were a lot of baked goodies to go around.

The base chaplain, William Sessions of Kearney, Nebraska, spoke on behalf of the large number of Christian soldiers and other Chaplains that were present. There were also a lot of war correspondents on hand from hometown papers. Just before we symbolically opened the door of Elijah, the Eternal Harbringer of good tidings, a refugee from Hitler's Europe, now in the U.S. Armed Forces, spoke and reminded us how fortunate we were to be able to participate in a Seder as free men in the armies of the American and Australian democracies, while our brethren were so cruelly persecuted in Europe. The Seder was completed by singing traditional Passover melodies, and closed with the singing of the Star Spangled Banner, our national anthem.

The squadron members finally solved the squadron's water problem. A pipeline was connected through the jungle with the main pipe of the 43rd Bomb Group, and as the water began to pour into the tanks, the unit began an era of having, for the first time, an adequate water supply.

Another thing that was established was continued training for the pilots and the R/Os. Lt. Elston Roady helped in the training of the Radar Observers. Through training of this kind the men learned how to properly operate their radar sets at Nadzab in the P-70s. Most of the time he would stand behind the R/O without a parachute on, which given the limited space in the P-70 is understandable. Communications between crew were done via throat mike and headsets. Roady would help the R/Os go over the right way to adjust the knobs and to correctly interpret the CRT screens on PPI (Plane Position Indicator) and their horizontal positions. One of the 421st NFS maintenance people, Sgt. Donald Knapp of Sauk Center, Minnesota, developed a device which made it possible for them to insure a constant signal to the airborne radar, which he transmitted during flights. Sgt. Knapp was in fact recommended for a medal for his development.

All through April the P-70s and P-38s flew missions whenever they could. The P-38 aircraft used by the squadron would finally be retired by the end of April, and the P-70 operations continued. Most of the missions were again routine, but occasionally one would come back with an interesting story to tell. On one such mission a 421st gunner had the following account of how their P-70 came back with a shot-up tail section:

> The area we were strafing was on the side of a steep mountain range that ran along the north coast of New Guinea. This sometimes caused us to be in some weird positions in order to strafe the ground. On this mission I was flying as the gunner with Lt. William Gill and his R/O, F/O Robert Clodfelter. In the middle of one of our passes I heard Clodfelter say in a very calm voice over the intercom, "Gill, you had better straighten her up and fly right." Gill, always wary of what prank Clodfelter was capable of, came back with "What the hell did you do now?" Clodfelter, in a very calm voice said, "I think I shot the rudder off." Gill immediately headed out to sea in a straight and level position. I scrambled out of the back end and got up beside Clodfelter in the open cockpit. He just grinned and pointed at the rudder. The rudder was vibrating in the wind because he had shot the top hinge on the rudder completely away. Only the bottom hinge was keeping the rudder on the plane. Gill was a good pilot, so the plane got home okay. All the turns were made by aileron only. Clodfelter always had that calm voice in talking to Gill when there was a problem. So, whenever Clodfelter would say anything in that manner, Gill would really start to worry.

The first of May was the 421st Night Fighter Squadron's first birthday. It had been one year since the activation of the unit back in Florida, which to some of the members already felt like a lifetime ago. The day was marked by a formation of all squadron members, at which some promotions were announced and medals were handed out. Most of these given were Good Conduct medals. That evening there was a party for the men in the recreation hall. Six Red Cross workers served light refreshments to the men and gave everyone a much-needed break from the daily routine.

One of the missions picked up by the 421st NFS was working in close coordination with Navy PT boats. Maintaining VHF con-

F/O Robert Clodfelter on left with Lt. William Gill. *421st NFS*

tact, attacks were made on coastal installations, with probable destruction of enemy searchlights and gun positions. This meeting began after a meeting between Lt. Howard Blanchard and Commander Davis of the 24th PT Boat Squadron.

During the conversation with Blanchard, Commander Davis made some disparaging remarks about the 5th Air Force's combat ability. He had recently lost a PT Boat near Point Aitape a few weeks back, and nearly lost another from the same shore battery, even though he had sent the location of the Japanese forces to the 5th Air Force to have it bombed. No action was ever taken by the Air Corps to destroy these targets, and it had taken its toll on the Navy. In defense of the Air Force, Blanchard pointed out that when you flew over the dense jungle you could not really see any targets, and furthermore, unless you have a direct hit, or one that was very close, there would be no real damage to the target.

There was an opportunity here for the 421st NFS to help the PTs. Blanchard asked him what their electrical power capability was, and he said that they had 28 volts DC. Since this was the same as they were using in the aircraft, Blanchard suggested that an SCR-522 radio and an AN-104 antenna be installed on their boats. When the boats were out on a mission they could arrange for one of the squadron's aircraft to be patrolling in that area at the same time. The normal "FRAG" (Fragment) Orders only directed the 421st NFS to keep two aircraft on patrol in the area from 6:00 at night to 6:00 in the morning. This schedule, with the nightly searches for "targets of opportunity" was not enough to keep the 421st NFS crews satisfied. Most of the men that made up the aircrews at that time were a pretty "Gung-ho" group.

After getting permission from Major Pharr the radios and antennas were installed and the final arrangements were made between the squadron and the PT drivers. Blanchard went out on the first such mission; after all, he was the Communications Officer and knew the Grid Authentication Codes used for security by the U.S. Forces at that time. The Commander felt that if Blanchard was crazy enough, he was welcome along for the ride. Out of this it was hoped that the pilots would be able to see the gun flashes and drop their bombs on the enemy.

At 5:00 in the afternoon the following day the PT left Saidor in the company of another. PT boats usually worked in pairs as they went up the coast. The Allies had been pushing the enemy back up the coast, and the Japanese 18th Army was in full retreat up the New Guinea coast. With the mountain range along the coast of New Guinea being steep, there were very few roads. The Japanese were using flat bottom barges with a low draft to retreat up the coast, staying very close to shore. This gave them some protection from air attacks by being hidden by the giant trees hanging out over the water. They also had the aforementioned advantage of hidden coastal guns that gave them some protection from sea-born attacks, such as PT boats.

Lt. Richardson, a 26-year-old, was in command of the PT boat and crew that Blanchard would join for the mission. He had the boats about three hundred feet off shore as they went up the coast. It was getting dark, but each PT had a small search radar used to pick up enemy targets on the water. They continued on until they reached the Bogia Bay area, which was about three hundred miles from Saidor, and it was a little after midnight.

Everyone on the PT's deck could see the side of the mountain with hundreds of Japanese signal lights flashing and all around campfires going. There they were, three hundred miles from their own troops and just off shore of what looked like an entire Japanese Army. The PTs were shut down to a low idle, and one boat moved on up the bay and around Manam Island. Blanchard's boat just chugged along the shore looking for enemy boats.

The moon soon came up and highlighted the entire side of the mountain. Along the roads scores of trucks and Japanese soldiers were moving along the shore. It was a wonder that the Japanese could not see the silhouette of the PT boat. Blanchard mentioned this to Lt. Richardson, and he nodded in agreement. He swung the boat around with the stern towards the shore. They had mounted a .75 mm cannon on the stern, which they had stolen from a wrecked B-25 bomber. Richardson remarked that it was time to let them know that they were there. As one of the crewmen was lifting a shell into the gun, the whole shore came alive. Richardson yelled at the crewman not to fire and hit the throttles, heading out to sea at top speed. The crewman dropped the shell, leaped up on the stern, and opened a valve near a tank that was sitting there. The tank released a dense could of white smoke. The first salvo of shells fired by the Japanese all went off near the boat, but somehow they all missed. The Japanese had spotted the second boat coming around the shore and fired their next salvo at it. The Japanese kept firing as the boats went out to sea. Blanchard had knelt down behind a panel, scared, since he felt that it would offer at least some protection. Lt. Richardson soon informed him, however, that the panel was only plywood.

The boats arrived back at Saidor around 6:00 AM, and they were met at the dock by a number of 421st NFS members eager to hear all about the mission. When they were told about the good meals the Navy guys had all of them wanted to go out on the next mission.

It was not too long before a number of men were joining the Navy crews on these missions. Sgt. Delagardelle was with a PT boat that spotted some smoke coming up from one of the small islands. Both PTs beached, and the men went to investigate. They found some small shacks and a camp that appeared to be completely empty. One shack seemed to be a post office for the Japanese troops. There was a lot of envelopes and rice writing paper, along with stacks of postcards. The campfire was still burning, but in a search of the general area no one was found. Under the circumstances, this was a very risky thing to do. The PT boats had a small group of about a dozen men with assorted weapons. A well-armed squad of Japanese troops could have ended their mission for good. The rest of the mission was un-eventful, and the boats returned to base.

Many members of the 421st NFS managed to go along with the PT boats and had other tales to tell about their experiences, such as the ride Lt. Blanchard went on:

> Despite the dangers, most men wanted to go on the missions because of the food. After a long discussion with my section chief about letting men go on the missions, I suggested

that those men who were in the worst shape, due to illness and lack of food, should be allowed to go first. As anyone who spent a few years in New Guinea knows, the men who were over 30 years of age were harder hit than the 18 or 19 year olds. I had one man who was 38, Corporal Haydon Hankins. He had false teeth and was slowly deteriorating. How he got in the Army I will never know. We let him go on a mission first. The next morning I went down to pick him up at the dock. He staggered off the boat, his face a pale green. He stammered to me that they could have their food, he was not going on any more PT boat missions. It turned out that the PTs had picked up four Japanese barges on their radar. The PTs peeled off and ran between the barges, firing out of both sides, and of course the barges were firing back. The gunfire was so severe that Corporal Hankins lost an eardrum and consequently was awarded the Purple Heart. This gave him an extra five points towards going home, which made him happy in a miserable way.

Larry Neville also got to go for a trip:

One of the PT boat missions I went on with the Navy used four boats. They were after barges that the Japanese would use to move their supplies. We went into Hayfield Harbor, all the boats cut their mufflers, and three of the boats backed into the harbor to wait. The other boat went down the shore a ways. The Navy guys spotted some barges by the shore and began to fire their deck guns. A few minutes later the Japanese began to fire back. The PT I was on kicked on their motor with the others to get out of there. The other boats also started spreading smoke to hide them, but for some reason my boat's tank would not work. We all made it back home safe.

Pilots, too, were not left out, as Lt. Malone recounts:

They would draw names of the pilots out of a hat to pick two men who would go on a mission with a PT boat. I happened to be one of the lucky ones. I thought it might be a nice trip, and maybe I would see some action. They operated out of Dreger Harbor. We went to the PT boat base that was one mile south of the strip. We got orders and went aboard PT boat #338. At 0900 we met Lt. JG. Gleason. He told us that we were to pull out in fifteen minutes from Saidor. The armament on the boat was surprising. This boat had one 37 mm, two 20 mm cannons, and eight .50 caliber guns. There were also four 2,000 lb. tin fish (torpedoes) on board. We ran through the rain all the way up to Saidor, got there around 1330, and stayed until 1830. We pulled behind two other boats and went out into the harbor, tested the guns, and started up the coast. The two boats ahead of us caught a Jap barge about 30 miles north of Saidor. They blew it out of the water with their machine guns, which you could see. We moved up north of Madang and went in about 1/4 of a mile off the beach. We could actually see Japs lighting cigarettes on the shore. We went back down to Madang harbor and right into the bay. We did not see any barges.

Lt. William R. Robbins and Rosie. ***421st NFS***

As far as the original purpose of these missions, which was protecting the PT boats from shore threats, there was only one case documented. On May 5th Lt. Al Lockhard flew a cover for the PT boats over Hansa Bay. Heavy fire was concentrated on a PT boat at the southwest end of Manam Island. During the mission two searchlights, one located 1/2 mile north of Awa Point and the other northwest of a native village, were illuminated when the PT boat opened fire at the shore. The PT boat started its engine with the mufflers open. The fire, plus the sound of the PT boat's motors brought the searchlights into play, followed by a barrage from three shore batteries. At this time air-to-ground contact had been made between Lockhard and the boat. Lt. Lockhard dove at the first searchlight position and strafed it with about 200 rounds of .50 caliber ammunition. Lockhard then made a quick turn and went after the other searchlight, where he dropped two bombs nearby. Lockhard and his crew noted no results, but both lights went out and were not seen again. No anti-aircraft was fired at the aircraft when they attacked, or when it left the target area. The PT Boat was not harmed and returned to base okay.

On another mission, Lt. Robbins, the "C" Flight Commander, was hit by light anti-aircraft fire as he attacked a suspected gun battery. However, no serious damage was caused, and the ship returned to base sporting nine holes in its tail surfaces. The results of his attack on the gun battery were not known.

In all, the bombing missions had mixed results, and most of the time the results were not observed. That and another important fact about the night fighter crews was later pointed out by Carl Bjorum:

The P-70 was an excellent airplane for low level bombing, but there was no instruction or bombing practice in the Night Fighter training program that the 421st pilots went through. We were not trained in that particular skill, and the results demonstrated that fact.

The teamwork between the 421st NFS pilots and PT boats would be used throughout the war, and as time went on the methods and dangers would increase for the boats and aircraft.

6

A Time of Changes: Wakde & Owi

With the conclusion of April and the beginning of May, decisions were being made to bring about changes for the 421st Night Fighter Squadron. Operations were still being flown out of Nadzab; orders, however, were soon received that a part of the squadron would be moved to Wakde Island around May 28th. Wakde was just off the coast of New Guinea, about 150 miles northwest of Nadzab. Four of the squadron's P-70s were to be transferred to Wakde to intercept incoming Japanese bombers that had been bombing the Allied bases in that area during the night. The Japanese planes came from Noomfor, Biak, and the Halmaheras, which the Japanese still controlled. At times they were quite accurate, and in the case of one raid on Wadke they managed to damage or destroy a number of aircraft. In addition, many personnel had lost their lives in these attacks. Wakde itself was an island made up of white coral, and the only refuge from the bombing was a series of caves near the ocean.

On April 21st Major Pharr received orders and was sent down to Brisbane, Australia, to see about four new P-61 "Black Widow" aircraft that had just arrived from the States. These would be the first P-61s assigned to the 421st NFS. A couple days after this Sergeant Bill Gorman got called into Headquarters:

A pilot's view of Wakde's landing strip. ***421st NFS***

> I was told to get ready to go to Australia the next day. I was not told where I was going, nor the reason for going. The next day, about fifteen of us boarded a C-47 transport and flew for hours to get to Brisbane, Australia. An Air Force Depot was there, and a brand new type of airplane had just arrived by transport. It was the P-61 "Black Widow" night fighter. None of us had ever seen one before. Anyway, we put the wings on them, put the engines on them, hung the props, and got these birds built. Of course, our pilots had never seen one, either, so it was quite exciting to go up in a plane on its maiden flight with a pilot who had never flown one before. Now, I know foolish boys are best to have in the service. We put four of them together and got pretty good at flying and maintaining them, and finding out what made them tick.

When the P-61s began flying, aircrews were sent down to check out in the new aircraft. At this time John Myers, Northrop's Chief Test Pilot in the P-61 program, arrived with Scott Johnson, Northrop's Service Expert and Maintenance instructor. When they arrived they found that the 421st NS personnel had not only assembled the aircraft, but were actually flying it. All this without any factory assistance and almost no technical data to go by. John Myers would later say of the 421st NFS crews:

> It is forever to the credit of men of the service squadrons that they had both the will and the ingenuity to do this. And it's as much credit to the boys, who got in and flew the ships without even an instructor's book. Naturally, there were some misunderstandings all around, and in most cases they were not to get the most out of the ship. It did not take long to iron out these minor difficulties, and the boys went for the Widow in a big way.

The P-61 would bring about great changes in the 421st NFS, both in the attitude of the squadron, and of course their fighting ability. Changes unforeseen by anyone in the squadron would also have a deep impact on the personnel of the unit. While in Brisbane, for reasons still not completely known, Major Walter Pharr suffered a mental collapse and was promptly hospitalized. It was reported to the squadron that his condition was serious and that he would not return. On May 15th, 5th Fighter Command relieved

Captain Bill Bradley beside the nose art of his P-61A #42-5521. ***421st NFS***

Major Pharr as the 421st NFS Commander. Major Pharr had commanded the squadron since its activation in May 1943. Squadron personnel would later say that he had worked hard and given a lot of himself to build the organization. The squadron as a whole keenly felt the loss of Major Pharr, but did not let it hamper the work that still had to be done.

Captain William T. Bradley, the squadron Operations Officer, assumed command of the 421st NFS following the release of Major Pharr. 1st Lt. Paul Zimmer was appointed the Operations Officer, and 1st Lt. Tom Malone became the new commander of "A" Flight.

On May 16th a plan came out of 5th Fighter Command for the possible use of Hollandia as a base for the 421st NFS. However, the newly captured strips were not yet equipped to handle night fighter operations. Captain Bradley left Nadzab with both "A" and "B" Flights and a total of forty-five officers and enlisted men to check out Hollandia. Upon reaching the field and seeing for themselves the conditions there, the group was forced to return to Nadzab on the 18th. Hollandia was not set up in any way to handle the night operations of the 421st NFS.

On May 28th, as scheduled, four P-70s took off for the flight to Wakde to stand alert. Captain Bradley, Lt. Malone, Lt. Mott, and Lt. Bjorum were the assigned pilots, along with their R/Os and necessary maintenance personnel. Upon their arrival it was obvious to all those concerned that they would be there for a while.

With the coming of June the 421st NFS would finally rid themselves of their old P-70s and complete the transfer over to the P-61 Black Widow. The first three P-61s arrived at Nadzab from Australia on June 1st. The fourth aircraft had a bit of a mishap on the way and would be delayed. Lt. Paul Zimmer was flying the fourth P-61 back to Nadzab with Bill Gorman as a passenger. Gorman was riding in the back compartment, which was the R/O's position on the P-61. Gorman had brought two puppies named Fertile Myrtle and

Lt. Paul Zimmer's P-61 "Chris Couldn't Wait" at Wakde. ***421st NFS***

Left to right are: Charles Lindbergh; Col. Guthrie; and John Myers at Mt. Cyclops. ***Myers***

Sterile Gerald along for the ride. Lt. Zimmer made a stop at Rock Hampton, Australia, and made a landing on the grass strip located there. Near the strip there were some good-sized boulders, and the plane hit one during the landing roll with its nose gear, which collapsed. The plane came to a grinding stop, and some boxed supplies on the plane fell and landed on the two puppies, killing both instantly. Neither Zimmer or Gorman were hurt, but the plane was going to need some work to get it back into flying condition. Lt. Zimmer caught another plane and went back to Nadzab, leaving Gorman alone with only a small toolbox. In looking over the situation, Gorman, armed with few tools and a plane on its nose, did not have a bright outlook. Gorman spent his time there in a small hotel sponsored by the Australian Comfort Fund—their version of the American Red Cross. He spent ten days there, and then received instructions to head back to Nadzab. He hitched a ride on a C-54 transport to Port Moresby, New Guinea, and a B-24 bomber the rest of the way. A full repair crew was later sent down, and the P-61 was lifted and repaired. The plane was flown into Nadzab a short time later.

John Myers, who had been in Australia, went on to New Guinea and then to Wadke Island to demonstrate the ability of the P-61 to the rest of the 421st NFS pilots. As at previous bases, the Widow's ability to turn inside any aircraft, its single engine performance, and short take-off and landing capability won the confidence of the on-looking flyers. Col. William Odell, a night fighter commander, would later recall the feelings that pilots had about the P-61:

> At last the USAAF had the ideal night fighter. The first of its kind, the P-61 was designed with a single purpose in mind, making it the most powerful and deadliest fighter plane ever produced. It became the prototype of a new species of aircraft built around radar. Predecessor planes had been retrofitted with radar as an accessory.

The pilots and R/Os immediately set out to get more transition time in the new ships, and flying was pushed to the maximum daily. Two more P-61s arrived on June 8th, and three more went to Wadke that same date. Lt. Zimmer, Malone, and Forrester flew these planes up, and on the night of the 8th, Lt. Forrester and his R/O, Lt. McQuire, flew the first 421st NFS P-61 combat mission. They flew a standard patrol mission and made no contacts. They returned to base without incident.

John Myers was still on New Guinea demonstrating the P-61 to the 421st NFS, while Charles Lindbergh, of "Spirit of St. Louis" fame, was with a P-38 day fighter squadron. He was teaching them to stretch out their fuel while on combat missions. Captain Bill Bradley just happened to know Lindbergh and sent an invitation invit-

Natives standing around 421st NFS P-61 at Mt. Cyclops. ***421st NFS***

Left to right are: Lt. Isadore Nachman; Sgt. Mike Hancher; Sgt. George Schwedler; Sgt. Aurthur Hagen; Sgt. Alto Munn; and F/O Daniel McGuire at Wakde Island, June 1944. ***Stevens***

Left to right are: Pfc. Wade Mitchem; Sgt. James Oxley; Sgt. William Powers; and Pfc. Emanuel Lesowsky. Taken at Wakde Island, June 1944. ***Stevens***

ing him over to the 421st NFS. With the combined efforts of Bradley and John Myers, Lindbergh was soon taught the ways of the P-61. On one of his flights Bill Gorman was again the passenger, and again he was lucky:

> Taxiing out on the runway, we met a B-25 coming in and had to pull to the shoulder of the taxiway. I noticed that we stirred up quite a bit of dust and rocks, but did not pay too much attention to it. We took off, and he flew straight and level while he got the feeling for the plane. After a while, Lindbergh told me to buckle in good, and we would see what this new-fangled airplane would do. For the next half-hour, he put the P-61 through maneuvers that it was not designed to do. He did everything that was ever been done to a fighter plane and then some. Then he cut off the right engine and feathered the prop. We were flying around on one engine, and that was the side where we had seen the dust fly as we were taxiing out. We did not realize it at the time, but each of the four blades of the prop were bent back about twelve inches from the end. The rocks that we hit did more than we realized, and we were flying in a very precarious position. When we landed and cut the engines, we noticed what had happened and nearly went into shock.

A few days later John Myers, Lindbergh, and Colonel Guthrie took off for Mt. Hagen, in the heart of the Owen Stanley Mountains. 5th Fighter Command insisted that another 421st NFS aircraft fly with Myers on this trip. The landing strip that they were heading for was nothing more than a short grass strip, approximately 2,800 feet long, and at an altitude of 6,500 feet. The 421st NFS pilot, however, landed too far down the runway, running his fighter right off the end. It had been raining there just before their arrival, and the P-61 came to rest in some deep mud. Fortunately, with no equipment available to help, John Myers got the help of a group of natives, who pulled the plane out. Myers later rewarded the tribal leaders for their help with a flight in the P-61.

Around the 8th, Lt. Zimmer had returned to Nadzab from Wadke to supervise the remainder of the transition flying. A sixth P-61 had just arrived for the 421st NFS, and more were on the way. On June 11th orders were received by the squadron's ground echelon to pack up and move by water to a secret destination. The squadron equip-

Left to right are: Pvt. Robert Wessig; Pvt. Earl Bogart; Pfc. Richard Scoles; and Sgt. Harold Ernst ready to go to work on Owi Island. ***421st NFS***

The first P-61 arrives at Owi Island making a pass up the runway. ***421st NFS***

Clifford Grider on left, along with Luther Meadows man the jeep-powered water pump at Owi. ***421st NFS***

Natives on Owi, which in some cases were half-Chinese. They all lived on the mainland and came over to the islands in canoes. ***421st NFS***

ment was transported down to Lae and then loaded aboard the U.S.S. *Thomas Nelson*, a converted Dutch freighter. The ground echelon, under the command of Executive Officer Captain Townsend, moved that afternoon from the camp at Nadzab into the Lae staging area. After remaining at the staging area until the 13th, the squadron boarded the transport at 5:00 that afternoon, but the ship remained in anchor overnight in the harbor. One hundred and twenty-six men were included in the ground echelon, including the officers; Captains Townsend and Govoni, and Lieutenants Buchanan, Pitzer, Wilson, and Eynon.

The transport finally sailed out of Lae at 3:00 in the morning on the 14th. Officers and several non-commissioned officers were assigned auxiliary cabins on the deck, whereas there was a space in hold number five between decks for the remaining men. Many men preferred to set up makeshift quarters on deck, using trucks and other vehicles that were parked topside. This resulted in a number of ingenious shelters and lean tos that provided comfortable shelter and relief from the heat in the lower hold. The squadron mess was also set up on deck, and the mess personnel did their best to provide some good meals. Despite the discomforts and lack of facilities, most enjoyed the trip thoroughly, and it served as a needed rest after their recent exertions. There were other reports from men that life below deck, as with the *Sea Pike*, was unhealthy, but none of those were ever substantiated. One enlisted man stated with a grin that they had to expand the toilet facilities to include a long wooden trough. The whole thing was around 30 or 40 feet long, and slightly elevated at one end with a constant flow of sea water being pumped through a hose on the upper end, so as to float everything down the trough and into the ocean. On one side a man could sit and extend his rear end into the trough. This was the ultimate in an outside toilet. It is estimated that ten to twelve guys could be lined up in one sitting.

Whatever the conditions on the ship may have been, it was in fact a pretty short stay. The ship arrived at Finschafen at 8:00 in the morning on the 14th. Here, a convoy and escort assembled, and the whole group sailed at 6:30 that evening. The convoy would arrive at Humbolt Bay, Hollandia, on June 17th and drop anchor. Though not known by the men at the time, the good ship *Thomas Nelson* was to remain in the harbor at Hollandia until June 30th. The ground echelon settled down for its wait on the water.

In the meantime, at Wakde the squadron's detachment continued with normal operations, both flying patrols and intercepts. Not forgotten by the Japanese, enemy raiders were now a nightly occurrence, making the caves and few foxholes on the island receive considerable attention. On the night of June 5th an enemy raid consisting of "Betty" bombers flying at about 17,000 to 18,000 feet bombed and demolished the squadron's camp. Enemy bombs also landed in a nearby bomb dump, and several Army bombers were destroyed by the resulting explosions. Miraculously, two 421st NFS P-70s received slight damage from fragments, and tents and equipment were blown away, but no one was seriously hurt. A number of squadron members were treated for minor injuries and nothing more. Lt. Preston Wilson was treated for hemorrhages of the inner ears, while Sgt. Wilfred M. Smith and Lt. Dorrie Jones were hit by schrapnel. Sgt. Lewis Thiede and Cpl. Walter Sikorsky were both treated for a minor concussion.

One interesting visitor at Wakde was Bob Hope, who was in fact flown to Wakde in a P-61 because a C-47 transport was not considered combat cabable. On stage Hope would say of Wakde:

> This is a beautiful island you have here. If you go to the extreme end of it and looked under one of the small cliffs you will actually find one of those palm trees down there that still has all the branches on it.

Wakde Island itself was not very big. The full length was about 6,000 feet long and about 3,000 feet wide. The island basically was a coral reef that had a runway that went from water at one end to water at the other. The 163rd Regimental Combat Team, 41st Division, on May 17, 1944, had taken it from the Japanese. The troops had landed in good shape, and it took two days of fighting to clear the island of Japanese. Two and half days after the landings, engineers and aviation technicians had the field operational. When the ground fighting had ended Army bulldozers buried the Japanese

Lt. Owen Wolf on left is joined by Lt. Byron Allain and Lt. Ralph Hulsey on their right. Wolf and Allain, along with their gunner, S/Sgt. Trabing, would shoot down the first enemy aircraft for the 421st NFS. ***Stevens***

dead as they formed the runway and parking ramps for the planes. After a month or so they wanted to make improvements to these ramps, and in doing so dug up bodies of dead Japanese. Men all over the area would say how badly it smelled for a while.

As the P-61s were being introduced into the 421st NFS a few pilots still flew some memorable missions in their P-70s. During one raid on Wakde, Lt. Frank G. Mott and his R/O, F/O William H. Hartsock, were up on an intruder mission. Lt. Mott filed the following report:

> At 2235 hours Fighter Sector called and gave a bogie 35 miles northwest of my position over Sawar airdrome. Dropping my four cluster fragmentation bombs, I began climbing for altitude. At around 6,000 feet my left engine cut out momentarily, and I took it down to approximately 5,000 feet and attempted to clear the engine. Sector then gave me a call that the bogie was three miles from Wakde. As I attempted to gain altitude again the left engine quit once more. I called Sector and notified them of my engine failure. At that time I turned toward Wakde Drome, at which time the island ack ack opened up on us. Evasion of the ack ack forced a sharp turn into the failing left engine. I was called by Sector again and told to head for Hollandia for a landing. I tried one more time to get altitude and get the engine going with no luck. I headed into Hollandia strip at about 1:00 in the morning. Me and Hartsock caught a B-25 back to Wakde the next day. An examination of the plane by the 4th Airdrome Squadron at Hollandia the next morning revealed that the wires leading to the generator in the left engine were almost completely burned out.

Not long after this the last of the P-70s were released from the 421st NFS, and almost to the man, not one tear was shed. By now all the crews had gone through their transition training for the P-61 and were ready for some action. By the end of June the squadron had acquired thirteen P-61s, and it was time to put this training to some good use.

At the end of June the air echelon at Nadzab and the ground echelon on the *Thomas Nelson* both arrived at their new base, Owi

Japanese "Sally" bomber parked between missions in the Pacific. ***421st NFS***

Lt. Dave Pahlka on the left with Lt. Ralph Hulsey during a break in the action. ***421st NFS***

Island. The squadron settled quickly into its new area and immediately began flight operations. The 421st NFS was assigned an area on the beach, on the south side of the island. The jungle was soon cleared, a road was cut through to the runway, foxholes were dug, and tents were put up for personnel and equipment. The work taxed both the officers and enlisted men, for besides setting up camp, the daily burden of running operations took its toll. The operations consisted of regular night patrols, or CAPs (Combat Air Patrols), with another crew on alert at the end of the runway all night. This spare aircraft would be launched only in the event that a Japanese raid was immanent. The control tower would show a green light, which would be a signal for the P-61 crew to immediately start their engines and take off. This system seemed to work pretty well, as far as the combat aspect went. Later, after a number of Japanese raiders were shot down, the raids would come to an end.

Owi itself was a very small island, much like Wakde. The island was across a strait about a half-mile from the much larger island of Biak, where thousands of Japanese troops had concealed themselves in caves and had fiercely defended their stronghold from the invading American soldiers. The Owi airstrip had been used extensively at this time by fighter and bomber aircraft involved in attacking the Japanese forces still on Biak. The Japanese collapse would come as a result of not being able to get supplies and reinforcements to their troops. By the beginning of July the Japanese on Biak had been blasted and burned out of the jungles and caves, and Biak was now securely in American hands.

The landing field at Owi was directly in the middle of the island. The bivouacs, or living areas for the supporting troops and various personnel were located in the small areas on either side of the runway. This is where the 421st NFS troops, as one of the advanced echelons here, had to hack through the mass of jungle to establish an area for the dispensary, mess hall, living quarters, and squadron headquarters. With picks, shovels, hoes, machetes, and whatever they could get their hands on, they began to clear the jungle. Owi was located almost on top of the equator, so conditions were very humid and moist all of the time. Clothes were most always soaked with perspiration, and they would begin to develop severe skin rashes all over their bodies. Most of the troops became known as the "Blue Brigade," because the medics would paint a blue solution on the infected areas of the body. This blue ointment helped somewhat, but it was by no means a cure. Men with a lot of hair seemed to suffer the most. After clearing the area of the jungle vegetation the balance of the squadron arrived. Owi actually be-

Dave Pahlka's "Bright Eyes" P-61A #42-5504, named after his wife. ***Harding***

came one of the 421st NFS' best bases throughout the war. They discovered an artesian well near the bivouac area with good drinking water. The water was located in the coral soil a mere 50 yards from the ocean, both remarkable and unheard of. While clearing out brush they found a small puddle of clear gushing water. The pool was soon enlarged, and the men dug deeper. The water was tested by the squadron's Flight Surgeon and declared safe. When word got out about the squadron's water supply, other units from the entire island began securing their drinking water from this source. The squadron eventually rigged up a pump system using a jeep for power. This system supplied the water to the squadron, as well as to showers that were built down by the ocean. The showers were built out on the beach and had ten shower heads, so the men of the squadron now had one of the missed comforts of home.

One problem with Owi Island, which was soon learned from the Indonesian natives, was that Owi was a Voo Doo island and people died here often after visiting, according to legend. The natives in the surrounding areas had actually used Owi as their burial island for generations. In clearing out the area, two 421st NFS enlisted men, Private George Bryan and another unknown member, became sick and died. It was found that they had been bitten by a small mite, which resulted in a high fever, and as one died the body would actually turn black. Thirty-seven other members of the squadron were also infected, but eventually pulled through. Doctor Vincent P. Collins, the 421st NFS Flight Surgeon, called it Island Scrub

Japanese "Helen" in flight. ***421st NFS***

Left to right are: Lt. Williams; Lt. Bjorum; and S/Sgt. Bobo relaxing after a mission. ***421st NFS***

Typhus. When it was discovered the Army Medical Staff mandated that all clothes worn, including shoes, socks, leggings, and underwear, with no exceptions, was to be soaked in a solution of DDT, GI soap, and other disinfectants. After soaking for a while the clothes would be hung out to dry and worn by all personnel. It did appear to stop any further cases of typhus, but it was itchy and hard on the skin.

By the end of June, both detachments of the 421st NFS were well established. Owi was secured, and operations were being carried out with no problems. At Wakde, the squadron's operations were also proceeding smoothly. There were a couple incidents that should be noted at Wakde. First, was the loss of Corporal Michael J. Gillian, who had worked with Lt. Roady and the Radio Section of the squadron. Gillian had a fair complexion, and the intense sun at Wakde made him sick. He reported to Doc. Collins, who did what he could, but in the morning he was found floating in the surf just off the beach. Apparently, he had collapsed and fallen in the water. The squadron also lost Corporal George Reese of the Communications Section at Wakde. Reese came down with Silicosis of the lungs. This was a lung disease caused by the inhaling of silica particles, a dioxide form of silicon that occurred especially from quartz, sand, and flint. This usually showed itself as a chronic shortness of breath. Reese was shipped home due to his illness, but died in the transport on the way. He was the only noted case of this to happen on Wakde during the American occupation.

One other incident that happened at Wakde happened to Lt. Dorrie Jones on June 28th, who was out on a test flight of one of the squadron's P-61s. Jones, on his return after the mission noticed a bunch of men in canoes and makeshift boats off Wakde. Military personnel would take old drop tanks and make boats out of them to use for recreation on their off-duty time. Jones was at about 5,000 feet and decided to "buzz" the men in the boats. He stuck the nose straight down and went down to around 1,000 feet. The P-61 built up an airspeed of about 428 mph by the time Jones pulled it up. As he did, part of his canopy flew off the plane. Jones had control of the plane and made it back to the field in good shape. There were no injuries to anyone on board, but the end result was that the "buzzing" of boats, or anything else for that matter, was not to be practiced much after this incident.

July would become a memorable month for the personnel of the 421st NFS. It would be this month that the squadron would chalk up its first aerial victory in the P-61 Black Widow, finally putting the squadron into the scoring column of the war. During the month both detachments would continue to perform well, regardless of the split of the squadron. Also, the existence of Wakde and Owi were not completely ignored by the Japanese. One raid at Wakde caused considerable damage to both men and machines, as Lt. Elston Roady later reported:

> I was on the flightline with two Sergeants calibrating and tuning airborne radar and the CRT monitor in the Radar Observer's position. The red alert sounded, and we ran for the caves at the end of the runway, but before we got there the bombs were starting to fall on the runway. I had flown into Wakde in a new B-25 alongside three others. All four B-25s were destroyed, as well as some other aircraft. I can remember the Lt. Colonel, who was the pilot of my B-25, and the Commanding Officer were fit to be tied.

The Japanese did not overlook Owi, either; there were raids on the 5th, 6th, 7th, 8th, 9th, and 13th of the month. These were small attacks of one to three planes, but several bombs were dropped on the island, resulting in a number of casualties and damage. One of the problems that the men had on Owi was trying to dig foxholes. The ground on Owi, as with Wakde was solid coral, and in some cases explosives were used to make the holes. Lt. Olley came up with the idea to take 55 gallon full barrels and cut the tops off them. They would then fill them with coral as a little bit of protection from the bombing. One of the pilots suggested taking a cutting torch and cutting the tops off, which was quickly dismissed because of the obvious danger of explosions from fumes and left over fuel.

Lt. Bjorum and crew cruising over the Pacific in their P-61A #42-5498. At the time of this photo Bjorum's crew had two confirmed kills. The small Japanese flags are barely visible near the nose of the aircraft. ***421st NFS***

Olley ended up taking a hammer and chisel, took the tops off all the drums, and left the filling to the others. Such measure did help and were completely necessary in view of the limited cover.

On July 7th, Lt. Owen Wolf, his R/O Lt. Byron Allain, and gunner S/Sgt. Donald Trabing would get the first "kill" for the 421st NFS. The victory followed an attack on the field by two enemy bombers. Lt. Wolf filed the following report on the action:

> Scrambled by fighter Sector, we took off immediately after the sounding of the red alert and stayed at a minimum altitude on a course southwest from Owi strip to avoid friendly AA. We climbed rapidly to 10,000 feet on a south-southwest heading. GCI (Ground Control Intercept) called in a vector, and we proceeded on this course, but bad weather obscured the radar scope so that no contact was made. Next I was vectored on a course parallel to and almost ahead of the bogie. At the direction of the Radio Observer (Allain) I throttled back, turning slightly to port so that the enemy plane, if it continued on its course, would cross the nose of my plane. By this time my plane was out of range of the GCI Controller, but I requested and received permission to continue the search visually and through my own radar equipment. On a generally westerly heading I searched the area for about five minutes, with slight rain hampering the sighting. GCI then ordered me to return if I had no contact. I asked for a few minutes more and received permission. Suddenly, a blip appeared on the radar scope at 0055/K, and the Radio Observer took control of the course of the "Queen." He directed the ship in a gentle turn to port and then to starboard, bringing my plane directly behind and below the tail of the enemy plane. At that time we were one mile behind the bogie at 6,500 feet. Throttling back at the direction of the Radio Observer so that we would not overshoot, I closed quickly on the enemy plane. The plane was a twin engined bomber with tapered wings and a thin fuselage, apparently a "Sally" or "Dinah." The exhaust pattern (bright orange) was distinct and visible. It extended below each nacelle at an angle of 45 degrees to the rear and 65 degrees in width as viewed from behind. Upon obtaining a visual on the plane, I throttled slightly forward and opened fire with all eight guns. At a range of 150 yards, the first burst scored a direct hit on the starboard engine of the Japanese plane. The engine flamed, and part of the fuselage exploded, throwing fragments into the path of my ship and slightly damaging the underside of my fuselage and port spinner. I continued to press the attack, firing long bursts. I could see the 20 mm exploding against the enemy plane, and the tracers of the .50 caliber entering its outline. The aircraft suddenly flamed and fell off into a steep dive. I followed directly on its tail, continuing to fire, until my airspeed indicator reached more than 400 miles per hour. The enemy plane crashed in the water along the beach on the southwest side of Japen Island. It exploded when it hit the water, and I could see that both the engines were thrown on the shore. There was no return fire from the enemy plane, as it was apparently unaware of my presence until the attack. None of the enemy aircrew was seen to parachute.

P-61A #42-5502 "Skippy," piloted by Dave Corts, having its radar serviced by Sgt. Robert A. Bittenbender. "Skippy" was named after a girl Corts knew at Orlando, Florida. ***Wendlinger***

Japanese "Betty" bomber sitting on ramp. ***421st NFS***

Lt. Owen Wolf and his crew were credited with the destruction of a "Sally" bomber, and its crash was confirmed by various sources.

Lt. Wolf took over the Wakde detachment on July 10th, relieving Lt. Dorrie Jones, who was going on leave. He remained there until the 25th, at which time Lt. Robbins took over. Wolf then returned to Owi to handle operations there in the absence of Captain Zimmer, who also was going on leave.

In the beginning of July, the Commanding Officer, William Bradley, returned from leave in Australia, ferrying up a new P-61. He had to leave this ship at Wakde for some minor repairs, and continued on to Owi in one of the detachment's other aircraft. This additional P-61 brought the squadron's number of available aircraft up to fourteen P-61s. This, however, would also change by the end of the month. On the 5th of the month Lt. Malone, flying P-61A #42-5494, came in for a landing and his nose gear would not come down. Malone was forced to make a crash landing, and the plane was badly damaged. The propellers broke off, and one of the blades came through the fuselage six inches behind Malone. None of the crew was hurt, but the aircraft was written off later on in the month. Another of the squadron's P-61s, #42-5510, was in for maintenance at the 10th Service Squadron on July 27th. A B-24 that was taking off crashed near the hardstand, and the bomb load exploded, wrecking several ships. Among them #5510 was damaged to such an extent it also had to be salvaged. By the end of July the squadron's total aircraft went back down to twelve.

With the closing of the moon period enemy activity ceased, only to start again with the new moon on the 25th. One raid occurred that morning, and another on the 30th was the extent of their activity for the remainder of the month. On the 30th the raid consisted of four planes dropping numerous bombs that landed near the runway on Wakde. Several hit in the area adjacent to the squadron's camp, killing several men and wounding a number of others. No one in the 421st was hurt.

Combat patrols on most of these nights resulted in no contacts with the enemy. Sometimes the P-61s were unable to locate the bogies that GCI had guided them to. There were other times the chase had to be abandoned because of low fuel. Other times a bogie would also turn out to be a friendly aircraft that had not been identified. There were some cases where aircraft were fired upon by friendly anti-aircraft. In most cases nightly patrols did guard against some enemy attacks, while in others it offered an awareness that the squadron was doing its part to protect American lives. No matter what was going on, though, there was always hope by most everyone that the victory score would soon be on the rise.

On August 1st, two of the squadron's aircraft were sent out to stand alert duty on Noemfoor under the 309th Bomb Wing. These two aircraft would remain there until the 3rd when they were relieved by P-61s from the 419th Night Fighter Squadron. In the meantime, patrols continued at Owi, and the detachment at Wakde also maintained its regular combat patrols and alerts. The squadron got a break from the routine on the 8th when pilots of the 421st NFS from Wakde were assigned a dawn patrol to cover a convoy heading for Sansapor. On the 31st the squadron was again assigned another escort mission over a convoy. Both missions went smoothly, and no enemy aircraft were sighted.

Early in the morning on the 5th, the Japanese again raided Owi, causing limited damage and no casualties. On the 12th the Japanese initiated a new tactic that they had developed in an attempt to thwart the night fighters. They would send in their bombers in a high formation while a couple fighters would come in low over the area to strafe. They hoped to divert the attention of the American defenses and make a surprise run on the base. The ruse worked for the Japanese pilots the first time, but the Americans, suffering only minor damage, learned very fast.

"Nocturnal Nemesis" is actually the other side of "Skippy" P-61A #42-5502. ***Wendlinger***

Lt. Dave Corts standing by his P-61 "Skippy." The nose cone and radar have been removed for servicing. ***Davis***

Also on the 12th the 421st NFS had an aircraft up on patrol early that morning. Lt. David Pahlka, his R/O Ralph Hulsey, and T/Sgt. Harold Cobb were on routine patrol near Owi when a red alert was sounded. The P-61 was vectored on the enemy by GCI at 11,000 feet, and immediately began its pursuit. Closing rapidly, the R/O, Lt. Hulsey, took over the controls when they were four miles from the enemy aircraft. He brought the ship on the tail of the bomber, but the P-61's speed caused it to overshoot on the first pass. Lt. Pahlka orbited and again came in on the enemy's tail. The pilot and gunner established visual contact, and closed in despite violent evasive action and heavy fire from the enemy's tail gun. T/Sgt. Cobb opened fire at 300 feet with his turret, and as they closed to 50 feet, the pilot opened fire with the 20 mm nose guns. Tracers were seen striking the enemy plane, and it went into a steep dive, crashing into the sea and exploding at 4:15 in the morning.

The downing of the Japanese bomber became instant headline news, and by the look of the two following articles one might have thought this was the squadron's first kill. The first information about the destruction of a Japanese "Helen" bomber appeared in "YANK" Magazine:

> Dutch East Indies—Out there they are calling it the Nipponese Nightmare. Call it what you will, the P-61 "Black Widow" or "Nightmare," it's still double-engined trouble for the Jap bombers.
>
> GIs by the hundreds had a grandstand seat recently when they saw a night fighter of the 421st Night Fighter Squadron down a Jap bomber.
>
> It was the seventh aircraft shot down by a Yank night fighter since the start of the war in the Southwest Pacific. At this writing the total is eight, and the score threatens to rise high in short order. The GI who staged the display for the boys in the slit trenches was T/Sgt. Harold Cobb of Evansville, Indiana.

He shot down a Jap "Helen" out of the skies while the men in the foxholes cheered like high school girls when the campus hero runs 90 yards for a touchdown. The combat report of the victory was typically laconic, and Cobb is not a guy to expand too much on the scrap. It was a pretty sight.

The night was warm, and the moon was skidding in and out of low scattered clouds. The Nightmare crews were alert on the strip. When Ground Control Interception picked up the approaching bombers, Cobb's crew was airborne in a matter of seconds.

Lt. David J. Pahlka of Bowing, Oregon, was the pilot, and his Radar Observer was Lt. Ralph B. Hulsey of Edmund, Oklahoma. Cobb was at his guns. After GCI steered the night fighter into the Jap, Lt. Pahlka brought the Nightmare in close.

There's his exhaust," he called out, and Cobb tensed. Closing in to 200 feet, Cobb opened up with his .50s, and the night was ripped with ragged red flashes. The Nip's right engine burst into flames. Lt. Pahlka blasted away with his 20 mm cannons and down went the Helen.

Lt. Robert Buchanan, the 421st NFS Intelligence Officer, also sent in his own version of the event:

Kawop! Kawop! Kawop! Three shots from the heavy guns transformed the tiny, moonlit island in the Netherlands East Indies from a movie travelogue version of the South Seas paradise to a melee of dashing, scrambling soldiers. Before the echo of the flak bursts reached out from the cloudless sky, the sleepers, rubbing their half-opened eyes with one hand and tugging on GI shoes with the other, scurried for their foxholes. Continued Jap raids, aimed at the field packed with bombers, fighters, and search planes made "believers" of them. The coral island in equatorial moonlight made a target that was all bull's eye.

The throbbing of Nip engines pushed the stragglers into the holes. "There they are!" "Sounds like a twin-engined job to me." "He's comin' right in." Silence from the men in the foxholes. "Hey, there's another one!" "Yeah…no, that sounds like, by golly, that must be a night fighter." "We got one up?" "Sure, they've been taking off all night."

Cautious heads popped from holes, sand-bagged corners, and coral filled 50-gallon drums forming barricades. The night fighter, roaring ahead was gaining on the Jap, and there might be a show. Soldiers will "sweat out" the ack-ack before hitting their holes, if they can see some fireworks. From the east the pulse of the Nip's motors bored into the island. And right behind him came the roar of the night fighter's two powerful engines.

"There he is!" "Where?" "Right there," the Corporal pointed, "comin' in fast right up there.""Is it a Jap or a night fighter?" "It's a Jap, but the night fighter's right behind him." "Boy, I'll say he is!

Roman candle blobs of tracers sliced the sky and machine gun fire chattered. Again, delayed sound of airborne firing reached the men on the island, now so intrigued by the fight that they climbed out of their shelters for a better look. Except for the tracers it was almost impossible to distinguish the aptly named Black Widow, the Army's P-61 night fighter, even in the brilliant moonlight. But fireballs still arched across the sky, and this time splattered against the Nip like raindrops on a puddle. The Jap bomber answered and tracers spat back. Spurts of flame furtively darted from the bomber as it dived into view now, close to the island. Then it was all flames, rolling into a ball and streaming a comet's tail as the Jap screamed towards the water with the night fighter right on top of him.

Guns and men were silent and the air was still. The flaming fuselage, leaving a blur like a whirling sparkler on the 4th of July, smacked the sea. Fire bounced high as the gasoline exploded and then faded into blackness as the water sucked in the wreckage.

A Notre Dame crowd shouting at the winning touchdown would recoil in shame at the cheers that rent those shores as the night fighter pulled out of his dive just above the sea and slid proudly away from the island. To be on the winning side in a game of life and death is a wonderful thing.

On the airstrip, easy-going, unruffled, Lt. David J. Pahlka, the night fighter pilot, just grinned as he pushed his way through the group of crewmen, flight chiefs, and Seabee construction men who jammed around "Bright Eyes," the P-61 named for his wife.

Well, guess you'll have to do some reporting work now," he kidded Isadore Nachman, who was there to question him. S/Sgt. Harold Cobb, the gunner credited with the actual kill on a 20 degree deflection shot, did not say a word. "It wasn't because I didn't want to," he says, "I was just too doggone happy to talk."

Night fighting is not glamorous, but it is specialized in every degree, especially in the seven-league-boots, island-hopping war in the Pacific. Pilots must be able to take and land without strip lights and on fields which are so new that construction is still in progress and Seabees are still working.

Left to right are: Lt. Bjorum; S/Sgt. Bobo; and Lt. Williams standing beside their P-61 after their second victory. ***Bjorum***

The pilots also face an enemy more dangerous than the Japanese, weather. In the daytime you can see thunderheads, a flier's nightmare, huge cumulus clouds encompassing a turbulence which will rip a plane to bits. Without a bright moon at night you are in a thunderstorm before you see it. And then it is too late. Or, in darkness, weather may sneak in to lay a blanket of rain or haze on the airfield so that the night fighter cannot see the base.

To be caught on the airstrip by a red alert is the worst problem of the ground crews. Coral strips in the moonlight shine like a shavetail's first gold bar, and you would swear that the Nip can't miss you, even from 20,000 feet. You can't dig holes in the coral unless you have a friend with a steam shovel, so the only thing to do is run for the nearest shelter. On the warning shots you dash a faster hundred than you ever ran in your life and plunge into the first depression or mound of dirt, which is heaven compared to the strip surrounded by planes. You feel a little foolish, however, as did a couple of radio men at Wakde, when the all clear was sounded and you discover that your protection was a revetment filled with 1,000 lb. bombs.

One last note on this mission came from Lt. Hulsey, the aircraft's R/O, on trying to get back home after the crew's victory:

> We were close to Owi Island, and everyone on the ground saw the plane go down. They said the whole island was cheering. We were getting low on fuel, so ground radar vectored us to an area to circle. While we were circling our own anti-aircraft opened up on us as we were caught in the spotlights. Cobb started screaming, "they are shooting at us!" Lt. Pahlka turned the plane out of the light. Cobb was a good gunner, but very nervous. He had been in five actual crashes; the last one had almost killed him. We were advised that there were un-exploded personnel bombs on the first 1/2 of the strip, and they said we would have to bail out or land in the water. We chose to land in the water. Owen Wolf was the Operations Officer, and he called the strip operations and talked them into letting us land on the other half of the strip. The red alert was still on, anti-aircraft guns were ready, and the strip lights were off. We flew in hoping the anti-aircraft crews would not fire on us. The landing crew had left their posts, so Wolf gave us instructions. He would hold a light across the strip to show which part was clear. We came in with landing lights on. Ordinarily we would use only the strip lights. Anti-aircraft did hold off, and we landed. We were glad to get on the ground, but we were feeling low because we did not think we got the Jap plane. It was good news to us when we heard that ground crews and others had seen the Jap plane go down. It was not quite daylight. We were advised that we were the only flight crew available and we might have to go up again. We did not think much of that idea. Luckily, we did not have to.

The excitement of the morning turned negative all too quickly later that morning when one of the squadron's planes crashed coming into Owi. Lt. Joseph Pritchard, returning from a patrol in P-61A #42-5503 was coming in for a landing at 5:35 in the morning.

John Myers had once said:

> The weather over the Pacific was for the most part marginal and fit only for the P-61. Add night time flying conditions to this and a moonless night, and there was no darker place on earth.

It was pretty much these conditions when Lt. Pritchard, flying in the mist just below a 700-foot overcast, was trying to get a heading back to base. He was unsure of his exact position, but he figured he was at least ten miles out from Owi. Pritchard later reported that he passed over what might have been a ship, and in the next moment his port engine exploded. He thought the engine had been hit by flak. Whether from a well-aimed ack-ack shell or an internal failure there was little or no time to make an analysis. He had at least enough control to ditch the plane in the water. He managed to get the plane down smoothly and in one piece, but the P-61 sank rapidly. Lt. Pritchard and the R/O, Lt. Crawford, managed to escape with only minor injuries. Their gunner, S/Sgt. Norman Bartlett, however, was unable to get out of the wreckage and was lost. Pritchard and Crawford crawled into a one-man raft and floated around the area for eight hours. A couple 421st NFS aircraft were sent out to find the missing crew as soon as it got light out. Lt. Al

Lt. Preston Wilson and an unidentified Japanese airman at the crash site of Bjorum's second victory. ***Bjorum***

Lockhard in one of the search aircraft found Pritchard and Crawford adrift just off Biak. He circled the crew and waggled his wings at the waiving, smiling pair bobbing along in the shark-infested waters. The crew was picked up and the search was called off.

The rest of the month the squadron's aircraft flew patrols and pulled regular alert duty in both locations. On the 23rd, two 421st NFS P-61s participated in fighter sweeps over Babo and Sagan. These flights continued for three days, ending on the 26th. These patrols, however, resulted in no contact with the enemy.

On the 25th the squadron would lose P-61A #42-5518 in an accident. Lt. Edward L. Tingen, coming in for a landing on Mokmer Field, Biak, crashed his P-61. The accident was caused by a collision with a B-25, which was coming in for a landing at the same time and just underneath the P-61. Unseen by Tingen, the B-25 was in the same pattern below him, and when both were a few feet off the ground the P-61 landed directly on top of the B-25. Amazingly, no one in the B-25 was hurt. Lt. John Olley, the squadron's Engineering Officer, who came along as a passenger was burned as he was getting out of the plane. Lt. Tingen and a Technical Representative from Pratt & Whitney engines managed to get out of the wreckage without a scratch. The accident was caused by a P-38 that was coming in for a landing against the traffic pattern. The tower was so busy trying to contact the P-38 that the B-25 and P-61 went completely unnoticed until it was too late. Lt. Olley, who had a front row seat to the accident, related the story later:

> On that day a Technical Representative from Pratt & Whitney engines, who had been sent into the Theatre of Operations to check on the performance of their engines, asked me to request the Commanding Officer to permit a P-61 to be flown over to Biak from our station on Owi Island. He explained to me the purpose of the request was to try out a piece of equipment that had been delivered to a Service Squadron at Biak. I understand the equipment was an engine oil-to-pump-and-filter device that could act as an auxiliary oil supply while the engine was running. The filter on the device was supposed to effectively remove all foreign matter not removed by the regular engine filter.
>
> Captain Bradley granted the request and assigned a pilot, Lt. Edward Tingen. The Tech. Rep. rode in the turret gunner's seat, and I rode in the radar operator's seat. It was a very warm day and very hot under the canopy, so I removed my shirt to keep it from getting sweaty and wrinkled. Take-off and the flight over to Biak were routine.
>
> It is my recollection that we made a downwind pass past the control tower, opposite the strip, of course, and made a chandelle maneuver preparatory to landing. I theorized that the B-25 had been making a long straight-in approach at low altitude over the water. I had been facing toward the rear in order to better enjoy the flight. Just before what should have been touchdown I saw the right vertical empennage of the B-25 and almost simultaneously felt and heard the crash.
>
> I cannot recall the next ten seconds, but I then became aware of a roaring runaway engine below me and to my right, and fire broke out in that area. I tried to release the canopy, but it appeared that the framework had been distorted and jammed. I gave up the effort, sat back in the seat, folded my hands on my chest and prepared to die. In dropping my head my eyes caught the gleam of my wedding band, and I thought of my wife. That gave me super strength, and I beat the canopy open with my fists. The heat from the fire possibly helped free it.
>
> I climbed out of the cockpit and onto the wing of the P-61 away from the fire, the wing being pitched at an angle of I would guess was about 20 degrees. I walked up to the wing tip and noted the horizontal tail surfaces of the B-25, then onto the ground.
>
> The next thing that entered my befuddled mind was that there had been a B-25 crash on the roll-out on the strip of Owi. I seemed to remember the crew running away from it yelling, "Get back! Get back! There are armed bombs aboard!" to all the personnel who had driven up to check out the crash. I took off running down the strip. About a hundred yards away there was a hole dug in the coral to get material to build the strip. I jumped in the hole, knelt down, and covered my head with my hands. Three GIs were walking leisurely down the strip to get a closer look at the crash. When they saw my burns they pulled me out of the hole and tried to get me to walk back to the crash site. I stuttered my fears about the B-25's bombs and jumped back into the hole. They pulled me out again and tried to reason with me. At about that time I think the guns from either the P-61 or B-25 started firing. This time they were first in the hole.
>
> An ambulance took me to the nearby field hospital. They tied my right hand behind my back and set me in a chair outside in the broiling sun. After a while they took me inside, undressed me, and laid me on a canvas cot, with a brown rubber sheet under my arm. They put a bunch of cotton batting around my arm in the burn area, slid a sleeve-bandage over the whole arm, and poured bottle after bottle of penicillin over it.
>
> On each of the following mornings I would wake up and look to see how much stinking ooze had slipped out from the bandage. On the fourth morning, in the dim early light I looked at the puddle and was surprised to see a small white object inching through the ooze. When it got to the clean rubber sheet it would turn around and go back through the ooze. "Hey Corporal" I yelled to the orderly. "Come look at this!" He came over, looked, and said, "Yep, they're working. Maggots!" They had set me out back to let the bowflies land on my burnt flesh, deposit their eggs, and develop maggots. The doctor later told me that he could never have cleaned out the burned flesh with a scalpel; the maggots did it well and would eat only the dead flesh.
>
> After about a week, the hospital had to release me to make room for other emergencies. Somehow I got back to Owi and the 421st Flight Surgeon; Doc. Collins looked at my arm and was afraid I might develop jungle rot. He sent me to a field hospital, I think it was at Hollandia.

The month of August ended quietly for the 421st NFS, with little or no activity on the part of the enemy. The squadron continued to stand alert and fly patrols at both Wakde and Owi, but with further successes of the Allied forces pushing back the Japanese, it appeared that the unit was in for a smooth period until a new forward base was selected.

In the month of September the squadron would raise its total to five Japanese aircraft destroyed, all of them since the squadron's move to Owi. Also, the quiet period enjoyed by the men came to an abrupt end as Owi would be hit with some of the heaviest raids yet sustained, one happened on the 9th. The alert started at 2:30 in the morning, and it was reported that approximately ten enemy aircraft participated. Bombs hit the island and caused damage, and the all clear did not sound until around 4:15.

A couple days earlier on the 7th a number of Japanese bombers attacked the Owi strip that evening. On patrol that night in P-61A #42-5498 was Lt. Carl Bjorum, his R/O Robert Williams, and his gunner S/Sgt. Henry Bobo. During this mission they would chalk up the next victory for the 421st NFS. Lt. Bjorum filed the following report on the encounter:

> While on regular night fighter patrol of Owi-Biak area with my crew, Second Lieutenant Robert C. Williams, R/O, and S/Sgt. Henry E. Bobo, gunner, I was given a vector of 70 degrees at approximately 0255/I. The bogie was then 40 miles from Owi Island at 17,000 feet. I closed in on the bogie, and at three miles the R/O picked up a plane on his scope. We closed to 3,000 feet as the bogie began evasive action, diving to the starboard and the port while making slight changes in altitude. I was unable to catch the enemy plane, however, because my port nacelle became so heated it appeared to be on fire, and I was forced to throttle back. Actually, the engine primer switch was stuck in the "on" position, and I burned off most of the bottom section of cowl flaps by the time I had diagnosed the problem.
>
> At this time GCI informed me that the bogie had entered the barrage of anti-aircraft fire coming up from the big guns on Owi Island. I was told to break off contact and fly a heading almost directly south of Owi, where I orbited. After making my second circle I was given a steer of 190 degrees and was told to drop from 17,000 to 15,000 feet. When I closed to three miles, my R/O again picked up the Nip on the scope and took over the interception.

Natives of the Semenoeari village look over the crash site. ***Bjorum***

> My indicated airspeed at the time was approximately 250 mph and, as I was closing in too rapidly, my R/O told me to throttle back about 20 mph. At 800 feet below and 100 feet behind I gained a visual on the "Sally," which was then 80 degrees above. Pulling up directly on the Nip's tail, I fired a 5 second burst from both the 20 mm and .50 caliber guns while dead astern and 250 yards behind the bogie. My gunner and I saw the bogie with the gunfire pattern, and tracers entered the enemy plane's fuselage. The bogie then went into a steep dive off the port side and I fired another burst, this time about a 15-degree deflection shot. Both my gunner and I saw the tracers hitting the wings and fuselage, and 20 mm exploding on the port wing of the Sally.
>
> Following the burst, the bogie returned fire, apparently 7.7 mm machine gun from the tail or dorsal turret, but the burst was low and to the starboard. After my second burst, the Sally went into a vertical dive, straight down into the water, at a point of 190 degrees and 56 miles from Owi Island, ten miles south of the center of Japen Island. The dive was so steep that I could not follow and passed over the Nip at 8,000 feet.
>
> I asked GCI if enemy planes were still in the area. The controller reported that he had two blips on the scope until the time of interception when one suddenly disappeared. He determined the remaining blip was my plane as he continued to direct me. I stooged around the area hoping to pick up a trace of the plane or its wreckage, but low clouds and haze limited visibility, so there was no sighting. I expanded 200 x 20 mm and 500 x .50 caliber, as both inboard 20 mm failed to fire.

The destruction of the Sally was confirmed by the GCI and Bjorum and crew were given full credit. The next victory was to be the most unusual that the 421st NFS would have during the entire war. With the same crew, Lt. Bjorum was scrambled in the early hours of the 9th, just before the sounding of the red alert. The enemy planes dropped a load of fragmentation and demolition bombs on the field. GCI vectored Lt. Bjorum on one of the bombers that was coming out of the anti-aircraft ring. As he started his pursuit, he observed a ball of flame as another enemy bomber dove into the sea and exploded on impact. Lt. Bjorum had been instructed to stay clear of that particular area, because Lt. David Corts was being vectored in to meet this threat. When Bjorum witnessed the explosion and flames he called out "Way to go, Dave!" But as it turned out, Lt. Corts had not fired a shot. Another Japanese bomber in formation with his countrymen shot down his own man, and Lt. Corts had scored an unusual victory.

At the time of the raid Lt. Corts was already on patrol, orbiting over Japen Island in his P-61A #42-5502 "Skippy." Lt. Corts and his crew Lt. Alexander Berg, the R/O, and S/Sgt. Millard Braxton, his gunner, were vectored in to intercept a number of bogies that had attacked Owi just a short time before. Under the control of the GCI they were on a course to come up behind one of the bogies, when suddenly their cockpit was lit up by tracer fire. Lt. Berg could see the tracers coming from behind and passing below to the right of their P-61. He in turn warned Corts of the danger, who in turn orbited and turned into the enemy at his rear. Confused by this maneuver, the bomber continued firing forward, where his fire scored hits on his wingman, and inadvertently shot down Cort's target. The leading Japanese plane burst into flames and crashed into the water at 03:05 AM. Lt. Corts, again, had not fired a shot at either bomber. The victory was officially credited by 5th Fighter Command and the 5th Air Force, but the award was rescinded by headquarters, Far East Air Forces in March 1945. So, the 421st NFS only got to keep this victory for about seven months. About the same time Corts was achieving his own bit of historical glory, a second Japanese plane had left the anti-aircraft ring around Owi Island. Lt. Bjorum was vectored in, and for the second time that month Lt. Bjorum got to write out another great combat report:

> My crew (William & Bobo) and I were scrambled in to investigate an enemy plot of two planes. The GCI controller told me to orbit north of Japen Island until the bogie emerged from the A/A ring. Through VHF communications I heard another airborne night fighter "Asphalt 16" (Corts) inform his R/O that he had observed a light on the wing of his bogie and was closing in. GCI told him to break off, however, since he was approaching my orbit position. I did not see the light, but my gunner and I sighted tracers and assumed Asphalt 16 had opened fire. The tracers were followed by a ball of fire which dove straight toward the water and burst on impact as the plane crashed.
>
> Meanwhile, the Nip for whom I was waiting came out of the A/A ring, and GCI vectored me on a heading of 80 degrees and then gave me a port turn to 220 degrees. At that time my R/O reported a bogie on his scope at a 5-mile range, but since I was dead on the bogies tail, he did not take over the interception until told to do so by GCI. At the same time that the R/O reported the bogie, GCI informed me of the same enemy plane. Then my R/O took over the interception, closing on the Nip at 220 mph in a climb as the bogie was 15 degrees above us.
>
> At this time my R/O said the scope became "clouded," since the Nip was dropping "window" in an attempt to black out the scope. One blip, however, continued to show a bright beam, and the R/O vectored me behind the bogie, closing rapidly while flying through "window."
>
> The gunner and I obtained a visual at 1,500 feet as the bogie went into a gentle diving turn to the starboard from approximately 15,000 feet. I turned starboard inside the Nip and closed to 200 yards, identifying the plane as a "Betty." When the gunner opened fire with a burst from the .50 caliber machine guns the Jap leveled out, and I fired a three-second burst with my 20 cannon simultaneously with a long burst from the gunner. Both bursts were from dead astern.
>
> The Betty went into a steep diving turn to the port, and I kept on his tail in an almost vertical dive. The gunner and I again opened fire with a long burst. In the dive the P-61 had closed to 200 yards at an estimated air speed of 400 mph when I pulled out of the dive, almost blacking out. I believe I pulled out at 5,000 feet, and my airspeed carried me back to 10,000 feet before I leveled off.
>
> At 0310/I both the gunner and I saw a sudden bright flash, which we presumed to be the bogie exploding or burning in mid-air. The pilot and gunner of the other night fighter, Asphalt 16, observed a long burst of tracer ammunition from my plane and, as they completed a 180 degree turn, saw the Betty flame and dive to the shore of Japen Island at approximately 0310/I.
>
> After I came out of the dive I remained in the area and sighted what I thought was fire along the north shore of Japen Island (A later patrol sighted smoldering wreckage of the Betty just inland of Japen Island). I was again called by GCI and began a new vector toward another bogie. We were catching up to the enemy plane, but he went outside of the GCI coverage from the radar site on Biak Island. This left us "in the dark," so I discontinued the chase. We were already low on fuel, and when we landed we only had 40 gallons left. At approximately 4:05 AM Lt. Tom Malone and his crew sighted a fire near the north central section of Japen Island, near a Semenoeari Village, and thought that it might be Bjorum's crashed aircraft. Lt. Malone put in a call to GCI and had them pinpoint his position. He then returned to his patrol area until daylight when he asked GCI to vector him to the spot he reported the fire. At about 150 feet inland the smoldering ruins of a twin-engined bomber were seen on the shore. The tail section of the plane was intact, making positive identification as to the type of aircraft as a Betty. It had at first been reported as a Dinah.

More of the wreckage. ***Bjorum***

About two weeks after the night of the 9th several people from the 421st NFS, including Lt. Bjorum, Lt. Buchanan, Lt. Wilson, and Lt. Williams went out to Japen Island and into the Semenoeari Village near the Betty's crash site. Bjorum would later state that as far as he knew the 421st NFS never fired at an enemy airplane at night without a victory: this was not due so much to their skill and high state of training, but rather the impact of four 20 mm cannons and four .50 caliber machine guns and ample ammunition. All eight guns were located essentially on the centerline of the aircraft. With the turret locked straight forward and fired by the pilot it was pretty effective against enemy aircraft. Bjorum would admit, though, that this was a rather selfish approach, as it placed the P-61's gunners in a position of having nothing to do except sit there and sweat.

Bjorum would also say of the P-61:

After our first experience of firing the turret at night I was convinced that very little actual night firing could have been done during the test phase of the P-61, or something would have been done about the awful blast flames generated by the four guns directly over the pilot's head. One night my gunner ran out of restraint at about 200 yards as we were closing on a Japanese bomber and let go without any sort of conference with me. My first reaction was "I'm dead." For the previous few seconds it had been very quiet in the Widow, as we had had visual for some time: then being hit with that sheet of flame and racket sort of got my attention. However, he was obviously hitting the target, which was also absorbing the 20 mms, as well. To reduce the flame and illumination problem our armament section later came up with long flame arrestors for each gun.

One of the other missions the 421st NFS took part in during the month of September was that of search and rescue. Servicemen, as mentioned before, would take old drop tanks and make boats out of them for their own recreation. Sometimes these little boats would get caught by the ocean currents, and many a man would go on "unscheduled" ocean cruises. One such case happened on the 19th when Sgt. Lester Kaldenbach and Sgt. William Woelfel of the 15th Weather Squadron took their own little tour. The men had taken a Republic P-47 drop tank and had fashioned their own little boat. Soon after they had set sail, they were caught by one of the currents and took off across the ocean. Lt. Rudolph, the Weather officer, soon put out the word for help in locating his two missing men. Two P-61s of the 421st NFS were sent up to help search for the missing personnel. While on patrol R/O Lt. Byron Allain picked up a blip on his scope, and upon circling the pilot, Captain Bradley identified a small object in the water with a makeshift sail. Bradley pinpointed their position and asked GCI to call Air-Sea Rescue to send out a boat to get them. The men were eventually picked up some 20 miles from base. They had spent a total of ten hours on their boat trip.

Left to right are: Lt. Buchanan; Lt. Williams; and Lt. Bjorum. They flew over together to see the crash site of Bjorum's second victory. ***Bjorum***

On September 21st, the squadron discontinued the detachment that had been operating at Wakde. Lack of enemy activity in that quarter warranted the release of the night fighters from that area. Lt. Dorrie Jones, who had commanded that detachment, returned with the personnel and equipment to Owi on the 23rd. A total of four P-61s had been operating out of Wakde, and their return to Owi brought the squadron together for the first time in months.

On the 27th Major Richard Bong again made an appearance at the 421st NFS to try his hand at flying a P-61. According to Major Bong's Flight Logs he flew the P-61 for almost an hour. Personnel on hand mentioned that Major Bong did not care much for the night fighter's job.

On September 15th the 1st Marine Division landed on the island of Peleliu in one of the most costly battles of the war. This was to set the stage for the upcoming invasion of the Philippines. At that time it was felt the Peleliu would be an important staging area for the Leyte operations, especially the airfield there. But as it turned out after over 1,000 killed and 5,000 wounded, Peleliu proved only to be of only marginal importance at best to the Allies Pacific Advance. At the top of the plans sat General Douglas MacArthur, making good his promise, "I shall return!" At the bottom of the plans were the night fighter units in the Southwest Pacific. Of the Night Fighter Squadrons; the 418th, 419th, and 421st were all given advanced notice for future movement. Movement order #580 was received from the 5th Air Force on the 18th, and the 421st NFS began packing equipment and prepared for the relocation. Also at this time, all flying activities were suspended by 5th Fighter Command. It looked like the 421st NFS was going to get a ringside seat to the upcoming invasion of the Philippines.

7

Another Pacific Paradise: Tacloban

The month of October would prove to be a busy one for the 421st NFS. Momentous events were taking place in the Southwest Pacific, and the squadron would make its move from Owi Island to the Philippines. In fact, the move itself would be something that would never be forgotten. Coming in with the assault echelon of the Invasion of Leyte would be the 421st NFS ground personnel. Interestingly enough, a group that would join them would be the personnel of the 489th Fighter Group, a day fighter unit. They would be the first Air Force units to reach the island in MacArthur's invasion. The flying echelon, on the other hand, would mark time in temporary quarters at Owi until it was time to fly their aircraft to their new location at Tacloban, Leyte.

The movement of the ground echelon to Leyte in the Philippines would be made by LST. The squadron was assigned to LST #663. The loading of equipment began bright and early on the 13th and continued steadily until its completion at 1:00 AM on the 14th. An unforeseen delay in trucking arrangements prevented the squadron from breaking the record for this type of loading. As it was, the time record was closely approached, despite a three-hour loss due to the failure of trucks assigned to the squadron to report on time.

421st NFS troops going aboard LST #663 at Owi. ***421st NFS***

The squadron broke camp at Owi early on the morning of the 14th, and the ground echelon, under the command of Captain Charles Townsend, boarded the LST. The ship sailed out at around 2:00 that afternoon bound for Hollandia where it was to join with the convoy. When the LST made Hollandia on the 17th, the LST had to pull into a floating dry dock to repair a propeller that had been damaged back at Owi. The replacement was completed by that evening, and no delay was involved. The task did prove to be an interesting spectacle to the men on board, though.

At 4:45 on the morning of the 18th, in a convoy with 67 other naval vessels, the squadron sailed on towards the Philippines. The six-day trip proved to be rather pleasant and uneventful. One of the benefits of the trip was that the men of the squadron got a well-earned rest and were enthusiastic about the food and accommodations. It was the first time in their travels that they had comfortable bunks and tasty meals. The officers were well satisfied, also; being assigned the ship's officers cabins and eating in a more satisfactory mess in the ship's wardroom.

However, all good things do come to an end, and during the early morning of the 24th, which was four days after the initial landings, the convoy arrived at Leyte. LST #663 and the squadron personnel soon found out how fast their period of serenity would come to an end. The convoy was met by the first all out Japanese air attack against the American forces making their landings. The Japanese had planned to conserve their air and naval forces until the actual invasion was underway, then launch them at the invaders in an all out attack, to which the squadron arrived just in time. The Japanese flung everything they had at the attackers, including a new weapon known as the Kamikaze.

From the deck of the LST in the harbor, the 421st NFS personnel watched full-scale dogfights overhead, witnessed bombing and strafing, and saw dozens of aircraft brought down by American anti-

Loading equipment on LST #663 at Owi. ***421st NFS***

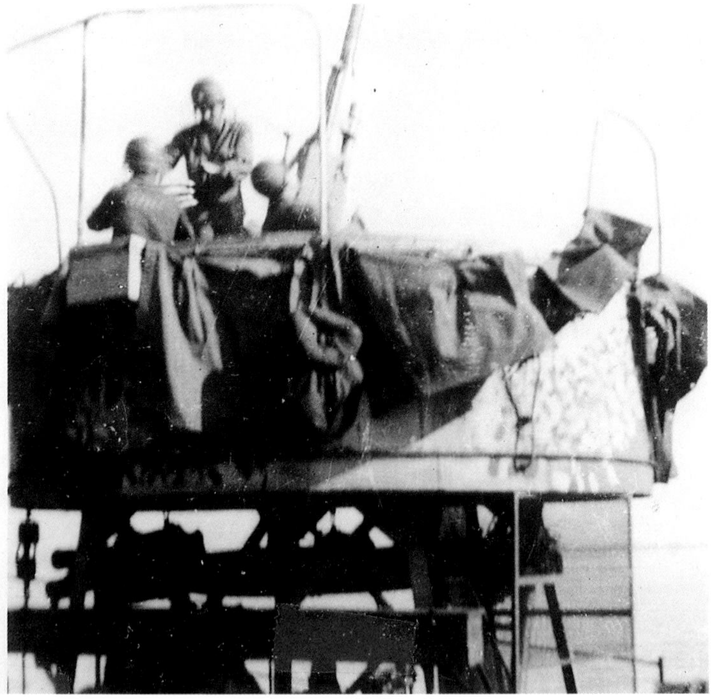

Navy gunners on LST #663 shooting at the Japanese aircraft overhead with their 40 mm anti-aircraft gun. ***421st NFS***

aircraft and fighters. Bombers and fighters seemed to be flying all around the ships. To the squadron members it seemed at times that airplanes filled the sky and one did not know where to look, there was so much going on. Fortunately, LST #663 was not hit, though there were several close calls. Flaming enemy aircraft crashed into several vessels nearby, and in the surrounding water. For the men of the 421st NFS there are many strong memories of this particular moment in time.

Sgt. Curtis Burgess logged the following in his journal:

> All hell broke out as a massive air strike by the Japs began. Dozens of planes were bombing and strafing, some at tree top level. I vividly remember standing on top of a load of supplies on a two-wheeled trailer and getting a ringside seat of what was going on. There were as many as six aircraft exploding, falling on land, or in the water at any given time. You could see a pilot eject from his airplane once in a while. These were mostly Jap planes. I came off the top of the trailer very fast when I saw a plane coming straight at me, the bullets picking up the water to the left of our LST. I skinned both knees and elbows getting under that trailer.
>
> The air protection we had, and it was outstanding, was almost all from carriers sitting several miles off shore. Thank God for the Navy! The most terrible thing to happen that day as I watched was a crippled Jap plane in flames flying treetop level, and it flew into an LCI (Landing Craft Infantry) loaded with 108 men headed for shore. Almost all the men were killed. We pulled one survivor aboard our LST. War was, and still is, Hell!"

Lt. Fred Kohl, one of the 421st NFS pilots along for the ride, wrote:

> The Japs had plenty of nerve. I saw several shot down in daylight, some by our day fighters and others by anti-aircraft. In one case a Jap plane was in a steep dive and had two P-38s on his tail, one on either side. He made a turn to the left and never made another. One of the P-38s gave him a burst and he went down in flames. I could tell a Jap plane by the sound of the engine. I can still remember it. It sounded like a hopped-up washing machine with wings.

Finally, of his experience there Lt. Howard Blanchard later said:

> On the LST I sat in the aft port gun turrets—multiple 40 mms—as the Air Recognition Officer, when a TBF "Avenger" came out of the dogfight trailing black smoke and letting down over a bay full of LSTs. We were the second LST in line for the beach. The first LST opened up with everything they had, and of course ours did, too. I took out my .45 and was banging on the helmet of the Fire Control Man, a navy enlisted man, trying to get his attention and telling him it was a friendly TBF. He had a headset on, and the noise was real loud from all the gunfire. He never paid attention to me. We had an Air Corps Officer in most of the gun turrets. Nobody was listening to us. I raised hell with the Captain on the way off the LST about their trigger-happy crew. His answer was that they had orders to shoot down anything that came over the fleet. My answer was where the hell else could they go? I saw them shoot down at least three of their own planes at the Invasion of Leyte.

These dogfights over the beachhead continued for a couple of days, with continued efforts by the Japanese trying to ward off the landings. Most of the air protection as mentioned came from a number of Navy carriers in the area, with help from some Army and Marine fighter units. Besides the day raids, the Japanese bombers were also up in the night trying to attack the hundreds of American ships that were unloading in the harbor, as well as the troop and facilities on shore. At night the anti-aircraft would light up the sky, and was reportedly bright enough to sit out in the open and read a newspaper by. The local area, as well as the airstrip at Tacloban had been bombed and shot up; with the arrival of the 421st NFS the airfield was in the process of being repaired by the Army Corps of Engineers and would be ready for operations in about a week or so.

When the squadron arrived at the beach, LST #663 was only able to pull up within 50 yards from the shore because of a sandbar that blocked the way. One story told that when the front door of the LST was lowered, M/Sgt. Goldstein got in a jeep and yelled out, "Men, follow me!" and proceeded to drive off the end of the LST into the water. There was a lot of laughter and somebody shouting "throw him an anchor!" (Note-M/Sgt. Goldstein still contends that this never happened!)

The rest of the troops proceeded to strip down and get in the water for sandbag detail. They began to build a wall of sandbags that went from each side of the LST's door to shore. The Americans also had a few bulldozers on the beach, and one of these was employed to push sand out into the space between the walls. Eventually, this would lead to the construction of a ramp to drive all the vehicles off the LST and onto the island. It must be remembered that while this was going on the Japanese kept up their attacks, and the men would often have to flatten out to protect themselves. There was also a great number of ships all doing the very same thing, so there was a lot of activity, as well as confusion happening everywhere you looked.

It was a slow, laborious process, but was finally completed, and the first truck rolled off the LST at 4:30 that afternoon. Due to the constant Japanese attacks the ship had to be unloaded at once, so work continued without respite for most of the night. Some of the equipment was taken to assigned areas of the squadron, but most of the bulk was just piled up on the beach. The unloading of

Squadron members unloading equipment from LST #663. ***421st NFS***

the ship was completed by 3:00 the next morning on the 25th, and as the men had to be off the ship by 5:30 they only received about an hour of sleep before disembarking. By 5:30, with a cup of coffee provided by the ship's galley under their belts, all personnel were on shore and the next phase of the move began.

When the 421st NFS first got to shore their job was to contact the Beachmaster to determine squadron's area of location. All of these events so far had been a nightmare for the squadron. As if the other incidents had not been enough, eventually they got their own assigned area that turned out to be near two muddy swamps. Squadron members questioned the location, but there was no mistake, that was it! So they sloshed through the water and mud, attempting to put up tents and get some kind of mess tent functioning. The repairs were near completion and the runway at Tacloban was almost ready to go. During the repair process it had been overlaid with corrugated metal that was then being utilized by the Army, Navy, and Marines, and was called "Marston Mat."

The squadron also learned that it had a new enemy to deal with at Tacloban; the onslaught of mosquitoes. Without any kind of netting or protection these raiders always found their mark, as Lt. Fred Kohl later remembered:

> When the rain stopped the mosquitoes descended in hungry hordes, taking advantage of the situation, as some of us did not have our nets up yet. They say you can tell a Philippine mosquito every time by the white spot on his forehead about the size of a football. I could not swear to the truth of that statement, but I can say I heard them calling in for landing instructions and then dropping wheels and flaps on final approach. The other day a big mosquito, amphibious job, twin-engined, landed on the strip, and the mechanic gave him 400 gallons of 100 octane before somebody wised up to the fact

Squadron personnel wading ashore to the beach at Leyte. This photo shows how far from the beach the LST was. ***Stevens***

that it was not an airplane. The mosquito was burned up because they would not service his radar! This was told to me by the tower operator in good faith, so I know it is true.

As the squadron members were setting up camp the heavy ships were still shooting over the heads of the troops and exploding inland. It was hoped by all in the squadron that all the shells had enough powder in each load so they would not fall short of their target. The enemy troops had moved inland, but had left a number of snipers in the area. Between them and the ship's shelling, the men began to feel pretty fed up with the whole operation. The ground water was about six inches below the surface in the Philippines, and when the men began to dig their foxholes it was a whole new deal. Most men found that the best thing they could do was gather up coconut logs and build a bunker. For the first 48 hours ashore, however, most of the squadron personnel were busy and did not get any sleep, so they did not worry too much about it.

For the first week at Tacloban the squadron was subjected to almost hourly attacks, both day and night. The bombing and strafing damaged squadron equipment, and several vehicles were hit, but fortunately none of the men were hurt. With the arrival of the first Army fighters on the 27th, enemy raids during the daylight hours eased off considerably, but the night raids continued with intense regularity. The Japanese averaged 18 raids per night, with 39 harassing raids thrown in for good measure.

With no sleep, continual enemy raids, and patrolling for infiltrating Japanese, the squadron set about preparing the camp. Work progressed, and within three days the area began to take on the semblance of a well-organized camp. The mess hall was set up and in operation, and housing tents, headquarters, dispensary, motor pool, shops, and showers were in full swing. The situation was complicated, however, on the third night when a typhoon hit the area and blew practically everything down. Forty-one of the fifty tents were blown down, and there was considerable damage to the motor pool and other buildings. The squadron spent a rather wet night after it finally ended. The next few days were filled with rebuilding and improvements that came along slowly. The squadron was aided, however, by the hiring of a group of Filipinos for a lot of the maintenance work.

Lt. Roland Forrester and his P-61, aptly named "Old Forrester." ***Bjorum***

The main road at Tacloban when the squadron first arrived. ***421st NFS***

During the Leyte landings the Japanese had introduced a new type of weapon into the war, just in time for the 421st NFS men to see them in action. The Kamikaze made their appearance in the Battle of Leyte Gulf. Kamikaze, which means "divine wind," refers to a typhoon which shattered the great invasion fleet of Kublai Khan in the thirteenth century and saved Japan. The Japanese concluded by this stage of the war that they were outnumbered and outclassed in the air, and that conventional air attacks stood little chance of success. Their only hope now was to turn their aircraft into human missiles by crash-diving them into American ships. Inexperienced pilots flying almost any kind of aircraft carried out most of these attacks. The new weapon took its toll on ships, equipment, and men, mainly because they were difficult to stop. The attacks also surprised and dismayed the Americans, but it did not slow them down.

One of the Kamikaze aircraft had crash-landed near the squadron camp a couple days after they had landed. Lt. Buchanan, the squadron Intelligence Officer, recruited Bill Gorman and several others to go check it out. The aircraft itself was a fighter that had apparently crashed just beyond the lines, but had not burned or exploded when it hit the ground. They found that the plane was in relatively good shape and had skidded into a nearby rice paddy. The pilot was still in the cockpit and looked to be a young teenager. He was dead and was wearing a funeral shroud. According to records of the Japanese military, the Kamikaze pilots took part in their own funerals before their last mission.

Along with the Kamikaze threat there were still many Japanese soldiers in the area, which proved to be a real problem and danger to the 421st NFS and other units that were not cautious.

The main road at Tacloban a few weeks later. *421st NFS*

Most of the men in the squadron were armed and posted to pull guard duty. Bill Gorman recounts one of his nights as a guard:

> We set up a perimeter around the campsite, and I was on guard duty one night. I hid under a bush, and the Officer of the Day came around and caught me hiding. He worked me over pretty good. This particular officer had been a technical advisor in the movie "Beau Geste," which was a French Foreign Legion film. It was rumored that he had actually served with the Foreign Legion at one time. He told me to march fifty steps, pivot, and march back. I told him that there were Japs all over the place, and I thought he was stupid. I should not have said that. He made me get up, march fifty steps, pivot, and march back. Those Navy shells were still going overhead and my nerves were about shot. He left, and I crawled back under my bush. As time went by the big guns quieted a little bit, and I began to get drowsy. If I had gone to sleep and had been caught, then I could have been shot. The Army frowned upon a guard going to sleep in a combat zone. I did not get to sleep, though, because just as I was about to snooze, a rooster, who was sharing the bush with me, crowed. I must have jumped ten feet. I got him, though, and he tasted good the next day.

While the ground echelon was getting settled at Tacloban, the air echelon was still sitting at Owi. With no operational flights scheduled for the crews they began to conduct tests involving gas consumption flights to see if they could increase the range of their P-61s. The war had moved on, and most of the aircrews were more than ready to get back into the action. A few of the pilots did get out and fly a few patrols when they could. Lt. Rolland Forrester found out one day that curiosity could be a very dangerous thing to flight crews, as well as the proverbial cat. Early one morning, while on a patrol with his R/O Lt. Daniel McGuire, they spotted a Japanese barge that was heading for its cover or hideout. Forrester dived on the barge, forcing the Japanese troops aboard to belly flop in the water. The sight was so amusing to Forrester that he watched them instead of where he was going. His P-61 chopped off the top of a nearby palm tree, but he made it back to tell the rest of the squadron of his mission.

On October 31st the first six aircraft flew from Owi to Tacloban. The ground echelon was then able to drop most of its infantry, engineering, and construction duties and get back into the flying business. On the first night of the aircraft's arrival, two P-61s were sent up on patrol, however, no enemy aircraft were sighted and they returned to base. A danger that became apparent at Tacloban to the P-61 pilots, and a great danger to the American aircrew's period, was the "itchy-fingered" anti-aircraft gunners. As the two P-61s approached Tacloban to get into the landing pattern, the anti-aircraft gunners, fearing another Japanese attack, opened up on them. One of the P-61s ended up with its fuselage holed by .50 caliber bullets, and the rudder was hit by a 20 mm shell. P-61A #42-5511 was damaged to such an extent that it would have to be salvaged, but luckily none of the crew was injured. With a bay full of naval vessels of all kinds and their commanders still paranoid from other attacks, the 421st NFS had found out that their planes had become good targets too. Because of this the squadron found that getting back to the field at night without the danger of being shot up was going to be rare. As a result of this potential danger, night interceptions by the P-61s were severely limited.

Another problem that confronted the squadron at Tacloban was the terrain, which proved to be unsuitable for their night operations. One of the main parts of night interception missions was the GCI station and their ground radar. These stations would pick up enemy aircraft and then help direct the night fighters on an intercept course to their targets. In the case of Tacloban the location of the GCI station was so restricted that its radar sweeps could only cover about a 90-degree area of the horizon. This also proved to limit the operations of the night fighter pilots. The squadron was later put on dawn and dusk missions, in which they provided convoy cover and again worked in conjunction with local PT boats.

Throughout the entire month enemy raids were almost continual, and foxholes claimed more time than most living quarters. The constant reports of infiltrating Japanese still kept the unit on alert, and some patrols continued to go out almost daily. Captain Townsend led a detachment that was fired on by a sniper, fortunately, no one in the patrol was hurt. The month of October would come to an end with the squadron all together and ready to carry on the war.

Most 421st NFS members will agree that Tacloban is one place that they will never forget. This was due to their first impressions of the mud and total destruction of the beach where they had landed.

Base control tower at Tacloban, Leyte 1944. *Stevens*

Lt. Dave Corts' P-61A "Skippy" on the flightline at Tacloban. ***421st NFS***

By this time the enemy had been pushed back some miles. Their air power was down, but still somewhat of a fighting force. Estimates have that the Japanese Navy had some 273 aircraft, and of these 149 were operational. The Japanese Army was reported to have 323 aircraft, with only 140 of these ready to go. This and the new environment are what the squadron had to face. Most of the area around the squadron was a picture of total destruction of all the trees and plant life for miles around. Most of this was again due to the massive shelling from the Navy prior to the first troops setting foot on the beach.

Since they were near the swamps, most of the area was mud and muck, with hundreds of shell holes filled with water. To make matters worse the first couple weeks there it rained every day, sometimes very heavily. Until things were in order many men had to go days without a decent shower, and for a time without a decent meal. At one point there were so many Japanese raids that a lot of guys got a little careless, and being exhausted they would sometimes remain in bed after an alert was sounded and at the last minute make a dive for their foxhole. In some cases men slept too long and in their semiconscious state during a raid, when they could hear the whistle of bombs coming down, they apparently would go right through the side of their tents. During the daylight hours to the humorous delight of the squadron members, they could see sides of tents or grass buildings torn or shredded after a night's raid. That is how it was quickly learned who slept during these attacks.

Still others learned that the foxhole had become a necessity in life. Even the aircrews wasted no time to get to work on shelters of their own. Lt. Fred Kohl remembers his:

> I arrived at Tacloban about D-10 or D-11, and I was very rudely awakened to the fact that there was a war going on. We promptly dug a nice deep foxhole. My R/O, Bob Kunzman, dubbed it our "pill hole fox box." It was about 4x6 feet high, enough to sit in. We lined it up with bamboo on all sides and the floor to keep us out of the mud and to keep the sides from caving in. Above ground it had logs for sides and a roof, and the whole business was covered with sandbags. It had two crawlways for quick entrance. (frequently necessary). We thought it would stand up to anything except a direct hit. We did have a lot of laughs in spite of the Japs. When we first got there we never we took our clothes off to sleep, but later on when the raids became less frequent we took a chance. I will never forget the night the Japs sneaked in on us. We heard anti-aircraft and were promptly in the foxhole with blankets and mosquito nets trailing behind, still half asleep. It had rained the night before and the foxholes were like a bathtub, only dirtier. There were six of us squatting bare naked in water eight inches deep, and everyone was slapping those dive bombers they call mosquitoes like mad. The mosquitoes would wait until you put your arm or other exposed part of your anatomy against the net, and then they would stab you. I learned to move sideways and break their beaks off, which made them very angry.

On the flightline, though, it was business as usual. One thing that became standard practice at Tacloban was that if an aircraft could not be repaired within a 24-hour time frame it stood the chance of being "bulldozed" into the bay. The 421st NFS had one documented case of this happening to an aircraft while they were at Leyte. P-61A #42-5502 "Skippy" was hit during a bombing raid on November 15th and was damaged beyond repair. It was salvaged for needed parts, and the remaining hulk was bulldozed off the strip. The strip at Tacloban was singular, and there were a lot of aircraft stationed there. A number of fighters, including P-38s and other aircraft, would also meet this fate. The strip had to be kept open, and space was an important commodity on the Tacloban flightline.

The personnel of the squadron faired pretty well considering the enemy continued to launch heavy attacks. Day raids were more and more infrequent, but the night attacks continued on a regular basis. Captain Townsend and Sgt. Lavern were wounded slightly on the morning of November 1st. On the 2nd Sgt. Harold G. Krust was wounded in the thigh during a raid. The motor pool suffered some slight damage, also. The night of the 3rd proved to be the heaviest, however, with some forty raids made during the night. With all the supplies being dumped on the island there were bound to be some lucky hits by the Japanese. In one case they had an area

Left to right are: Mende; Cunningham; Cown; Foster; and Hall beside a crater where one of the Japanese bombs fell. ***421st NFS***

containing a thousand fifty-five-gallon drums of fuel and a Japanese bomb hit it. This particular fire lasted for about a week.

Personnel of the 421st NFS also took on some extra duties. Lt. Blanchard was told by the AACS (Army Airways Communications Service) that the 421st NFS would have to take their turn and man the control tower to handle some of the air operations, as they were not manned for a twenty-four hour operation, especially at night. So, Blanchard and a number of others took on the new chore. The Corps of Engineers had done a good job in getting Tacloban ready for any kind of operations. Most of them worked day and night and through countless Japanese attacks. The strip itself at Tacloban was a narrow peninsula that jutted out into the sea. The Corps of Engineers had to make it longer and laid the Marston Mat for the runway and aircraft operations. On the east side, a short distance from the mat was the shore, with just enough room to park the aircraft between the mat and the bay. The tower was on the west side of the strip. It was built on marshy land that was on the inlet side of the peninsula. It was about 150 feet from the runway. One reminder of the war was a Japanese tank almost at the foot of the tower. It had a shell hole in the turret and had been left there when the Japanese retreated inland.

One evening when Lt. Blanchard was heading up the tower one of the AACS sergeants came over and asked if he could come up in the tower with Blanchard to see how the night fighters operated. Blanchard agreed, and they both made their way up. There were no stairs on the platform, which stood about 30 feet above the ground. There was an 8 X 8-foot platform, with 2x4s as railings. They put up a corrugated tin roof over the platform to provide some shelter when it rained and from the intense sun.

It was not long after dark that the first raid came. There were three Japanese fighters, which came in low over the water through the strait between Leyte and Samar. Neither of the men saw them until they opened fire on the aircraft parked on the side of the ramp. When they opened fire the sergeant did not hesitate, and over the side he jumped. Blanchard curled up on the platform and tried to become a small target. When the planes had left Blanchard headed down to check on the sergeant. He was moaning, but appeared to have been lucky. He had landed on the soft ground, but his leg was obviously broken. The doctor was called, a splint was put on his leg, and he was taken to the hospital.

Interestingly enough, about three weeks later when Blanchard was again going to head up to the tower, the sergeant came over to talk to him. He had Class "As" on with his leg in a cast, but was walking with the help of a crutch. Blanchard noticed that he had several ribbons pinned on, including the Bronze Star and Purple Heart. Blanchard asked him where had gotten them. He told Blanchard that while he was in the hospital he had been presented the Bronze Star for being in the tower during a heavy enemy attack and the Purple Heart for the broken leg. Blanchard pointed out that he and his men were up in the tower every night during attacks and none of them got a medal to show for it. The sergeant grinned and thanked Blanchard for letting him come up that night, as he was also being sent back to the States. His parting words to Blanchard were, "Lieutenant, you have got to jump!"

At 7:45 on the morning of November 4th, the darkest day in the history of the 421st NFS would transpire. The squadron would lose six of their men in a Japanese attack. There would be no alarm given, and at that time of day many of the men were still at breakfast or taking showers. The personnel killed would include: F/O George Garenger (R/O); S/Sgt. Rubin J. Kaplan (Engineering); Sgt. Eldon Farmer (Engineering); Sgt. John Efstathiou (Mechanic); Sgt. Lynn Ballard (Mechanic); and Cpl. Albert T. Bloomgren (Engineering). A number of men were seriously wounded and sent to be hospitalized, including: Sgt. Armand Giarrusso; Sgt. Eric C. Sandstrom; and Pvt. Luther E. Meadors.

The attack began as four low flying Japanese "Zero" fighters came in from the west at about eight to ten thousand feet up. They were obviously making a bomb and strafing run on the airfield while all the American planes were still on the ground. What they did not know was that Captain Bob DeHaven and his wingman, Lt. Walter Leaf of the 7th Fighter Squadron, were up on patrol that morning in their P-38 fighters near the strip. As the Japanese began their attack run the P-38s cut them off, splitting the Japanese into two groups of two. The Japanese fighters, armed with bombs, dropped them im-

M/Sgt. Herbert Goldstein is awarded the Silver Star. ***Goldstein***

The Flight Surgeon, Doctor Collins, is also awarded a Silver Star. ***Collins***

Captain Bob DeHaven and his P-38 just after his 14th victory. ***DeHaven***

mediately and made a run for it. The Japanese bombs struck near the squadron's mess area and among the tents located nearby. Most witnesses in the 421st NFS saw two of the Japanese planes as they came over and then headed off in separate directions, with the P-38s on their tails. The bombs that struck the 421st NFS camp caught the squadron completely by surprise and gave them no time to take shelter. Captain DeHaven chased one of the Zeros, and in firing a burst hit it mid-fuselage. The aircraft rolled, and the pilot of this plane jumped out and opened his parachute. The Japanese pilot landed near the village of Jaro and was captured by U.S. troops a short time later. DeHaven, who had now achieved his 14th victory of the war, returned to Tacloban after about an hour. His wingman, Lt. Leaf, had been separated and had tangled with another group of Japanese fighters. His P-38 was shot up during this engagement, and he also headed back to Tacloban. He was lined up to make a landing, but another aircraft squeezed him out of the pattern and he was forced to go around again. Leaf's plane did not make it, and he crashed in San Pedro Bay during the attempt. The pilot and aircraft were both lost.

Meanwhile, on the ground at the squadron's campsite the experiences of those few minutes were many, but the war as a whole became very personal and closer to each and every one of them.

Curtiss Burgess later wrote:

> The bombing raid killed six of our men, one within an arm's reach of me while I was hugging the base of a palm tree. I was knocked coo-coo for two or three hours. There was not a drop of my blood lost, and that same day I was given a "shot" of combat whisky and they offered me the Purple Heart, which I refused. It sounds hard to believe, but I had my hand on Harold Bloomgren. He was from Harrington, Kansas, and he was 37 years old. We called him "old man." One of the kindest, gentlest, and best men I would ever care to know. We were clutching the base of the tree when the bomb hit and I got knocked out. A large fragment hit him in the head. I remember he gave a loud groan and went limp as my hand grasped his. Oh God! What a loss.

Jake Loran was also lucky on that day:

> I was in the chow line near a wall of cases of C-rations about five feet high. A bomb hit about 40 feet away, and the blast knocked me to the ground. I think the wall of C-rations saved my bacon, as it was between me and the exploding bomb.

Ray Eynon remembers his close call:

> I had not slept much that night because the Japanese came over on their raids throughout the night, and by morning I was pretty tired. I went to the chow hall to have breakfast and was sitting with George Garenger, one of the R/Os in the squadron. He had just came back from patrol, and after breakfast he got up and went toward his tent to get some sleep. I got up just after him and went to my tent. Inside my tent was a General Electric Tech. Rep., who I sat and talked with a bit. I went back outside to the latrine, and as I was heading out I heard the sound of an airplane engine that I was sure was not ours. It sounded like it was about to dive or turn. About the time I was coming

Lt. Frank Mott's P-61A #42-5509 is seen running up its engines at Tacloban. ***421st NFS***

421st NFS pilots from left to right are: Lt. Roland Forrester; Lt. Al Lockard; Lt. Paul Zimmer; and Lt. Tom Malone in front of a P-61. ***Malone***

back out to take a look I heard the first bomb hit. The next bomb hit seconds later, and it sounded about half as far away, and I proceeded to hit the dirt. I found George, who had been killed by one of the first two bombs; he had a bad wound through his back. The third bomb hit came right down very close to the showers, and a number of men were killed there. People were running around all over the place trying to get things together at a near panic. I went back to my tent and found 28 shrapnel holes through the mosquito netting. This was right at the spot where I had been sitting just a short time before, so it was a good thing that Idecided to go to the latrine.

Doug Ponsford also later wrote down his memories:

I had just left the mess hall when all hell broke loose. I heard the screeching of bombs and a passing of mud and schrapnel. I looked at my hand and saw that it was bleeding. I looked up and saw Corporal Cerio coming out of the showers covered and speckled with blood. After that I went and had my hand looked at. I remember Yando the medic asking for help with the bodies; they had been brought to his tent and put on the ground. I then helped carry a stretcher with Ballard's body to the Seabee campsite, where there were ambulances to take the bodies to the hospital. My eyes were filled with tears for the boys we lost. If anyone ever deserved a Silver Star it was the boys that came off the line and went to their death. I know the boys never knew what hit them. I also remember Sgt. Goldstein taking charge of some of the commotion and directing help for the wounded.

Another witness to the bombing was Howard Blanchard:

I was returning from the strip after working all night, walking down the road to my shack. I saw the Japanese fighters coming in from the west. As they neared our camp two P-38s made a crossing pass at the Japanese, and I expect they dropped their bombs in order to do battle. They may have dropped them to bomb the strip where the aircraft were, who knows? The planes looked like Zeros to me. They did not shoot on this pass, but just after that I heard the bombs coming. I stopped and watched, and then started running to the pillbox. I was between Garenger's tent and Pitzer's when the bombs came. I was also about 30 or so feet from our pillbox. I saw Mickey McGuire reading a pulp magazine in his tent, and I yelled at him to get in the hole. The last I saw of him he was struggling to get out of his mosquito net. I got down to enter the blast shelter and the first bomb hit. What felt like a heavy weight knocked me flat. I thought for sure I had been hit, until I heard Mickey say, "Jesus Christ! That was close." If I had stayed to watch, I probably would not be here now.

I scrambled out to see how Pitzer and his tent mate Jones were, and saw that the bomb had landed near Garenger's tent across the road. Garenger was lying on the ground near his cot. I went to see how badly he had been hurt. He had been hit in the chest with shrapnel and it had made a big hole coming out his back. He was dead, and I assume killed instantly. His tent was closest to where the bomb hit. He was a newly assigned R/O that had joined the squadron. He was very young, maybe 19.

I had seen Pitzer sitting on the edge of a little trench they had dug next to his cot. He had his helmet on with the straps dangling and biting his fingernails staring straight ahead. I asked him if he was ok, and he did not answer, he was in shock. Ray Wilander, the General Electric Tech. Rep., had been reading in his cot. A piece of shrapnel had hit him in the kneecap, so I used my first aid kit to bandage his knee. In checking on my men I found that Eric Sandstrom had been hurt badly, a piece of shrapnel though the chest and out his back. Lugara was hit with shrapnel also, but not vitally hurt. They were up on the shower platform when the bombs hit. I guess that's where most of the wounded were.

And finally, from John Dew the following memory:

A tent-mate and I had just gotten inside our tent from breakfast when we heard a plane coming in toward us. He looked at me and I looked at him, and then we both headed for the foxhole. We could feel the concussion from the bomb against our backs as we entered the foxhole opening. We both knew it was a Jap plane from the sound of its engine. We both knew that constantly listening and identifying all sounds day and night while in the combat area was the best way to stay alive. This listening kept you tense at all times.

Japanese "Tony" fighter in flight. *421st NFS* 156.

The actual attack only lasted a matter of minutes, but the impact it left lasted for a lifetime. As in most cases in war the men of the 421st found themselves in a situation that brought out unrestrained fear or super-human strength to deal with death face to face. Herbert Goldstein, the squadron's First Sergeant, chose the latter. According to those in the area where the bombs hit, Goldstein took control and tried to help the people that were wounded and organize the others. One squadron member commented that Goldstein was all over the place at the time he was needed most. For such actions M/Sgt. Goldstein was later honored with the Silver Star.

Along with Goldstein, many others, such as Captain Govoni and Doc. Collins, the squadron's Flight Surgeon, rose to the occasion to help out as much as they could. The actual damage to the camp was minimal, with no aircraft, fuel, or ammunition hit. In fact, the biggest material loss to the squadron that day was the showers, which had been constructed from a couple of auxiliary fuel tanks resting on top of a wooden framework. The squadron was forced to go back to bathing out of their GI helmets for a short period of time. After a few days life, as it was, went back to normal, and the squadron concentrated on getting back at an enemy that had now touched them all personally.

Lt. Owen Wolf on left, with Lt. Dorrie Jones at Tacloban. ***421st NFS***

Japanese "Zeke" fighter in the Australian War Memorial. ***McDonald***

A couple days later a great cheer rang up from one end of Tacloban to the other. A couple more squadrons of P-38s from the 49th Fighter Group arrived from Biak. Captain Bradley had brought most of the P-61s that had been at Owi at the beginning of the month, with three more coming by way of Palau a little later. By now there was a substantial fighter force of day and night fighters stationed at Tacloban. But even then some Japanese raiders still made it through and managed to bomb the runway and put it out of commission for a day or two at a time. On one of these occasions a group of Navy fighters came in for an emergency landing. Low on fuel, their carrier had been damaged in a naval battle and Tacloban was the closest sanctuary for them. As they tried to land on the strip they found that the longest open area without bomb craters was only about 100 yards. Each plane landed with its brakes on, and they nosed over one by one. Most of them were damaged so badly they had to be bulldozed into the water, but none of the Navy fliers were hurt.

As mentioned before the Japanese Army, although very limited now, were still out in the jungle setting up snipers and small attacks on U.S. personnel that were not cautious. Sgt. Burgess later told about a strange incident he had been a witness to while the base was on alert for Japanese infiltrators. On this particular morning a local native had come into camp and spread the alarm, "Jap!" "Jap!" Some of the squadron personnel took off with the native to find out where he was. By this time Burgess had gotten to where the Japanese soldier had been located. The soldier had been shot while trying to conceal himself under some bushes. His body had been dragged out, and a number of the men present raised their carbines and fired more bullets into the body. Burgess asked them why shoot a bullet into one already dead and watch it flinch. One man simply said, "I can say when I get home that I shot a Jap." As time went on the last of the Japanese were eventually killed or captured, bringing an end to this potential danger.

With the flight crews getting into operations, new things began to come up to make the flying out of Tacloban all the more interesting. One was the local anti-aircraft, and the other could be

Lt. Bjorum and crew flying near Tacloban in their P-61A #42-5498. ***Davis***

just landing at Tacloban after a mission, as one of the 421st NFS pilots, Lt. Mack Ballard, learned:

> One night on Tacloban, early in the Battle of Leyte, we had been scrambled, sent on a wild goose chase way the hell and gone. I don't know how many miles we were sent, but there was nothing there. At least we could not pick it up on our radar. Then they vectored us some place else, and we chased there. Then we chased back another direction. There was nothing in the skies that we could pick up on our radar. I flew to where they said they were supposed to be. They were not there! We were in bad weather and nearly out of fuel. We headed back to the strip. We had learned early on to make a straight-in landing, no pattern at night. So this particular time, while we were out chasing ghosts, the Japs had come over and bombed our strip, knocking out the lights (strip lights). When the tower told me that, I said "Well, put a jeep down at the end with the headlights on, we can pick it up." The only thing is, they put the jeep at the wrong end of the strip. So I came in, out of fuel, coming in over the top of the jeep and set her down. It was raining like hell, and there was a bad cross wind. Started setting her down, and finally decided to look out. All I could see were big waves out there. So, anyway, I bend the throttles, suck up the gear, bend round, get back, line up again. Meantime I do a little cussin. "Get the jeep to the other end!" So, as I was banking around in the turn to get back and to line up the runway, the red lights are flashing "No Fuel." I line up. The crosswinds are blowing at about 60 mph, which is a pretty tough crosswind. So, when I set it down, I came over the jeep and the strip lights, which of course are out, but I missed it far enough that, as we slid down the runway, which was a metal mat, I could just hear these lights going "plink, plink, plink." I was knocking them out as we rolled down the runway. The starboard landing gear is hitting every one of them, right down the row. When we got to the end of the strip, both main tires blew out. I had been skidding all that way; it was wet, but it still did enough to blow the tires.

The use of a jeep only happened a couple times while the squadron was at Tacloban because of the strip lights being inoperative. It may be noted that there was some talk about a jeep being a good target for Japanese bombers. But in looking at the reality of the

Japanese "Oscar" fighter owned by the Flying Heritage Foundation. ***McDonald***

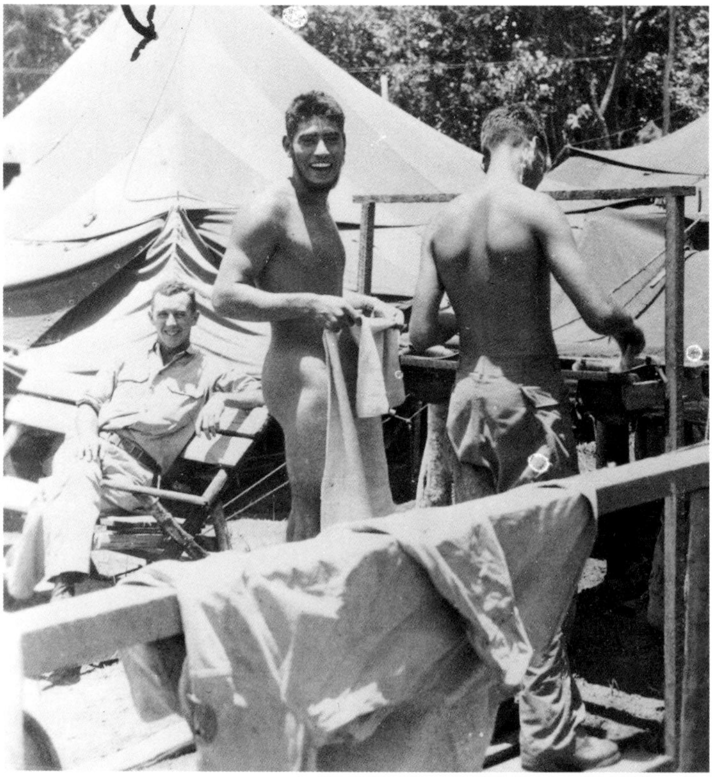

Larry Neville on the left, with Efraim Lopez and Joe Cox in front of Neville's tent. ***Neville***

scenario, Tacloban had been a Japanese airfield for most of the war before the Americans arrived. They were familiar with the layout of the strip to every detail. Also, with over 300 ships in the bay, one jeep would rate pretty low on the target list. When the lights were down at any time, there was always a major effort to get them back up and going, especially if squadron aircraft were up and coming home from patrols.

On another mission Lt. Lloyd Partridge would also have an "interesting" landing experience. When returning from a patrol mission he was deviated to Dulag, a strip about 50 miles south of Tacloban. Partridge did not know the reason for being sent elsewhere, whether it was because of a raid in progress or damage to the runway. Whatever the reason, he headed for Dulag as ordered. Dulag was even smaller than Tacloban, and the runway ran from east to west. As with Ballard's landing, he was coming down without the benefit of strip lights to aid him. Along the runway at Dulag, lined up in neat rows were P-38s, which were parked just off to one side of the strip. Partridge landed his P-61 a little left of the center of the runway. As his plane touched down his left wingtip struck a couple of P-38s in the nose. One of the P-38's guns went off upon impact, and several rounds were fired into the P-61's left engine. Lt. Partridge and his crew parked the plane and had to catch a ride back to Tacloban. A new engine with a maintenance crew were later trucked down from Tacloban and installed. Needles to say that the 421st NFS leadership, as well as the P-38 squadron, were not happy about it. Lt. Partridge, however, was not reprimanded, and the record later viewed it as an accident.

One of the problems that the 421st NFS had was the lack of good engines. A large shipment of engines came in for the squadron's P-61s and were stored in depots at Finschafen and Biak. As it turned out, the engines had not been "pickled" when they arrived for storage. Over 400 engines were lost because of the rapid corrosion. Because of the engine shortage now faced by the 421st NFS, the squadron would be limited to only six operational aircraft at a time. So, with Lt. Partridge losing another engine even by accident, it would seriously impair the squadron's mission capability.

The next victories for the 421st NFS would come on November 10th by Lt. Albert Lockhard, nicknamed by his squadron mates as "The Detroit Fat Boy." Lt. Lockhard, accompanied by his crew Lt. Stuart A. Thornton, R/O, and S/Sgt. Joseph Mazur the crew's gunner, would score a double-kill, downing two Japanese "Tony" fighters during this engagement. Lockhard was flying a cover patrol near Ormac Bay. The patrol had been in two sections, one around the north and one south near Leyte, providing protection to PT boats on their missions through the Surigao Straight. Lockhard later recalled:

> About 30 minutes before the PT boats released us, my wingman, Lt. Rollo Forrester, developed a problem and departed for Tacloban. After the boats were in open water I headed home. About halfway to Tacloban, over Kikilo, my gunner, Sgt. Mazur, spotted two aircraft crossing from left to right at about 11 o'clock, about 100 feet off the deck. At first we thought that they were a couple of P-51 mustangs, but soon it was obvious that they were Japanese. I radioed my sighting and requested that a couple day fighters be sent up to intercept the incoming fighters. I was asked to repeat the message, which was done as per request. I was then asked to repeat the message again, because the transmission had been cut off by another aircraft, at which time I shouted "Goddammit! I'll get the bastards myself!"
>
> I began a 270 degree turn, cleared the 20s, and Mazur cleared the 50s. In activating the turret one of the actuator motors burned out and the turret locked in the vertical position. To this day I do not know why I continued the closing maneuver. We closed on the two Tonys, who were flying almost in trail. I fired a short burst at the trailing plane and could see hits on his left wing root and fuselage. He rolled over to the

Peleliu Island taken from the air. ***Sykes***

left and went straight into the ground. The leading plane continued on a straight flight. I lined up and fired a long burst and could see hits all over the wings and fuselage. He went straight in.

Both of the Tonys crashed into the Valley just west of Kikolo. Lt. Lockhard orbited and strafed both of the burning wrecks. Lockhard had fired three bursts from his 20 mm cannons, totaling just 150 rounds from a minimum range. These two victories brought the 421st NFS score up to seven.

Al Lockhard would have another victory a short time later that would go unconfirmed. Lt. Dorrie Jones and Lt. Lockhard were on a patrol over Ormac Bay with two other 421st NFS pilots. They were about 40 to 50 miles out, and Jones instructed the flight to head for home. Lockhard called over the radio that he was after another Japanese fighter, later identified as a Zero, and told the flight "I've got this bastard!" Lockhard was just above and behind the Japanese fighter, who was trying in vain to dive away. Lockhard stayed on the Zero's tail and watched as the Japanese pilot crashed into the side of a hill as he tried to evade the P-61. 5th Fighter Command, however, would not give him credit for the downed fighter.

Lt. Dorrie Jones downed another Japanese fighter on November 16th. A flight of four P-61s, led by Lt. Owen Wolf, was patrolling west of Dulag and south of Ormac Bay. Flying with Wolf and Jones that day were Lt. Lloyd Partridge and Lt. Frank Mott. Somewhat to the surprise of the 421st NFS pilots, they ran into an enemy formation of some twenty Japanese fighters. The P-61s were at an altitude of 12,000 feet and the Japanese around 11,000. In the ensuing dogfight that followed, the P-61s were joined by a few P-38s. The Japanese fighters were all carrying bombs, and were observed to jettison them and split into two flights. During the battle the Japanese used slow rolls, followed into split-esses, and sharp dives. In the opinion of the American pilots these Japanese pilots seemed well trained and aggressive. Lt. Jones fired a burst at a "Frank," which burst into flames and went straight down, and soon had another in his sights. However, as he pulled into a tight turn at about 350-mph, his P-61 lost the entire rear gondola. He was able to complete his turn and fire at three more Zekes, which all out turned the crippled P-61 and made their escape. Lt. Jones' plane was buffeting violently by this time, and Jones felt that he was losing control. The P-61's controls locked, and the aircraft dove to 1,500 feet with the elevator jammed in the nose-up position, and the plane tried to loop. Lt. Jones had to wrap his arms around the control wheel and brace his knees up against the control panel. By dropping his flaps he was able to recover the aircraft. His crew was preparing to ditch, but Jones regained control and they all flew safely back to base.

During this same engagement Lt. Owen Wolf scored hits on another Zeke, which would be listed as "damaged." Since the plane again was not observed to crash, 5th Fighter Command would not confirm it. Lt. Lloyd Partridge and Lt. Frank Mott each hit a Zeke, but again they were listed as only "damaged."

Just a couple days later on November 18th, while on a mission to protect returning PT boats from their night patrol west of La Paz near San Agustin, two P-61s of the 421st NFS, piloted by Lt. Tom Malone and Lt. Chester Craft, were flying at around 7,000 feet. Above them was a flight of four P-38s. At the same time a flight of four "Oscar" fighters were spotted approaching from the American's 9 o'clock position and quickly swung around to their 6 o'clock position. The Japanese fighters made a firing pass at the P-38s, at which time one P-38 was hit and went down. Three of the four Oscars continued their attack, going after the P-61s at the lower altitude. Lt. Malone took evasive action and then turned to go after the Japanese aircraft. Lt. Craft was unable to follow Malone, and the three Oscars got on his tail. The first, second, and third dove below the P-61, but the fourth went after Craft. Lt. Moore, Craft's R/O, had spotted the incoming aircraft. Lt. Moore was heard on the radio back at the base, where they were monitoring the battle, yelling over the intercom, "Give me the guns, I can see his gold teeth, he is so close!" Taking over the .50 caliber turret Lt. Moore managed to hit the Oscar in the engine. Smoke was seen trailing behind the cockpit of the crippled fighter as it went into a steep vertical dive. A P-38 pilot who had witnessed the plane going down also called it out over the radio. Sadly enough, again 5th Fighter Command would not give Moore a confirmation on his kill. Headquar-

Lt. Blanchard in one of the VMF-(N)-541 Hellcats. *Blanchard.*

ters eventually also listed it as "probable." Of the four Oscars that attacked the American planes, the one single fighter pressing the attack on Craft to around 300 yards failed to fire his guns. Both Lt. Craft and Lt. Moore expressed the same questioning thoughts on why the Oscar never got off a round. The Japanese pilots again appeared adept at maneuvering their aircraft and were particularly skilled at aerobatics, a sign of a well-trained pilot. It was also felt that the Japanese may have mistaken the P-61s for P-38s and were not aware of the P-61's turret. Lt. Malone pursued a couple of the fighters out of the area, but did not make contact. Both Craft and Malone returned to base and did not encounter any more enemy aircraft. On the way home they did spot three P-38s in a rice paddy west of Hinunangan Point. The planes appeared to have bellied in and were in good condition, and no personnel were observed in the area. It was determined that these may have run out of fuel and crashed landed there, but nothing else was ever found out about them.

Corporal Bill Sykes on left with Sgt. Jim Cardis. Two of the Marine ground crew. ***Sykes***

The action in the November skies still had one more round to go before it was over. On November 28th "D" Flight was on an evening patrol under the leadership of Lt. Owen Wolf. Again the 421st NFS was on a PT boat escort mission covering them from Panaon Striaght to Baybay. Wolf's flight encountered a formation of seven enemy fighters, six of which were "Zekes" and one "Hamp." The Japanese were flying at about 7,500 feet at about the 10 o'clock position from the P-61s. The P-61s were at an altitude of 1,000 feet when the Japanese were spotted. Closing in for the attack, Lt. Wolf had Lt. Allain as his R/O, and S/Sgt. Emil K. Weishar was his gunner. Weishar destroyed the Hamp with his turret .50 caliber using a deflection shot. The tracers were seen entering the fighter's cockpit, causing it to catch fire, blow up, and crash into the ground.

Another Zeke was destroyed by a burst from the turret of S/Sgt. Ralph McDaniel, Lt. Pew's gunner. Lt. Hoke Smith destroyed a fourth enemy fighter, with Lt. Robert H. Bremer, his R/O, and his gunner, Sgt. James W. Pilling. The three Japanese fighters that remained came up on the 6 o'clock position of the P-61s; again, there is speculation that the Japanese mistook the P-61s for P-38s. One came in on Hoke Smith's tail, and Lt. Bremer noted that the guns in the fighter's left wing were not working. This failure may have saved the Black Widow, for Lt. Bremer also noticed tracers from the right wing firing past his gondola. Bremer took over control of the turret from the gunner, and with a steady burst into the Zeke destroyed the attacking enemy fighter. The few remianing fighters turned and fled, and the 421st NFS flight returned to base.

VMF-(N)-541 squadron sign. ***Sykes***

Lt. Carl Bjorum was in the fourth P-61 and later talked about his experiences that day:

> The P-61 was never intended as a day fighter, but our squadron had several occasions to mix it up with Japanese and their Nakajima KI-43 "Oscars." Although the Black Widow was maneuverable for its size, like most American airplanes it was no match for a Jap in a turn. One of our pilots met two in a head-on pass in the morning coming home from a lone sortie. He ended up diving out of the fracas after he found them shooting at him when he completed only 90 degrees of a turn.
>
> About this mission on November 28th, 1944. The Flight Leader was Bud (Owen) Wolf. I was the second element leader. The other pilots were Hoke Smith and Robert Pew. It was about 0400 in the afternoon—maybe earlier. We were flying out of Tacloban, Leyte, on PT Boat cover. When it all started we were down at about 1,000 feet looking for a bogey as directed by GCI. We never found the bogie, but soon got a call from GCI of bogeys at about 1 o'clock high at about five or six miles. I looked up and initially saw two or three Jap fighters above us quite a distance away. They kept popping out from a cumulus cloud, and there were seven of them flying in trail formation. They must have seen us about the same time, as they immediately went into a steep climb. My thoughts at the time were that they would be at an altitude of several thousand feet above us when we joined, but they were not, which proved that we were out climbing them. They were about 300 feet above us, turning from port to starboard, and as we were already at a pretty steep climb angle no one could get a shot with the 20 mms except Wolf. Bud Wolf's gunner later fired a short burst at what I believe was the last one of the batch and took the cockpit area right out of the airplane. The airplane rolled to the left in flames, and that was the last I saw of it. The rest came

around to make a pass at us, diving somewhat. This was okay with us, because they were going to meet 16 .50 caliber guns. I was watching the gun barrels on my turret as Williams, my R/O, tracked them around. As the Jap leader started to shoot, I told Williams he had better open fire. He responded with "The guns won't fire!" By this time the lead Jap plane had disappeared behind me, and I again told Williams to start shooting. This time he said, "Bjorum, the guns won't fire!" Whenever he called me "Bjorum" I knew he was serious, because everyone called me "BJ." The three other turrets were firing like mad. I could see Bud Wolf's turret firing because I was tucked in very close by then, and I could hear the others. The other three R/Os shot down one each, which left three Japs who broke off and left. We had been in a typical "tucked in" four aircraft formation, with two elements of two. My element on Bud Wolf's right wing and his wingman on his left wing. There was no 20 mm ammunition fired during this engagement, and none of our planes were hit. Shortly after the Japs had broken away, my wingman called to say he had lost an engine and had feathered it. That meant that my element had one airplane on a single engine and one airplane without a functioning turret. The circuit breakers on my turret had not been reset after the last servicing, and the guns would not fire a single round. All this when the Oscars came around firing like mad and leaving me with a bad case of the "puckers."

Back at Tacloban the Japanese bombers still continued to attack at night and inflict damage on the Americans. Lt. Nachman, the Intelligence Officer, was wounded slightly in the head the night of the 18th. Sgt. Orien Gown was hit in the back on the 27th, as was Lt. Edgar Crawford, who received a slight wound in the arm when the Japanese bombs struck near the strip. Lighting for the camp and runway was also still a problem and had to be repaired continuously. Whenever the Corps of Engineers did repairs on the runway, the caterpillars, as before at Nadzab, tore up the electrical wires that were laid along the runway. Most men who worked on these systems would later say, "We were our own worst enemy."

The excitement up in the skies did not mean that life on the ground was boring by any means. One night Lt. Blanchard, S/Sgt. DelaGardelle, and Sgt. Lochman were in a dugout with some crews in case there were any problems with the alert aircraft. Lt. Zimmer was ordered to scramble, and his R/O Lawrence "Squeak" Carr said that they could not take off because the intercom system was not working. Zimmer went after the communications guys figuring that they should have had the plane ready to go. Blanchard asked Carr if he had written it up after the afternoon test flight, to which he replied he had. Carr insisted that the intercom was still broken, and Blanchard and his men ran across the steel mat to the plane. DelaGardelle got in the gunner's seat, Lochman in the R/O's position, and Blanchard in the pilot's seat. Blanchard turned on the switches, and they called each other with no problems. Not ordinarily that exciting of a check, but at the same time the Japanese were dropping bombs close to the ramp. The three men made it back to the dugout and out of harm's way to let Lt. Zimmer know that he could take off.

The month of November ended with the traditional arrival of Thanksgiving to Tacloban and the 421st NFS. This was one holiday that the squadron would not soon forget, thanks to M/Sgt. Herb Goldstein:

> General MacArthur had his headquarters up a hill past our makeshift camp, and he and staff had turkeys, beer, liquor, and the works sent up there. I was told to send up cooks, bakers, and men to help out. Captain Govoni was to be in charge. He was from the old school and knew the tricks of the trade. He arranged to sneak out everything he could land his hands on, and what a good job for me he did. We had turkeys and beer for days afterward. The main ringleaders were Larry Neville and Efraim Lopez, as well as a few others.

November ended as it began, with a tragedy. Early one morning at the strip a loaded B-24 started down the runway on its takeoff run. A C-46 transport started to land from the wrong direction, and it was obvious that they would meet on the runway. The tower saw what was happening and a red flare was fired. The B-24 was about three feet off the ground, and the pilot tried to swerve to the left. All of the 421st NFS aircraft, as well as others were parked along the runway, but all were missed by the B-24. He went ahead and hit the C-46, which at that time was loaded with wounded. Both aircraft burned to the ground. The end result was that over fifty men burned to death. It was again realized by all present that peril did not always come with the Japanese.

VMF-(N)-541 camp at Tacloban. ***Sykes***

In December one of the strangest turns in the 421st NFS' history took place. According to many reports General Douglas MacArthur was dissatisfied with the dawn and dusk protection he was receiving from his night fighters. In some ways MacArthur was right for all the wrong reasons. The main reasons for poor night fighter support included: for starters, the pre-mentioned GCI station's limited search range; the lack of spare parts; poor operating conditions; and the 421st NFS was forced to use only limited aircraft at one time. Because of these problems the Japanese had kept up their bombing at night, and that among other things bothered the General. But in looking at the overview of the situation the 421st NFS had been able to shoot down seven Japanese aircraft, along with a number of "probables" and "damaged" fighters on their record. Compared to the other night fighter squadrons in the Southwest Pacific during the month of November: the 6th NFS had one kill; the 418th had three; and the 419th none. So, for the month of November at least the 421st NFS was on a roll. This, however, was brought to an end by MacArthur. MacArthur approached Admiral Nimitz concerning a trade for a Marine squadron flying night fighter F6F Hellcats. MacArthur's reasoning for this was that the Japanese had employed their "Oscar" fighters, and the P-61s were not able to contend with this aircraft. However, in looking back over the 421st NFS record and their battles with Oscars and other Japanese fighters they were at eleven and 0; the P-61s holding their own, not to mention that the Oscar was used as a day fighter only. There was also mention that the Hellcats had longer range, and as brought up by one Naval Liaison, had folding wings that could save precious space on the crowded Tacloban strip. The Hellcats did have longer range than the P-61s, but the missions that they would fly would not require this. As for folding wings, this particular model of the Hellcat did not have this ability.

In looking at the three principal aircraft, one can see just how they matched up:

KI-43-111 "Oscar"
(Operated by Japanese Army Air Corps)
Max Speed- 358 mph at 21,920 feet.
Cruising Speed- 275 mph.
Ceiling- 37,400 feet.
Range- normal 1,320 miles. Maximum 1,990 miles.

F6F-5N/E "Hellcat"
(Operated by VMF- (N)-541 "Bateyes")
Max Speed- 376 mph.
Cruising Speed- 238 mph.
Ceiling- 38,400 feet.
Range- 1,085 miles. (Internal tanks only)

P-61B "Black Widow"
(Operated by 421st Night Fighter Squadron)
Max Speed- 366 mph.
Cruising Speed- 229 mph.
Ceiling- 34,000 feet.
Range- 1,010 miles (Internal tanks only)

In looking at the statistical information here speed was not an issue. The F6F could outperform the Black Widow in some areas, but each fighter was more than a match for the Oscar or any other Japanese fighter. The Oscar could out turn a P-61 in a dogfight, but the P-61 made up for it elsewhere. It has not been documented where the General and his staff came about their information. There is one important point that can be argued by the 421st NFS and most of the other night fighter squadrons, and that, of course, was how the night fighters were used in actual combat. Being still "Day Fighter" oriented, most, if not all of the higher headquarters' policy makers had little or no formal knowledge in the deployment and utilization of night fighter forces. The lessons learned from the RAF and Luftwaffe night fighters over England were completely lost to the leadership in the Southwest Pacific. This was obviously true from the Wing Commanders right up to MacArthur. Or maybe the reason was more simple than that, as one former member of the 421st NFS later said, "Maybe 'Dug out' Doug got wind that we dined well on Thanksgiving with him supplying the 'un-authorized meal.'"

The squadron that was picked to come to Tacloban and take over was VMF-(N)-541, the "Bateyes." Their Hellcats were scheduled to arrive at Tacloban on December 3rd. The plan was that they fly out of Tacloban for a period of two weeks, while the 421st NFS would send a detachment of its aircraft to Peleliu for the same amount of time. The actual length of time, however, turned out to be a period of over five weeks.

One interesting view of the Army and their P-61s was recorded in one of the Marine flyer's journals:

> We soon learned why the P-61 "Black Widows" had not been effective against the enemy night raids. The plane was designed to combat large multi-engine bombers, but the Japs were using fighter-bombers to do their dirty work. These nimble planes would bomb and strafe the strip at will and return to their bases, mostly in nearby Samar, unharmed—almost unchallenged. The pilots and gunners of the Black Widows told us, almost with tears in their eyes, that they felt completely helpless trying to maneuver their big twin-engined planes against Jap fighters. The P-61 lacked the characteristics necessary for that kind of operation, such as agility, range, speed, water injection for quick bursts of speed, and adequate radar. I believe it was the first American aircraft specifically designed

421st NFS P-61s lined up at Peleliu. ***421st NFS***

Sgt. "Red" Brown beside Lt. Fred Kohl's P-61A "Sleepy Time Gal." ***Kohl***

as a night fighter, and it was an impressive looking plane, but it was not capable of handling the duty required of it in the Philippines Campaign.

The radar of the P-61 was installed in the nose, with the antenna facing forward. The antenna rotated horizontally for 360 degrees, at a relatively slow rate, so that a large portion of each scan was blocked out by the fuselage. With these limitations, it is easy to understand why the crews told us they had never seen a Jap plane on their radar, much less shoot one down.

To say this to any former member of the 421st NFS is sure to get a bit of a smile, but there has never been a documented case where a 421st NFS crew, or any other P-61 crew ever had "tears in their eyes" because of what the P-61 lacked.

Whatever the case may be, the Marines came. Their Commander, Lt. Col. Peter D. Lambrecht, would arrive at Tacloban with twelve of his F6F Hellcats, twenty-three pilots, eight ground officers, and one hundred and eighteen enlisted men who came the 602 miles to trade bases with the 421st NFS. After they arrived, however, they found that what they had been taught under the Marines and how they were going to be used would be two different things. Colonel Lambrecht came up with a plan to fly sixteen three-hour sorties each night, as they did at Peleliu. But the Army Commander of the 308th Bomb Wing had other ideas for the Marines. He wanted Lambrecht to do his patrols during the dawn and dusk, much as the P-61s had done. He felt this was the time when his planes needed the most protection. Lambrecht pointed out that this operation was more fitting for Army day fighters. There was no need for radar direction and interception on this type of mission. But the Commander informed Lambrecht that his pilots were not trained for predawn take-offs and after dark landings. Lambrecht felt that he was being used in a manner that was a waste of his squadron's time. And, of course, there were numerous other problems, as descried by Col. William Odell:

> The worst of several handicaps was the absence of the squadron's own well trained GCI controllers. On those occasions when the pilots were sent out on true night missions, they were likely to find themselves in the position of Lt. O.K. Wilson, who was chasing two bogies at 0430 on 10 December when Army GCI vectored him in the wrong direction and caused him to lose not only the enemy planes, but also himself. Listeners on the ground heard some violent expostulations from "O.K." when he discovered he was lost—but then, it is not a nice feeling.

One Marine pilot also noted:

> The doggone Army is not only fouled up, but don't seem to know how flyers operate. With twenty-three pilots, they expect us to carry out 20 to 50 sorties a day. Not only that, but they forgot the function of night fighters and leave the airfield wide open for attack, keeping all of our pilots on dawn and dusk patrol, many of which seem unnecessary. It is a miracle to me that the Army in the Pacific have not lost all that the Marines and the Navy have taken.

The major problem with some of the Army GCI stations was again the lack of experience and understanding of night fighting. One of the stations, "Blue Eyes," just south of Tacloban, was having the most problems. Its radar was being directed toward the east and had only 75% coverage to the northwest for only 40 miles between Leyte and Samar. The GCI sight was partially blocked by 4,000-foot mountains on the one side, and its best function was assisting instrument approaches of U.S. aircraft. The station at Baybay also covered only about 75% of the sky. There were two Marine controllers attached to the Army, and they protested about the location of the site. The Army eventually moved the site, but to an even worse position. The site was located next to native huts with metal roofs that weakened the radar's signal. At this position the site could only pick up enemy aircraft below 10,000 feet at a distance of only about 20 miles. As much as the Marines protested, the Army, confident with their decision, would do nothing to remedy the situation.

In addition, and seemingly on cue, the lights on the Tacloban strip would work only 10% of the time on the first three nights of the Marines' visit, and were never available when needed. In some cases returning Marine aircraft had to orbit from fifteen minutes to an hour. Once again jeeps had to be rounded up alongside the runway to show the Marines home. Lambrecht finally sent for his own light set up and field lighting crew, and this particular problem was solved.

In most cases there was both good and bad passed between the Army and Marines. Both groups would say they got along pretty well and had a healthy respect for each other. The problems mostly surfaced between the Marines and the powers that be in the Army Command. The Marines definitely had no love for General MacArthur, who they felt, among other things, helped the Army take all the glory assignments and gave the Marines the tough battles without recognition. They also felt that "Dugout Doug" was a publicity hound and a super egotist. Whatever their feelings were, however, they were still under Army management for at least five weeks.

Meanwhile, at Peleliu, Captain Bill Bradley took 32 officers, 63 enlisted men, and half of the squadron's aircraft to the temporary base. Bradley got the men squared away and started an alert schedule for the following night. The squadron also had the help of some of the Marines left at Peleliu for aircraft maintenance and to keep the flying operations going. Back at Tacloban the Marine detachment stationed there had the help from the remaining 421st NFS members. One thing the squadron personnel noticed right away was that there was a distinct line between the enlisted and officers in the Marines, more so than in the Army. This also included Marines that served as non-commissioned pilots who flew with their units. Within the 421st NFS detachment, they held their own views of the Marines and the island.

Lt. Fred Kohl later wrote:

> I remember the island as being a mass of white coral, and being issued a 5th of whiskey along with the Marine Corps officers. I was not much on booze, so I saved it and later gave it to a guy to paint a picture of a scantily clad (of course) gal and "Sleepy time Gal" on the side of my airplane. It was not a very good job, however.

Curtiss Burgess wrote the following in his journal:

> About my so-called 40 days of R&R spent on Peleliu Island in the western Pacific. Those 40 days turned out to be the most miserable time I spent in the war. When we arrived on the island, it had only recently been secured. Around the mouths of the caves on "Bloody Nose Ridge" were strewn the many Japs slain in those terrible battles. Their bodies were torn to pieces, head here, torso there, legs and arms everywhere. The Japs had been buried in mass graves, which were scooped out by bulldozers and then covered over by another bulldozer. The island stank terribly because of this. There were also millions of land crabs everywhere. They would keep you awake at night, scurrying about. But the worst thing was the sand fleas. During the 40 days I kept my collar buttoned up, my cuffs on my shirt tied, and my pant legs were also tied. I had a solid sore around my neck, wrists, and ankles. I was glad to give up R&R.

Bill Gorman remembered it, also:

> The worst part of it was having to live with the Marines. The 421st was not a Gung-ho outfit. When it came to saluting, dressing up, knowing the differences between officers and enlisted men, and other junk like that we were not as duty-bound. We all worked together and got along good. The Marines did not believe in that. One mess served officers and enlisted men with a screen wire down the middle of it. Officers on one side had fresh eggs, real meat, lettuce, and other good food. The enlisted men sat on the other side and ate rations out of a can. The Marines expected you to salute them even when you were on the flightline getting ready for flights. We spent over a month there, and it was a very long time.

P-61A #42-5512 showing damage to tail booms from debris after the Japanese transport was shot down at Tacloban. ***Bjorum***

As far as air operations the 421st NFS only ended up standing their regular alerts and flew occasional test flights, but unlike the battles of November they had no contact with the enemy. VMF-(N)-541, on the other hand, was credited with 924 combat hours flown, 22 enemy aircraft shot down, and 5 more destroyed on the ground. In releasing the squadron General MacArthur informed Nimitz that the Marines had performed magnificently during their temporary duty. MacArthur went so far as to award the Marines the Distinguished Unit Citation, the only Marine unit so honored during World War II. The original reasons that MacArthur insisted on the swap in the first place never really transpired. The missions flown and kills by the Marines were in itself commendable, but none of them were true night fighter kills under radar control. VMF-(N)-541, as stated before, flew dawn and dusk missions, so MacArthur's clamoring for night protection for his forces was unsound to say the least. Japanese aircraft, in fact, continued to bomb Tacloban at night with or without the Marines there. On January 11th, 1945, the Marines returned to Peleliu, and Bill Bradley and the 421st NFS returned to Tacloban.

During the Marine visit on December 6th a Japanese "Tabby" transport aircraft, which looked similar to the American C-47 got into Tacloban's traffic pattern in an attempt to land. One report stated that an English speaking Japanese pilot called for permission to land on the airstrip using a call sign of one of the P-38 units stationed there. Realizing that the P-38 was on the ground and the other plane was marked with Japanese "meatballs," a twin .50 caliber position, as well as others opened up on the aircraft. The plane swerved and skidded onto the beach parallel to the landing strip, plowing in between a PBY aircraft and a P-61, and hitting a cletrack where it exploded. Upon impact one of the Japanese engines rolled across the beach and over a trench. Corporal Harry Ellwanger and Corporal William Wolfrom were both burned when the plane crashed. Both were in the small slit trench when the plane exploded and a gasoline fire raged all around them. Their clothing caught fire, and they ran into the ocean to put out the flames. Two GIs in a jeep picked up Wolfrom. He was transferred to an ambulance to go the field hospital. Ellwanger was nowhere to be see. The roads to the hospital were so muddy that Wolfrom's ambulance eventually bogged down, and with little choice on the matter he walked the rest of the way. Soon afterwards, Ellwanger, burned but alive, also showed up at the hospital. Both Corporals were burned pretty badly, and in visiting them later squadron members reported that they both looked like mummies.

As for the crash itself, it was discovered that the transport had been filled with Japanese Marines, who intended to land and attack the field, however, not one on the Japanese plane survived the crash. The cost of the attack was one cletrack, a PBY Flying Boat destroyed, plus damage to the tail booms on P-61A #42-5509, which was repaired to fly again. P-61A #42-5512 was also damaged and later salvaged. Other then the two 421st NFS members no one else was hurt or injured. There were some scattered reports that the Japanese had tried this at other American bases, but no documents have been found to substantiate this.

Upon their return to Tacloban the squadron was again asked to escort Navy PT boats on their missions, as well as having a squadron representative go along on the boat. The 7th PT Boat Squadron approached the 421st NFS, and it was worked out between the two units to participate in joint missions. The PT boat Commander felt that this was a good idea to have some kind of air cover when they had to go down through the Surigao Straight and up into the Ormac Bay area.

By this time more of the squadron's pilots wanted to go on these missions. On one particular evening Lt. David Youker and Lt. Robert Pew got aboard on a mission to Ormac Bay, in which they would both be observers on this trip. This particular mission was one that Youker and Pew would always remember and regret. Lt. Youker later shared his memories of that ill-fated mission:

> This mission was to be one of the most frightening experiences of my life. We were operating out of Tacloban in the Leyte Gulf. Our planes had been stretched to the limit, and many were grounded requiring extensive repair and maintenance. Bob Pew and I were bored with inactivity and decided to pay some of the Navy crews a visit. Our flight crews had been in radio contact with them during numerous missions.
>
> When we arrived we were royally received and learned that two boats were going on a search and destroy mission that evening. We were invited to go along and enthusiastically accepted. The two officers in our boat were both family men and needed to complete two more missions before going home.
>
> We proceeded along the coast of Leyte in the early evening, though it was still daylight. When we were approximately 30 to 45 minutes out, two enemy planes were spotted at about 2,000 feet. They passed directly overhead, and suddenly peeled off and began to dive toward us, each heading for one of the boats. Our skipper went to full power and began evasive action. Bob and I were standing a few feet behind him, and thinking we were going to be strafed, we soon hit the deck. Our gun crews commenced firing and continued to man the guns throughout the plane's dive. I considered them very brave men.
>
> The plane that had targeted us came down at a slight angle and struck our boat on the portside, in the cockpit area, midway between the torpedoes and the fuel tanks. There was a tremendous crash on impact, and then I remember complete silence. Bob and I were covered with debris, but managed to stand up simultaneously. We looked over at the Skipper, who had been standing at the helm, and all that remained was the torso. His head had been decapitated, and his legs were gone. The second officer had also been killed. I deeply regret that I do not remember their names. Most of the crew had been thrown into the water, some dead and some with various degrees of injury. Fortunately, the other plane missed its target and dove harmlessly into the sea. The other PT Boat came up alongside and picked up the survivors and casualties.
>
> On the return to Tacloban, the crew administered medical attention to the injured. Bob had several facial lacerations, and I suffered a deep gash in my left leg. Many of the crewmembers were severely injured, and needless to say, we were grateful to be alive. I spent two months in a field hospital recuperating from my leg injury. Bob and I were awarded the Purple Heart medal. To this day I have the utmost admiration for the Navy PT boat crews during the war, who endured extremely hazardous duty and, in my opinion, were the unsung heroes of the war.

Life back at camp went on, and the men faced both the good and bad of the war in stride. For entertainment Sgt. Henry Simacek got a 16 mm Bell & Howell movie projector for the troops. During one of the raids it was hit by a bomb fragment, which took out the light. Bradley issued an order for a new projector, realizing the need for something for the men to take their minds off the war, even for a little bit. It was clear, though, at the time that movies were not a high priority item. Simacek and a fellow squadron member decided to find a substitute. The rest of the projector seemed okay, so it was just a matter of a light. Some crashed Navy fighters that were sitting near the 421st NFS were the first to be looked at. While removing the batteries out of the aircraft, they discovered that the gunsight bulb had similar dimensions. The bulb was a little large, but they finally got it in position and wired it to one of the dimmers in a series with a battery so they would not burn the film or photocell out. That evening the squadron personnel got to enjoy movies once again. The sound was not perfect for a Betty Grable film, but it did not seem to matter. That first night the squadron also had five air raids, so with the breaks in the movie it did not get over with until about 2:00 in the morning. This was used for a couple of months until the squadron received a brand new RCA movie projector.

Other people had different priorities for their own peace of mind. On Christmas Eve around 10:00 in the evening, Corporals Joe Heeb, Larry Neville, and Efraim Lopez were going to walk to evening church services near Tacloban. Neville talks about this memorable walk:

> Jap bombers, evidently trying to catch us off guard, gave us a busy night. We were in and out of foxholes and muddy ditches most of the night. We decided to sleep in our last mud hole. We finally made early mass at 0800 Christmas Day, but

Lt. David Youker at Tacloban. ***Youker***

The Squadron latrine burns in the background, causing interest and amusement for the personnel at Leyte. ***Goldstein***

the memorable night is what I remember most about Christmas 1944. Efraim dirtied his shorts, claimed it was a load of mud; Joe Heeb swears he saw St. Peter, and I never made another attempt to go to church again.

One final incident occurred with the ending of 1944, and that was the famous "latrine burning" that took place at Tacloban. One of the squadron's enlisted men had been given the duty to clean out the latrine. Using an extra amount of aviation fuel the man intended to clean it out the best he could. A spark from a still unknown source ignited the fuel, and the latrine created quite a spectacle to the squadron members for a couple of hours. The negative part of this was that the squadron had to build a new latrine, a duty that no one really cared for.

The month of December ended with the loss of some of the squadron's original members and key figures. Captain Bill Bradley, upon his return from Peleliu received orders to return to the U.S. He would remain the Commander of the 421st NFS until January 2nd, 1945. Also leaving the squadron was Lt. Frank Mott, Lt. William Gill, Lt. William Hartstock, and Lt. Robert Clodfelter. The squadron did pick up some new personnel and three new P-61s, including #42-5555, #42-39380, and #42-39443, which was the squadron's first P-61B aircraft.

Enemy bombing resumed on the 24th with several raids that night and renewed activity continuing for the balance of the month. The squadron suffered no further damage, however, despite several close hits. The 421st NFS was gearing up for the New Year and all that it would bring to the future of the men and machines of the squadron.

8

1945: San Marcelino & Clark

The beginning of 1945 brought numerous changes to the 421st Night Fighter Squadron. The New Year would include a number of command changes, a change of station, change of personnel, and a change in the squadron victories. The rotation of flying personnel and the assignment of numerous replacement crews considerably altered the make-up of the unit, which had been practically a family that had served together overseas for almost a year. The month of January began with the relief of Captain Bradley, who handed the command over to Captain Paul Zimmer. Zimmer in turn got orders home and left the squadron on the 15th, and the command went to Lt. Dorrie Jones. Jones would be the 421st NFS Commander for a total of five days until the new commander came to the squadron on the 20th, Captain Richard Kiick.

On the 11th the detachment of the 421st NFS left Peleliu and headed back to Tacloban, again switching places with VMF- (N)-541, which returned to its own base at Peleliu. The 421st NFS aircraft had been there since December 3rd. This brought the squadron all together once again, and flight operations began again at Tacloban. Coming back for the 421st NFS ground echelon and Bill Gorman proved to be an adventure in itself:

> Finally, after six weeks (Christmas 1944 included) we returned to Leyte and the rest of the squadron. We took off at about 4:00 in the morning in a C-47 transport loaded with about twenty of us. After about an hour out, there was a slight explosion and the right engine caught fire. We were going down fast, for you could feel the wind and whine of the plane. The worst part was not knowing how high we were above the ocean. Finally, we began to level off and the fire went out. We limped back to Peleliu and landed just after dawn. We were told that we had dropped 9,000 of the 10,000 feet that we were flying.

On another transport Curtis Burgess had the following memory:

> Before I left Peleliu and went back to Leyte, I'll tell you a couple times I thought my life would be lost in an airplane crack-up. The first time being when 30 of us boarded a C-46 to make a trip back to Leyte. When taking off, both engines began backfiring so badly that flashes would light up the whole inside of the plane. I really felt that the plane would lose all power and crash into the coral below, but somehow the pilot

Lt. Dorrie Jones was the 421st NFS Commander from January 15, 1945, through January 20, 1945. ***421st NFS***

Major Richard Kiick was the Commander of the 421st NFS January 20, 1945, through December 15, 1945. ***Kiick***

circled back to the end of the strip and landed. The next time was on a C-47 transport we boarded to make the trip back. We ran into such a bad storm that I did not see how we could get through it. There were only seven or eight on this plane. The distance was about 700 miles, and we had made about half the distance when the storm struck. We placed all the rafts and other equipment as near the side door as we could while waiting for the "bellying-in" we thought would come. We were jumping and swaying around so badly that the altimeter read 50 to 100 feet. All of a sudden we were clear of the storm, and into the bright sunshine. Did it look and feel good? You bet!

When most of the personnel got back to Tacloban they found that many of their fears had come true. Fred Kohl had just gotten back from Peleliu and found that the Marines had made themselves at home in his hut. He found that many of the walls had been knocked down and things were missing. He felt that he had definitely come home to a pig pen. There were bottles, cans, and trash in the hut, under it, and all around it. He felt that the Marines definitely took things a little too far.

Cover missions, patrols, and ground alerts again became the order of the day for the 421st NFS at Tacloban. With the reduced enemy activity in the area, most flights for the crews almost seemed routine. The squadron lost another P-61 on the night of the 16th, when a B-24 coming in for a landing blew one of its main tires. P-61A #42-5500 was parked just off to the side of the runway, but right in the path of the incoming bomber, which struck the P-61's nose with its wing. The crew of the bomber all got out of the aircraft, but #5500 had its nose torn off and was a total wreck. The squadron would also lose P-61A #42-5521, which was sent to the 10th Service Squadron as "War Weary."

On the 20th, Captain Richard D. Kiick took over command of the 421st NFS. He had come to the Southwest Pacific flying the P-38 with the 432nd Fighter Squadron. While with the 432nd FS he shot down two Japanese "Tony" fighters on November 10th, 1944, and had flown over fifty missions. Brigadier General Frederic H. Smith picked Captain Kiick to go to the 421st NFS to be an "organizational" leader, since the squadron had been left with only temporary commanders since Captain Bradley left. Kiick, a day fighter pilot at 24 years of age, was not a night fighter pilot and had not been trained with a crew to fly night missions. In the long run, however, Kiick proved to be a most able and excellent leader, and just what the squadron needed.

Kiick relates his first days with the squadron:

> I knew nothing about the P-61 when I took over the squadron, don't believe I had ever seen one. Anyway, early on I made it to one of Dorrie Jones' Operations briefings for that night's activities. I found myself explaining how by sight you could synchronize your propellers' rotation with the rotation of the aircraft ahead of you, thereby minimizing throttle movement. After a slight pause I realized the props are behind the pilot on the P-61! Extremely embarrassing!
>
> I sneaked into another Dorrie briefing through a back flap of the tent and heard Dorrie say, "The 'old man' wants it done this way." Moments later I realized that he was talking about me, his 24 year old Commander! I sneaked back out.

The 421st NFS again suffered a major setback during the month of January. On the 20th Lt. Robert H. Reynolds was taking off in P-61A #42-5499 from Tacloban when his port engine blew up. Lt. Reynolds ditched the aircraft, and the crew, including F/O Robert Van Sant as R/O and Pfc. Raymond F. Curren as gunner, made their way to get out of the sinking ship. The crew cleared the aircraft, but F/O Van Sant's Mae West did not inflate, and despite the efforts of the other crew members to save him, he was drowned. Search teams recovered his body several days later, and a funeral was held by the squadron. Reynolds ditched his plane at 4:49 AM, and it sank almost immediately. One possible reason for the engine to explode was turned up by an investigation of other P-61 engines also having similar problems. Research showed that a flat washer installed as a pressure seal on the fuel line would sometimes have scratches on the surface. By not getting a good seal on the line, it was shown to cause a fuel and vapor build-up under the cowl until heat or a

Studio photo of Major Richard Kiick in 1945. ***Kiick***

421st NFS P-61s leaving Peleliu to return to Tacloban. ***421st NFS***

spark caused it to explode. This happened a number of times on the P-61, and a full inspection was ordered, with many of the washers being replaced.

Orders from 5th Fighter Command were issued for the movement of the ground echelon of the 421st NFS to Luzon on the 22nd. One flight of the squadron's P-61s were also scheduled to go to the new location, while the balance of the flight echelon remained at Tacloban with a required number of maintenance personnel. Camp was struck, and the loading of LST #606 was begun by the squadron at once. By working through the night the loading was completed on the morning of the 23rd, and the LST, with nine officers and one hundred forty-five enlisted men aboard, pulled into Tacloban Harbor. The ship stood by until the 24th, when the convoy finally set sail at 9:00 the next morning. The LST arrived at Mindoro on the 25th and dropped anchor off shore, where it remained for several days before resuming the voyage. In the meantime, back at Tacloban on the 24th, Lt. Owen Wolf downed his fourth "confirmed" enemy aircraft. This brought the 421st NFS to the "official" score of thirteen kills.

Wolf's next victory occurred while on a patrol over the Ormac Bay area, in the vicinity of Natag-og with his regular crew, R/O Lt. Byron N. Allain and gunner S/Sgt. Trabing. Wolf was given vectors on a bogie heading west of Ormac toward Burauen. Wolf was flying at 10,000 feet and made a 180-degree turn when the GCI told him to fly a heading of 90 degrees. Lt. Allain called in that he had a blip on his scope and he took over the interception, only to have the bogie disappear. Wolf was given a starboard turn by GCI, and again Lt. Allian made contact on his airborne equipment with the bogie at approximately 8:30. Lt. Allain got the enemy on his scope and guided his pilot to close in. The night fighter was doing approximately 250 mph, having climbed to 12,000 feet, and closing in on the bogie with a 20-mph advantage. At about 1,500 feet S/Sgt. Trabing sighted the bogie, a Japanese Zeke (type 32) off the port side of the night fighter. Wolf throttled back and made a gentle turn, closing to 1,000 feet, to a point where the pilot and gunner opened fire simultaneously with the 20 mm and .50 caliber machine guns. Tracers and high explosive ammunition were seen to hit the fuselage, wings, and engine cowling of the fighter, parts of which flew from the plane. The Japanese fighter split-essed into the overcast, bursting into flames, and crashing on the east side of the hills a short distance east of 5th Fighter Command at Barauen. Lt. Wolf reported that the Japanese pilot had no idea there was a night fighter in the area, so no evasive action was taken.

Another bogie contact was made later that evening, however, problems with communications between the P-61 and GCI, as well as the time lag which resulted, caused the night fighter to lose what little chance he may have had for contact.

On a third occasion that same evening another 421st NFS P-61 was crossing the southern tip of Biliran Island. The pilot took up a direct heading south when the GCI station "Bearded" reported a bogie in the area seven miles from the night fighter's 2 o'clock position. The bogie was approaching from the south. A request by the pilot for altitude was not answered by GCI. A short time later, however, the station said they could not read the bogie's altitude. The P-61 was at 10,000 feet, and he dropped to 5,000 feet, indicat-

P-61A #42-5500, or what's left of its nose after a B-24 struck it after losing a main tire on landing. The aircraft's radar assembly is visible at the bottom of the photo. ***Burdue***

ing approximately a 300-mph airspeed, when the R/O reported a blip on his scope. The bogie was about five miles out and 10 degrees starboard. The night fighter was still flying on a southerly course, and the bogie was approaching on a straight west heading. The blip was lost by the R/O, and at that time the GCI station reported that their equipment had gone out and there was no further GCI or R/O radar contact with the bogie. The pilot did notice two flares burning off his starboard side and below the night fighter, followed by four distinct streams of tracer ammunition, apparently from anti-aircraft fire near the village of Tinago on the northwest tip of Leyte Island, just north of San Isisdro Bay. The pilot and gunner believed that the bogie dropped flares to light up the area and to strafe along the beach from the bay to the vicinity of the village of Taglanigan. There was red tracer fire from the ground anti-aircraft, which trailed the bogie on his attack run across the beach. The bogie itself was never hit, and eluded the night fighter that was hunting for it.

Crews begin to salvage #42-5500 for parts for other aircraft. ***Burdue***

Enemy activity during this period for the squadron was at a minimum, in sharp contrast to what the squadron had to face during previous months. There were a few nightly raids and alerts, but most of the raids on Leyte pretty much came to an end. The ground echelon on LST #606 in the convoy sailed along in peace, and there were no attacks made against them during the course of the trip. The Philippine campaign was progressing apace, with isolated pockets of Japanese being systematically eliminated. The possibility of renewed activity on Luzon was always a prospect, but developments there were still in the immediate future.

At the end of January the ground echelon was still aboard LST #606 anchored off Mindoro. The ship sailed for Luzon on February 2nd, arriving at Subic Bay the following day. The 421st NFS members beached at 10:00 that morning, the LST pulling right up on shore at Subic and greatly facilitating the unloading in comparison with the previous experience at Tacloban. Unloading of the LST was completed the same day, and the squadron moved inland about twelve miles into its new area at the San Marcelino airstrip.

Even with the relocation of a part of the squadron, flying would continue at both Tacloban and at San Marcelino. After the tense and active period the squadron went through at Tacloban, the 421st NFS was surprised to find Japanese activity over the new area almost at a standstill, but the uninterrupted nights were quite welcome, if not an unexpected relief.

A new member of the squadron had also made the journey with the 421st NFS, and that was "Gizmo," a monkey that had been adopted by the squadron at Tacloban. The squadron did have a pet dog named "Rosie," but she came to a sad end at Tacloban. Marines racing along the flightline in a jeep had hit her. This did not improve the already strained relationship with the squadron and Marines, to say the least. Because of this, squadron members constructed a line of sandbags across the road to slow down traffic in the future, maybe a testament to one of the world's first "speed bumps." Gizmo, like all pets, had his good and bad sides. One noted adventure of Gizmo was a run in with Lt. Forrester. Forrester had a carton of cigarettes inside his duffel bag, which was in his tent and tied securely. Gizmo managed to untie the bag, drag out the carton of cigarettes, and proceeded to open every pack and break each and every one. In the Southwest Pacific area of fighting cigarettes were hard to come by and were considered as good as gold. Forrester was none to happy about losing his cigarettes, and let the monkey know it with a good swat. Gizmo was also famous for his knack of knowing there was going to be an air raid. Squadron members say that you could watch him head for the shelter and know trouble

Another view of #42-5500. ***Burdue***

The B-24 shows the damage sustained after hitting the P-61. ***Burdue***

was coming. He was usually the first in the dugout, even before an alarm had sounded.

The camp at San Marcelino began to take shape at once. The area was well situated, in country somewhat reminiscent of parts of the U.S., and the men began to feel that this new camp was a decided improvement over the jungles of New Guinea and the swamplands of Tacloban. In short order Filipino labor was again contracted to help construct buildings and make camp feel like home. It was only a short time until a well was dug and water was made available for showers and other facilities. This was a welcome addition to the camp, considering the dry and dusty days the men had to live and work in.

On the 8th, six of the 421st NFS P-61s arrived at San Marcelino from Tacloban, and flight operations were established. For the rest of the month the squadron would operate from both bases.

As Col. William Odell would later write, to the crews flying out of San Marcelino and everywhere else the P-61 would continue to show its value:

> It was at San Marcelino that the pilots came to appreciate the unique characteristics of their P-61s. In practice simulating an engine failure on take-off, 1st. Lt. Carl Bjorum had convinced himself that if there was sufficient forward speed for the main landing gear to leave the ground, he could continue to climb out on one engine as Northrop test pilot, John Myers, had repeatedly demonstrated. That remarkable ability, with turret and a full combat load, excluding external stores, was reassuring for those who flew from the short strip at San Marcelino. Its length was slightly more than 6,000 feet. The 421st often conducted operations from half that length, because the other half was closed for maintenance at night, so as not to inconvenience the day fighters, who needed all the runway they could.

Back at Tacloban on February 3rd, things were going down hill for the squadron, and mostly for Lt. Dorrie Jones, who would have to leave two planes on one day. Both P-61A #42-5504 and P-61A #42-5562 were lost, plus the additional loss of a crewmember:

> I had been out on a flight, and I landed the bird back at Tacloban so softly the tires went "chirp, chirp, chirp," and I rolled to a very gentle stop; then the son of a gun caught fire, and I had to bail out right there on the runway. That was not the end of the trouble, though.

Another view of the damaged B-24. ***Burdue***

Lt. Owen Wolf's P-61A "Dame de la Nuit" (Lady of the Night) showing four confirmed kills. Not all the kills were scored in this aircraft. Most were in CO Bill Bradley's plane P-61A #42-5521. The number of this plane is thought to be #42-5516. ***Owen***

> I got to the operations tent, and they told me the material people (supply) had discovered some badly needed radar parts at Biak, which was a base on a little island out there just on the north side of New Guinea. Somebody had to go down there and get those radar parts, and it had to be someone who could identify what we needed—guess who? They had a big rainstorm, and the papers got mixed up and didn't match the boxes the parts were in. Boy, that was the supply system for you!
>
> My leg, that had been hurt previously, was still not healed, and was giving me enough trouble that the doctors limited me to four hours of flying per day, so I could not fly down to pick them up. Anyway, I had to check out a new pilot, 1st Lt. Vincent W. King, who had just got in. He could fly an airplane all right, but he needed a "route check" from somebody who had been there before. I climbed in and sat in the gunner's seat, right behind the pilot, with the Radar Observer F/O RayMazalan at my back, and away we went! So, we get about 700 miles over water and land on another of the little islands to gas up.
>
> It was getting along mid-afternoon, and we were still 800 miles away from Biak Island, on the north shore of New Guinea. Well, it did not bother us, so off we go again. About halfway there we ran into the damnedest, biggest storm you ever saw, and the weatherman had not mentioned that any bad weather might be around. The bird bounced, and bounced, and turned us every which way but loose, but I had to act calm and collected so they would not panic.
>
> I was sitting there with my leg out on crutches and reading a book, and the R/O and this new pilot were having a conversation about which way to go, and I could not hear them with the earphones turned off. Well, they fooled around too darn long without asking me, and we got almost 160 miles off course, miles we could not afford to lose.
>
> Well, by then we were down by what they called the Gumic Bay area. They had a huge bay, really a great harbor, on the

The ground echelon of the 421st NFS unloads on the beach twelve miles from its new home at San Marcelino. ***421st NFS***

One of the squadron's P-61s taxis out to the runway in preparation for another mission. ***Davis***

New Guinea coast. The Japs still controlled this entire coastline, almost over to Hollandia. So, here we are over this bay, with Japs all around us, and the needle said empty! Not just "E" for empty, but "A" for absolutely!

We are flying at 11,000 feet and had gotten out of the stormy weather, but we were all soaked to the skin. It was not only us, but the parachutes and maps were soaked, as this darned P-61 leaked like a sieve. We knew we were going to have to walk, so ankles and elbows went flying around to clean up the cockpit so we could get out. During this process my R/O Ray says, "Look, fellows, let's not jump over the water, I'm scared shitless of water." "Now you tell us," I said, "when we have no 'go-juice' left." The plane had found its way over the jungle by now, and we all bailed at about 10,000 feet; Ray went first and drifted inland quite a ways.

Lt. Bjorum and the squadron's newest member, "Gizmo." ***421st NFS***

Struggling out through the canopy into 150 mph airflow I pulled my "D" ring, but my chute would not open. It was wet and soggy and had to be pulled out by hand. Flying down there I felt naked, but finally got the silk umbrella open above me. About 8 or 9 seconds later I went through the tops of the tall trees; boy, that was close.

I thought about the young pilot, who did not follow instructions and went over the side, which meant almost sure death. There were many snags on the fuselage that could get you, so I told him to slide back with me and go right over the wing. He did not do that, and I never saw him again. I never saw the plane again, either, and I did not know if the guns had gone off, but there was no gas to burn and no way to ever find it in that dense jungle.

In fact, years later King's airplane was located in the New Guinea jungle, and the wreckage is still there to this day. Lt. King's body, however, was never recovered. On the 26th Lt. Jones and F/O Ray Mazalan returned to the unit after being lost since the 3rd. Jones and Mazalan had landed in New Guinea just inland from the northern coast, roughly south of Japen Island. Though coming down some 200 yards apart, the dense jungle prevented their getting together, and they found their way to the coast separately.

Jones was in the jungle for four days, and finally he made contact with some natives who brought him to the Dutch Post at Soroei. From here he was evacuated and reached Biak, and from there he proceeded to San Marcelino. Mazalan, on the other hand, would spend ten days in the jungle. Making his way through the swamps and jungle growth he went without food for nine days. He eventually made contact with the natives, who also brought him to the coast to the native village of Wanti. Nica authorities took him to Soroei. He was picked up there with Jones on a boat back to Biak. From then on they made their way back together.

The P-61, as previously mentioned, was not a good plane to bail out from. Pilots such as Bjorum would later say that once you crawled into the P-61, maneuvered your way into the pilot's seat, locked it back into position, strapped in, and cranked up, you had it made. That is only, though, if you did not have to leave the plane in a hurry. Most of the pilots would say that bailing out of the P-61 "was a real bastard as far as the pilot was concerned." Both the gunner and Radar Observer had it made, if they had to bail out. There were three exit methods, two of which could be effective. The third, the top hatch, was not intended as an in-flight exit. Lowering the landing gear and leaving by way of the bottom hatch was one possible method. The other and only practical way (using "practical" only loosely) involved unlatching the pilot's seat, tilting the seat backwards, and clawing your way back to the gunner's escape hatch on the starboard side. This, of course, all depended on how much time you had.

Curtis Burgess on the flightline at San Marcelino. *421st NFS*

Part of the airstrip at Clark. Photo taken February 1945. *421st NFS*

Before the month of February was over the squadron would lose another P-61 in an accident. This occurred with Captain Beverly S. Bowers at the controls of P-61A #42-5520. During a routine landing at San Marcelino on the 21st everything seemed to go wrong with the brake system. #5520, or "Janie," had previously been piloted by Lt. William Gill before he was sent back to the States. On this particular flight Curtiss Burgess just happened to be the lucky passenger:

> I was in a plane crack-up while at San Marcelino, but thank God, it was on the ground. This is how it happened. I had taken the RO's seat to fly with Captain Beverly B. Bowers over to Clark Field. It was only about 40 miles across the mountains, 100 miles by road. We made it to Clark Field fine, and Captain Bowers took care of his business. We started our take-off, and a small plane pulled in front of us before we reached take-off speed. We returned to the end of the runway and took off. When we made our landing at San Marcelino, our hydraulic pressure failed, which left us only emergency air pressure for the brakes. At the end of the strip was a couple hundred yards of flat clay, and then there was a huge drainage ditch. Captain Bowers cut power to both engines, hoping the plane would roll to a stop before coming to the ditch. It did not roll dead, so the airbrakes were activated, which threw the plane forward on its nose and the two milling props. The plane rocked back on the twin booms, smashing them straight up in the air. I was out of the R/O compartment before the plane stopped rocking. We later salvaged partsfrom the P-61.

With the coming of March the 421st NFS would score another aerial victory, but the squadron's "official" tally would remain unchanged at thirteen. The reason for this was the loss of credit for the plane downed by Lt. Dave Corts on September 9th, 1944. This was the engagement in which one Japanese bomber shot down another trying to shoot down Corts, who was between the two.

Within the squadron, many replacements were joining the squadron as many of the "old hands" were rotated back to the States. One of the 421st NFS crews, with less then a month with the squadron, would add to the unit's scoreboard. Early on the morning of March 11, 2nd Lt. Carl Remington, on patrol with his R/O, F/O William B. Boze, and gunner, T/Sgt. Brady W. Swinney, encountered a twin-engine enemy bomber southwest of Lingayan Golf. A vector was given to Remington by GCI, and the Radar Observer got a blip showing the aircraft on his scope. The Japanese were using "window" extensively in the area, but despite this the P-61 was able to keep contact and closed on the enemy bomber. Coming within range T/Sgt. Swinney opened up with the .50 caliber guns on the bomber; the Japanese aircraft, which turned out to be a "Betty," burst into flames, went into a steep dive, and crashed into the ocean at 6:25 that morning.

Since the month was pretty quiet as far as enemy activity went, ground support was added to the squadron missions. Besides the usual night patrols and alerts, both squadron detachments did considerable strafing in support of ground troops. Throughout the month these missions were undertaken over the lines west of Fort Stotsenberg, and the Tacloban detachment attacked the island of Cebu.

Left to right are: Captain William Page; Sgt. Richard Barker; Sgt. William Rife; M/Sgt. Jake Loran; M/Sgt. Herbert Goldstein; Sgt. Richard Shepard; and Lt. Ralph Moore. Photo taken in front of the 421st NFS Headquarters building at Clark Field. ***421st NFS***

Squadron P-61s lined up at Clark Field. ***Natiello***

In special cases 421st NFS crews also became involved with other missions, as well. Such was the case of Lt. David Youker and his crew:

> Lt. Robert C. Pew and I were called in for a briefing on March 18th, 1945, with Major Richard Kiick, our Commander, and our Intelligence Officer, Lt. Isadore Nachman. We were informed that an urgent radio message had been received from the island of Cebu, that the Japanese were threatening to overrun and capture an important airstrip on the island. The plan was for me to lead our flight to Cebu early the next morning to pick up Colonel Cushing, a guerilla officer who would direct us to the target area (principally a Japanese Headquarters) for a low level strafing attack. I assume we were selected for this mission, as opposed to day fighters, because of the firepower of the P-61, which was four 20 mm cannons and four .50 caliber machine guns. Also, I believe they considered us because of our capability of landing on and taking off from the short landing strip at Cebu.
>
> We proceeded as planned and landed at Cebu shortly after daybreak. We were greeted enthusiastically by a rather large reception committee, and much to our surprise, we were escorted to a large dining area and served a huge breakfast, including fresh eggs (a real treat) and fried chicken. After breakfast we then boarded our aircraft, with Colonel Cushing seated directly behind me, and I prepared to take-off. This, in itself, was quite an experience because of the shortness of the runway. We lined up at the extreme end of the strip, applied full power to both engines with the brakes on, and 1/2 flaps before starting our take-off run. Lt. Pew and I were airborne with room to spare, and then the problems developed. The Colonel was trying to use a crude map that was on such a large scale it proved to be practically useless from the air at a speed of 250 mph. To make matters worse, the Colonel became airsick and had to use the barfbag. After a bit he finally collected himself. We then circled the area, using the airstrip as a reference point, to get him oriented. He was then able to direct us to the target area, which proved to be several barracks type structures. We went in fast at tree top level and strafed the area. We made

several runs, encountered return fire from small arms and machine guns, but at the speed we were moving they were ineffective. We then dropped the Colonel off at the landing strip and returned to base at Tacloban.

Subsequent radio contact indicated that we had been effective, but they would like a repeat performance, which Lt. Pew and I carried out on the 21st. Lt. Pew flew cover as I picked up the Colonel and later joined in during the strafing. Things went smoothly, and the only problem developed after we had completed our attack and were returning to drop off the Colonel. My .50 caliber guns were so hot they were misfiring every few seconds. I instructed my gunner, Sgt. Joe W. French, to aim the guns straight up so we would not endanger anyone on the ground. We returned to our base without incident. The following day, our radio contact reported that the enemy had retreated and the airstrip was out of danger. Other supporting missions were praised by the infantry, and it was felt that these attacks were eminently successful.

Japanese ground activity was now pretty much nonexistent, and at San Marcelino there were only two alerts throughout the month. No bombs were dropped, although nearby Clark Field did undergo a few minor bombing attacks. There was a tendency at this point to dispose of empty beer cans in foxholes; a sure sign there was little anticipation of enemy activity. The only combat the unit saw that month, aside from the strafing missions, was the discovery of a Japanese Marine, who was dispatched by Lt. Tom Malone.

Carl Bjorum and Tom Malone shared a tent at San Marcelino, and they were getting some sleep because they were scheduled to fly a mission that night. A young Filipino "house boy" came in and started telling them about a Japanese soldier. Bjorum told Malone to go check it out so he could get some sleep. Malone got up and grabbed a .45 caliber Tommy gun and a full clip, and headed out the door with the boy. A short time later Bjorum was awakened by the sound of nearby machine gun fire. Malone had in fact fired off a whole clip. When he returned to the tent he removed the clip and handed it to the boy to clean. He informed Bjorum that he had taken care of the Japanese intruder. What Bjorum later found out was the boy had come cross a piece of corrugated steel that had been pulled up over a hole. When the boy moved the metal he saw that a wounded Japanese Marine was in the hole taking cover. Malone had went out and fired the whole clip into the hole, killing the Japanese soldier. Malone then went calmly back to the tent and went back to bed.

A main street in Manila. Signs still warn of mines that have not been cleared. *421st NFS*

Another view of 421st NFS P-61s lined up behind a B-25 at Clark. *421st NFS*

On the 13th Captain Kiick flew P-61A #42-39380 to Mindoro for a meeting at Headquarters. A couple days later Kiick and his R/O for the flight, Lt. Robert L. Kunzman, made ready for their flight back home. At the end of the runway Kiick discovered that his hydraulic pressure was low and decided to taxi the plane back to the parking spot. While he was going down the taxiway, two A-20s were coming directly at him, so he took a quick left back to the spot. About that time he lost all pressure, and the plane kept going on a straight course until it hit a small drainage ditch. The landing gear was sprung backwards and the plane came to a sudden halt. The tail booms hit the ground, rupturing both. Kiick and Kunzman were both okay and walked away from the wreck. Both later went back to San Marcelino by transport. The P-61, however, was written off, and a crew was sent down to salvage any usable parts they could get.

On the 15th, Brigadier General Frederic H. Smith, Jr., Commanding Officer of 5th Fighter Command, visited the squadron for the presentation of decorations. A formation was held in a makeshift ball diamond at 10:00 in the morning and the ceremony went off smoothly. The squadron, for the first time in as many months, turned out in Class "A" uniform. Medals were presented to thirty-nine officers and enlisted men, totaling: one Legion of Merit; four Silver Stars; two Distinguished Flying Crosses; one Soldier's Medal; fifteen Air Medals; and twenty Purple Hearts. Captain Kiick was presented with one of the DFCs and an Air Medal. The officers then entertained General Smith to lunch before he headed back to Headquarters.

On the 19th, Fifth Air Force Movement order 66 arrived at the squadron instructing the 421st NFS to begin moving to Clark Field. The Tacloban detachment was to move first by LST, which started

In front of the San Lagaro Hospital in Manila left to right are: Munn; Moore; Burdue; and Brown taking in a little sightseeing. ***Burdue***

promptly on the 23rd. However, on the 19th Captain Govoni, with two enlisted men, left San Marcelino to establish a camp at the new area and work at once in anticipation of the Tacloban detachment's arrival in the next few days. By the 24th the entire detachment had arrived at Clark Field from Tacloban, with Captain Dorrie Jones leading the way. Tacloban was then reverted to the Filipinos for their use. The squadron was now divided between San Marcelino and Clark Field, with some 27 officers and 67 enlisted at the latter location.

At the end of March the squadron had eleven P-61s. Four new aircraft had been assigned, including #42-39448, #42-39452, #42-39465, and #42-39466. With only the loss of Kiick's plane at Mindoro, the rest of the squadron looked pretty good. By this time the detachment at San Marcelino was now standing by to move to Clark Field. Both sections of the squadron continued routine operations, though reduced enemy activity brought them down to a more minor scale. As usually happens after periods of quiet, there is the beginning of feelings of restlessness in anticipation of further moves and major operations in the future.

During the month of April the squadron saw many changes. Many original members of the squadron, including Captain Townsend, Captain Dorrie Jones, Lt. Howard Blanchard, Lt. Rolland Forrester, Lt. John Olley, Lt. Carl Bjorum, Lt. Edgar Crawford, Captain Elston Roady, Captain William Robbins, T/Sgt. Emil Weishar, S/Sgt. George Rees, S/Sgt. Joseph Barrosi, S/Sgt. Brady W. Swinney, and S/Sgt. George DeHaven were all transferred out of the 421st NFS.

The move of the San Marcelino detachment started on the 25th and was completed by 3:00 in the afternoon on the 26th. This was the first time the 421st NFS had been all together since January. Transportation of all personnel and equipment was accomplished in good order and without mishap. The San Marcelino area was policed and cleared, allowing the 100th Service Squadron to take over the old camp. The new camp was in pretty good shape, right down to a good water supply directly from a reservoir.

Materials were obtained for construction work setting up wooden structures with corrugated metal roofing. Included in this would be a mess hall, day room, headquarters building, PX, and a dispensary, as well as numerous workshops. Although the area was rather small, the layout was well planned and had ample room for all.

Plans were also put in effect to give the men more recreation, such as three day passes to Manila. Although the Philippines were in American hands, there were still some very real dangers left by the Japanese that could take lives. The Japanese had poisoned some of the local liquor before leaving, and quite a number of men died and some went blind. The Headquarters section actually put up a big billboard outside of town showing the statistics of how many had died. Unfortunately, even with the warnings many continued to drink the liquor anyway. Also, there were still some small pockets of Japanese in the local hills and snipers were a constant danger. Another peril came in the form of land mines and booby traps rigged in buildings and former Japanese equipment. It would take some time to finally make the whole country completely safe.

Liquor was a rather important item to the troops for relaxation and for something to trade. Lt. McCullough relates how important it could be. This took place just before the combining of the two detachments:

> Our squadron was split into two groups; we were at San Marcelino and the other was at Clark Field. After each mission you were to get two ounces of whiskey. The squadron doctor said that no one wanted to have a shot in the middle of the night or the middle of the morning, so they told us that when we had accumulated enough missions they would just give us a fifth, and we could drink it whenever we were not on duty. Most of it was used for trading. Anyway, several at San Marcelino had a fifth coming, and the doctor was at Clark Field.

Sgt. Loyal Males by Lt. Paul Zimmer's P-61 "Chris Couldn't Wait," which would meet an unscheduled demise. ***Burdue***

Lt. Clinton Gaston was to fly over to get the mail and the whiskey. Coming back to San Marcelino it was a beautiful day for flying, so he decided to do a slow roll. When he did, the whiskey fell out of the case and all the bottles broke. When he came back and into the tent he was sitting on his bed with the most unhappy face, so I asked him what was the matter? He told me that he was going to be over here forever, putting in enough missions to pay for all that liquor he broke. He said he almost got high from the smell in the cockpit. And no, he did not have to stay longer than the rest of us.

A training program was initiated for all the aircrews to give them additional training in strafing technique, night fighting operations, formation flying, and instrument flying. With the lack of any enemy opposition it was felt that continual training would keep the crews in a constant state of readiness.

On the 12th the 421st NFS engaged in its first P-61 bombing mission. At 3:00 that afternoon Captain Beverly Bowers took off with two 500-lb. bombs in support of infantry action north of the town of Infanta. Bowers dropped both his bombs on the target area, but no results were observed.

The mission of the squadron for the month had been principally night patrols, with most flight records showing no enemy aircraft encountered. There had been a number of bogies that had been run down, only to be identified as American. On one patrol Lt. Edward Tingen was vectored into a bogie and got a visual on him at about a half mile. Closing in to near gunnery range the enemy fighter split-essed, lost in some cloud cover, and dropped off the R/O's scope. After freelancing unsuccessfully for a time in the area the search eventually had to be abandoned.

The squadron also lost two planes this month. On the 8th three P-61s were taking off from Clark Field in formation. One of the planes, piloted by Lt. John Chew, was on the right side of the formation. Upon take-off his P-61 attained an altitude of approximately 50 feet. Without warning, however, the P-61 seemed to come straight down and make a crash landing. Lt. Chew would later report the actual cause of the accident. As he took off with the formation his aircraft cleared the ground and he raised the landing gear, but found immediately that he had no lift. He was caught in the prop-wash of one of the other planes, and as he got lower the tips of his propellers hit the steel mat. He then throttled back the engines and just brought it in. Lt. Chew and the gunner got out of the plane as quick as they could. The R/O, Lt. Heohn, was stuck in the back of the plane, but Chew was able to open the canopy and free him. The plane was wrecked when it hit the ground, and not long after it caught fire and was a total loss.

Squadron P-61 lifts off from Clark Field on a mission. ***421st NFS***

On the 22nd another 421st NFS aircraft, "Chris Couldn't Wait," Lt. Zimmer's former aircraft, was being cleaned by the crew chief, Sgt. Loyal Males. Sgt. Males was using fuel to clean the aircraft while smoking a cigarette. The fuel ignited, setting the plane on fire and burning it to the ground. Sgt. Males fortunately was not hurt. Harold Burdue, who was right next door, watched what was happening and later expressed what he felt at that moment:

> I could see what Sgt. Males was doing and when his plane caught fire. My plane was right next to his, and I immediately jumped in mine, fired it up, and moved it out of the way. I did not want my plane catch on fire!

Obviously, the true account never got as far as the commander. No action of any kind was ever taken over the destruction of the P-61, and it was written off "officially" as an accident.

During the month of April, even with the decrease in action for the squadron, the crews were still pulling alerts. Lt. Bob McCullough talks about one of the alerts he pulled at this time:

> I remember one time my pilot, Lt. Lloyd Partridge, was sick—appendicitis—and Lt. Hoke Smith needed a Radar Ob-

421st NFS P-61B #42-39682 at Clark Field. ***McLaren***

server, so I went to stand alert down on the airstrip. We did not take off that night as no "bogies" came in. As some B-24s got ready to take off we went to the jeep, loaded our chutes and everything, and I was going to drive. Just as I was about to put the jeep in gear a hospital plane was coming in and a B-24 was taking off. The tower was shooting flares, and it looked like they were going to meet right over us. Hoke had not gotten in the jeep yet, and I started to jump in at the same time I popped the clutch. The Jeep rolled just enough to roll over the tops of Hoke's shoes and pinned him down. The jeep stalled, and Hoke was waiving his arms saying bad words that he must have learned from the Tank Corps. I never heard them in the Air Force. Anyway, the hospital plane went around, the B-24 got airborne, the jeep started, and we got safely back to camp. I don't remember flying with Hoke again.

The concern about night fighter operations and how the P-61s were being used in combat was brought up again, this time by Major Richard Kiick. He contended that the patrol duties that the squadron was used for rarely provided opportunities to make use of the tremendous firepower of the P-61. But, as what usually happened in such matters, his voice reached 5th Fighter Command Headquarters, but fell on deaf ears.

One final note about April 1945. On the 12th the 421st NFS and the rest of America suffered perhaps their greatest loss with the death of President Franklin D. Roosevelt back in the state of Georgia. The President, who had been the leader of the nation for the past twelve years, had some of the toughest men on the flightline breaking down in tears. Interestingly enough, in Japan on that day an announcer for Radio Tokyo read the death bulletin to the Japanese people and unaccountably presented some special music, "In honor of a great man."

With the coming of May the squadron continued its training program for the aircrews. The only thing that hindered it somewhat was the lack of aircraft. The squadron began May with a total of ten aircraft and twenty-four pilots. By the conclusion of the month the squadron had lost two more planes, putting the squadron in the position of having almost three crews per plane. Even with the handicaps the training program improved the crew's performance in regular interception missions, and it also gave the men practice in radar bombing, in which excellent results were achieved.

P-40N #44-7788 assigned to Major Richard Kiick at Clark Field. ***Bjorum***

The Black Widow itself did not have a bombsight of any kind, since it was never intended to be used as such. But being the adaptive sort, the crews of the 421st NFS managed to hang bomb shackles on the wings of the P-61, along with a load of two 500-lb. bombs, giving the P-61 a new role. Most of the bombing raids were considered more harassment raids than anything else. Also, by no means was this considered in any way precision bombing.

Radar bombing itself was a system of bombing developed by the P-61 pilots. The system was based on the combination of how far it was to a target, your altitude, and your airspeed. Basing it on a triangular pattern, using the radar to determine your distance from the ground, the pilots and R/Os came up with a system that put the bombs pretty close to the target. Some pilots, like John Chew, worked out systems so good that he had marks on his windscreen to aid him on his bomb run. On one of his first bombing missions, Lt. Chew remembers some of the details:

> We had begun to carry out harassment raids on the Japanese. Most of the Japanese cities were receiving constant attention from the bombers, so we went in at night to keep them on their toes. I think the Japanese themselves were pretty much out of it. I remember on one mission looking down and seeing a man pushing his bicycle along and not paying a bit of attention to me, it was like I was not even there.
>
> The big thing I remember from my first mission is that we were always briefed to get rid of our drop tanks before we went into the target area. This was because when you got all the fuel out of the tanks, and they were full of fumes, the tanks were almost like a bomb. This was very true if ground fire should hit one of them. I never liked the idea of getting rid of my tanks, so on that mission I left them on. After I had hit the target and dropped my two 500-lb. bombs I headed back out over the coast. Not paying attention, I turned my fuel lever all the way down to the feed for the empty tanks. Not long after one of my engines quit. My gunner got excited and started yelling out that we had been hit. To add to it we could not get a hold of the my R/O in the back of the plane. My gunner got even more excited, thinking that they had hit Lt. Heohn. But everything got put back in order. I realized my mistake with the fuel control and got the engine going. Shortly thereafter my R/O checked in and told us that he had pulled out his mike cord and had some trouble getting it back in, and he could not talk to us. The rest of the flight was uneventful, and we made it back to the base okay.

Lt. John Chew had come to the squadron as one of the new replacement pilots, and he also remembered his first days with the squadron:

> I joined the squadron at Clark Field and was assigned to one of the Flights in the squadron (Different Flights had their own "hut."). There was a nice little Officer's Club. One of the prized squadron possessions at this time was the thick Mahogany outhouse seat. A folding, canvas chair was an individual's prized possession. He could then sit outside and

watch the movie in comfort. (The natives on one side of the screen and the Americans on the other.) One quickly came to know the little Barrio near Clark and the broiled chicken, comotes, and rice which were available there. A visit to Manila (the "Pearl of the Orient") soon convinced us that it no longer was a pearl. I flew night patrol missions around Luzon Island, PI, when I first got there.

On daylight orientation flights from Clark Field we would try to rendezvous with Navy and other fighter aircraft and practice dogfights. The P-61 would always do well, because other pilots had great difficulty in getting the nose of their planes ahead of us in a Luftbury. Additionally, in the P-61, we were able to stall the aircraft in a very tight turn with our flaps partially down and the wheels down and not snap roll out as some aircraft had a tendency to do. The gunner could then swing the turret around and confront the other aircraft with four machine guns.

Another bit of excitement happened to one of the pilots out on a gunnery mission. When the turret was fired directly forward the plexiglass canopy was shattered by the muzzle blast, and the pilot had sustained a minor head injury. As the canopy flew open the pilot received cuts on his face and head. To keep the canopy from tearing off completely and going into the propeller, the gunner came forward and held the canopy all the way from South of Bataan to Clark Field, where the crew landed safely.

The squadron also flew additional "Snooper" patrols in the Cagayan Valley, Luzon, where Japanese planes had been reported to be operating. However, no bogies were ever picked up in the area by GCI or aircraft. On one of these missions Lt. Partridge flew as a reconnaissance plane for a napalm strike. After the completion of the mission Partridge returned to base, and as his wheels contacted the runway his left engine cut off and froze cold. Expert handling by Lt. Partridge completed this hazardous landing without incident.

Lt. Partridge still remembers that mission well:

> The mission was to cover the bombing of the Nip positions northeast of Manila. If I remember right, the mission was about 3 1/2 hours long. The weather was good, and the airplane performed perfectly for most of the mission. During the last hour, the oil pressure on the left engine began to drop at the rate of a few pounds every fifteen minutes. I remember the engine quitting on final approach, rather than with the wheels touched down. The engine froze completely and never turned over again, necessitating an engine change.

On the 3rd the squadron lost P-61 #42-5501. As the plane was landing the main gear unlocked and folded up, causing the plane to belly in. Being damaged beyond repair, the plane was later scrapped. On the same day a crew chief was doing a preflight on P-61 serial number #42-5519 when the plane apparently collapsed on its nose, damaging the crew nacelle enough to warrant another salvage aircraft.

On the 5th the 421st NFS also lost its P-40N with Lt. Hoke Smith at the controls. The P-40 itself came to the squadron under "unusual" circumstances, as Major Richard Kiick related:

> When I was briefed by General Smith, the Commander of the 5th Fighter Command, before going to the 421st to assume command, he was emphatic about my not flying the P-61. He said I was being sent there to provide "organization" only, and that he believed that there were enough pilots there. Further, he pointed out that the P-61 was a three-man airplane and these men had been trained as a crew.
>
> Later, when I went to Mindaro to attend a Commander's Conference, he asked me how I got there. After an awkward silence, I admitted I had flown a P-61. After the conference he reiterated he did not want me flying the P-61, and asked if he could get me something else to fly around "in the afternoons." He suggested a P-40, which I eagerly accepted, since I had time in it and really liked it. He cautioned me not to let any of my crews fly it, because of the "torque" problem that the P-40 had.

Lt. Owen Wolf on left, with Lt. John Owen and Sgt. John Danko on right. ***Owen***

Two weeks later he called and said my P-40 was ready for pick-up, and I had someone fly me down to Mindaro. The aircraft had only 19 flying hours on it! Apparently, it had been assembled and ferried from Nadzab, New Guinea.

When I returned to the squadron, I was under immense pressure for "check out" flights in the P-40 by most of the pilots. I finally decided to check out my Flight Commanders, Mac Ballard, Tom Malone, Robert Pew, and Hoke Smith. After three successful launches, I took Hoke Smith to the end of the runway and went over the cockpit and settings with him. I jumped down, and he taxied out and took off. I could see a problem right away. He got off the ground, but it was at 1,000 feet before he remembered the gear. I waited around awhile, but then returned to OPs.

Sometime later, Hoke Smith reported to me at OPs, blood streaming down his face and said, after saluting, "Sir, I busted it up!" or something similar. After getting him medical help, I went out to look. The landing runway had been changed, which is why I never saw him come in. He had run off the end of the runway and through a lateral ditch, totaling the P-40.

Lt. John Leckie on left with Lt. Larry Lackey early in 1945. ***Lackey***

Lt. Smith suffered no permanent damage, fortunately. I don't know if General Smith ever heard about this, certainly not from me, but I never had the nerve to request a replacement.

Also during the month the squadron received a B-25J, which was soon named "Two Bits." Major Kiick was looking for a pilot to fly this plane, and Lt. Larry Lackey, who had flight time in this type of plane, was quickly elected to do it. This aircraft became the squadron "hack" plane, used to do supply runs and other sometimes "personnel" missions.

Closing out the month the squadron was looking forward to a future move and a hope of some new aircraft. A number of new P-61B aircraft had been promised to the squadron by 5th Fighter Command. The seven that were left in the squadron were getting pretty worn, and were harder on the maintenance crews to keep flying.

June found the squadron in practically a "Stateside" garrison situation, with very little activity outside the routine patrols. There were many changes in personnel, however, due to the arrival of new crews, which gave the rest of the "old men" a chance to get home. Captain Owen M. Wolf was at that time the only original 421st NFS pilot left in the outfit.

The training program continued in the squadron, with excellent work being accomplished despite very few airplanes available for use. They began the month with only seven P-61s, with two being taken away to a service squadron, leaving only five for the squadron's use.

Two red alerts without action were called due to Japanese reconnaissance over Manila on two different mornings. It was reported, to the delight of the night fighters, that it took the day fighters 35 minutes to get off the ground, while Captain Wolf scrambled one night to 10,000 feet in eight minutes.

One other mission that took place was flown by Lt. Lloyd Partridge:

> On one mission while we were at Clark Field, we received information that a Jap plane with several high ranking officers would be coming in from the north into the Cagayan Valley. This particular mission took place after midnight. My Radar Operator at the time was Bob McCulloch. We were flying low in the valley, and we thought we saw the target aircraft and went after it, approaching it from the rear. When we were within range I opened fire with the 20 mm guns. Unfortunately, one of the explosive shells exploded in the barrel of the gun, flinging it out and knocking off the pitot tube, which was located between the guns on the bottom of the aircraft. This effectively knocked out my flight instruments that depended on the pitot tube to work. Naturally, we ceased fire and headed back to Clark Field. Our main problem now was to navigate through thunderstorms that were lined up between Clark and us. Flying with just the needle-ball and compass was not fun, but we made it back to base.

The night snooper missions over Cagayan Valley were in conjunction with a break through of U.S. ground forces into the last enemy stronghold on Luzon. The P-61s flew missions with the intent to disrupt any possible enemy night air evacuations, and also to observe enemy troop activities. The squadron pilots also continued the task of strafing and bombing throughout the area. The crews saw minimal anti-aircraft fire over the targets, and no planes were hit.

The 5th Air Force gave the 421st NFS an Annual General inspection, which finally resulted in a realization higher up that they were in a bad way for airplanes and vehicles. They were promised about 100% new replacements, along with all new P-61s before their next move, which the squadron knew was coming. Within a week most of the equipment had been moved to a debarkation point. All of the buildings were taken down, equipment packed and ready to go, and a new fleet of trucks and jeeps joined up with the squadron.

On July 2nd the 421st NFS would again suffer a loss of an invaluable aircrew. Lt. John G. Leckie and his R/O, Lt. Charles B. Faust, while on a routine patrol crashed into Mt. Aryat. They were flying P-61A #42-5498, which at one time had been flown by Carl Bjorum's crew in shooting down two Japanese aircraft. Lt. Leckie's gunner, Sgt. Nicholas Natiello, luckily did not make the mission with them, and the two crewmen flew it to their tragic end. Funeral services were conducted the following day at a military cemetery in Manila. This loss was another keenly felt by all the members of the squadron.

Two more aircraft were lost, as well, during the coming month. On the 10th one P-61 was lost while having maintenance done at the 10th Service Squadron. A B-25 crashed nearby on the runway, and the debris hit the P-61, causing major damage and the aircraft to be salvaged. Another P-61 was lost on the 13th when it was transferred to the 10th Service Squadron as "war weary." On a good note, and none too soon the 421st NFS received eleven new P-61s from depot, fulfilling the promise made by 5th Fighter Command for new aircraft. The 421st NFS finished the month with 13 aircraft.

Lt. Leckie's grave at the military cemetery near Clark Field. ***Lackey***

9

The Last Dance: Ie Shima & Japan

July saw the squadron move from Clark Field, Luzon, to Ie Shima, in the Okinawa Group of the Ryukyus Islands. The ground echelon was loaded on LST #794 and left Subic Bay on the 13th. Loading was completed, and the convoy left for Okinawa on the 16th, but lost two days of travel because they were forced to stay near Luzon until a typhoon had moved out of the north. Rough weather was, however, encountered for several days, but very few men suffered, though the consistent rains were a sore subject for the more than 200 officers and men. The ship's crew was very friendly and generous, and the men enjoyed the same chow served to the ship's officers and men.

Just before the move one squadron member, Sgt. Kenneth G. Grayson, suffered a fractured spine when a truck on which he was riding, hauling bulk equipment to Subic Bay, went off a wooden bridge. He was hospitalized at the Navy Hospital at Clanapo and was moved as soon as possible to Manila for evacuation to the States.

Karemu Retto was sighted on the morning of the 23rd, and after a short anchorage at Okinawa, near Naha, LST #794 dropped anchor at Ie Shima at about 4:00 PM. After being advised that they would most likely stay aboard the LST until morning, orders were soon issued from Harbor Control to disembark all troops. This was done at 1:30 in the morning on the 24th, and all the squadron members were trucked to their new areas with equipment. A miserable night was spent in the mud and rain, and the first meal came from the 548th Night Fighter Squadron of the Seventh Air Force, who sent trucks after the men and gave them dinner and supper. The generosity of the 548th was very appreciated by all members of the squadron. The LST beached at 10:00 that night, and unloading began on the 25th and continued till 5:30 in the morning on the 27th.

Since the first night of their arrival, there had been constant red alerts with small raids by Japanese aircraft. No damage was done, and most of the bombs fell in the water well out from shore. The new camp was taking form, with all the men working hard getting ready for the arrival of the squadron's P-61s, which were scheduled to arrive in the near future.

While the 421st NFS ground echelon was on the move to Ie Shima, the flight echelon still continued to fly patrols, and they still managed to find themselves in some interesting positions. Lt. Mack Ballard got a rude awakening when he found out whose convoy he had been protecting:

> I was vectored out to cover a Navy convoy. It was about 300 miles away from Ie Shima. We went out, right on the nose where they had vectored us. There was cloud cover between 5,000 and 7,000 feet. We were flying at about 10,000 feet. Everything was fine. No enemy aircraft, no bogeys any place.

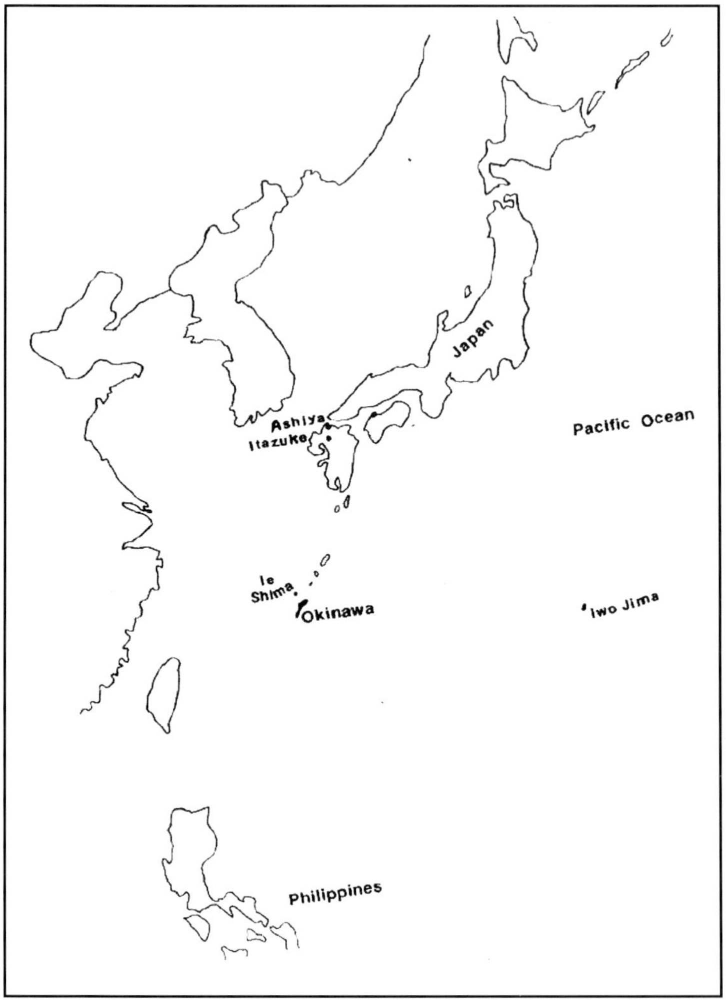

Loading the LST at Subic Bay for the trip to Ie Shima. ***Stevens***

Squadron camp at Ie Shima. ***421st NFS***

When daylight arrived, we spotted the flight of four P-38s coming to relieve us. I did the usual thing by going down through the cloud cover and buzzing the ships in the convoy. Waggling my wings, and taking off for home. The problem was, when I got down and looked across—they were Japanese ships! When we went down and waggled our wings at the convoy there was no indication that they knew that I was the enemy. We completely caught them by surprise, and I had been up buzzing around all night. I guess they thought it was one of their planes protecting them. And, of course they did not have the radar that we had. Here we were no bombs, we did have our machine guns and cannons, but I was out of fuel. The P-38s were still on their way to relieve us, so I radioed them and told them what had happened. They in turn said they would cover the convoy until the bombers got there. Then the P-38s and B-25s that came worked over that convoy of Jap ships.

Not long afterward the 421st NFS crews were recruited to do another unusual mission. Two P-61s were furnished to cover a B-24 one night at Mako Island, Formosa. The B-24 had a radar SNAFU, and the P-61s took them on over the target for a successful mission and then guided them home.

August 1945, as it turned out, was a month to be remembered by the world, and one in which the 421st NFS played a small, but important part. By the 18th the Japanese government was asking for peace; they could not stand any more of the unlimited hammering that the American forces had inflicted upon them. The revelation of the Atomic Bomb, coupled with the declaration of war against Japan by Russia, persuaded the Emperor and his war cabinet that plans for world domination were far from sane.

Ie Shima from the air. ***421st NFS***

At the start of the month the ground echelon on Ie Shima had been anxiously awaiting the arrival of their "Black Widows" and crews from Clark Field. Action by the Japanese at night had provided ample opportunity for the squadron to undergo new experiences in foxhole digging. At 10:00 on the morning of the 5th the thirteen P-61s of the 421st NFS, led by Major Kiick, left Clark for the flight to the new base. The trip took only five hours of flying time, with the formations landing at Ie Shima at 3:00 that afternoon.

The flight crews were taken to their new area and were settled into their new living quarters. Time for re-acquaintance, however, was cut short by order of 5th Fighter Command; something big was being planned for the P-61s and their crews. The squadrons were given orders to load up their P-61s and begin the bombing of Kyushu, Japan.

The first of these missions took place on the 8th, involving six aircraft and again carrying two 500-lb. bombs per plane. Crews were briefed, aircraft loaded, and the crews made their way to their planes. However, due to the late mission order the planes could not be bombed up in time for a one-flight take-off. Take-offs were staggered in time as the aircraft were made ready. Lt. Robert E. Savaria with his crew Lt. George A. Freeman, his R/O, and Sgt. Davis, his gunner, were the first crew to take to the air at 8:15 that night. Following them, more aircraft would take-off at 9:30, 10:25, 11:00, 11:05, and the last aircraft at 11:45. The stars were out in full array, an advantage for them in navigation and finding the target. As it turned out, this was not the case over the target area, however, which was covered with low clouds.

At about 1:10 in the morning Lt. Savaria's plane was heard calling the tower for landing instructions. It circled and landed without incident. Most of the ground troops were anxious to find out what had happened, but they had to wait until all the planes had

Another view of the camp. ***421st NFS***

421st NFS aircrew. Top row left to right are: Mack Ballard; Paul Boger; Richard Kiick; Clinton Gaston; and Raymond Daniels. The center row are Donald Macleod and Francis Gilmartin. The bottom row includes: Robert Schoonover; Bernard Faulstick; John Owen; and John Holmes. ***421st NFS***

returned and the crews had been debriefed. Two of the aircraft had been fired on by anti-aircraft over the target, one of which had three searchlights directed nearly to the night fighter. The crew felt that in this case they may have been radar controlled. The anti-aircraft itself was slight to moderate, and as far as Japanese aircraft, one of the P-61s had a bogie on his tail warning radar. The pilot dropped his belly tanks and started evasive maneuvers, after which the bogie disappeared. All six planes dropped their two 550-lb. bombs over Kumamoto City and Kyushu Airdrome. Solid overcast from 3,000 to 6,000 feet prohibited visual bombing or observation. Four of the aircraft bombed by radar, and the other two by estimations. All the planes bombed from about 8,000 feet and came in from different headings. On their way back home all the crews reported the entire

Lt. Mack Ballard standing by the engine of his P-61. ***421st NFS***

Miyakono area was burning heavily, causing each crew to believe that the B-29s had previously bombed this target. All the crews returned with pretty much the same reports, and they were informed by Headquarters that they were to continue these bombing missions.

On the 9th five P-61s went out on a mission again with staggered take-offs, at 6:20, 6:45, 7:15, 8:45, and 9:45. Each aircraft was again carrying two 500-lb bombs. Four of the aircraft dropped their bombs on Kumamoto and Miyakono with mixed results. Aircraft #4, piloted by Lt. Neal E. Reinerd, had to return to base because his nose wheel would not retract on take-off. Lt. Reinerd called "Hazel," the local GCI, informed them of his situation, and got permission to jettison his bombs 30 miles west of Ie Shima. Lt. Reinerd brought the plane back to Ie Shima and had to belly in when the gear collapsed. The aircraft was wrecked, with a good deal of structural damage to the tail booms, but the crew was safe and uninjured.

On the 10th, two missions of four P-61s each were sent out. One P-61 returned once again due to mechanical problems. All of the other aircraft dropped their bombs on Karasehara with no results observed. Only one P-61 reported that he had been fired on by moderate, but inaccurate anti-aircraft. All aircraft, however, returned to Ie Shima safe.

Lt. Larry Lackey was one of the pilots on these missions and recalls his memories then:

> There was one small incident that was somewhat amusing when looking back, but when it happened it was a little scary. When we were on Ie Shima we flew intruder missions over the Japanese mainland. To do this we carried two 500-lb bombs and two drop tanks. We would proceed to the assigned target, drop our bombs, and then proceed home. Before we cleared the south home island, the drop tanks would run dry and had to be dropped. The first of us to do this did not know that the tanks would trigger the tail warning radar, so you can imagine

the start when over hostile country, a single aircraft, and the radar signaled someone was on your tail.

These missions went on through the 15th, along with standard patrols and ground alert duty. In most cases the use of the P-61 Black Widow as a bomber faired about as good as the Messerschmitt 262 jet used in a bomber role in Germany. For the most part, the result of strikes as far as damage and effect were never known or recorded. As Major Kiick later recalled:

> Toward the end of the war the 421st NFS was sending missions up over Japan on an every 2 hour basis each night. I would label these "Nuisance" raids. We carried two 500-lb. bombs on external shackles. The Radar Operator would identify with his radar set on IP and give the pilot a run heading and drop notice. I flew one of these missions. We took off in a 500 foot ceiling from Ie Shima, flew 2 1/2 hours, dropped 2 bombs, and flew 2 1/2 hours home to another 500 foot ceiling. Never saw anything visually between take-off and landing.

The squadron lost one other aircraft during the month. On the 13th another one of the older aircraft was transferred to the 10th Service Squadron as "war weary."

On the 15th word came down through Headquarters that the Japanese wanted peace. On the 6th the B-29 bomber "Enola Gay," piloted by Col. Paul Tibbets, Jr., dropped the first Atomic Bomb on Hiroshima, Japan, at 8:15 in the morning, killing around 80,000 people in a single blow. Three days later on the 9th another B-29, "Bockscar," with Major Charles W. Sweeney as the pilot, dropped the second Atomic Bomb on the city of Nagasaki at 10:58 in the morning, killing over 40,000 people. To add to the problems for the Japanese, on the 8th the Russians declared war on Japan, and the Russian Army poured over the Manchurian border and began a rapid occupation of territory.

The Japanese accepted the unconditional surrender being offered by the United States, and the details were worked out for peace emissaries to fly into Ie Shima and onto Manila to formalize

Lt. Neal Reinerd's aircraft, which he had to belly in. The crash caused structural damage to the airframe and booms. The aircraft was salvaged. ***421st NFS***

Lt. Larry Lackey beside his P-61 at Ie Shima. ***Lackey***

Two 500 lb. bombs. These were the last two bombs dropped by the 421st NFS in the war. Both were dropped over Kyushu, Japan. *421st NFS*

The Betty taxis into its assigned position on the field. *421st NFS*

the surrender. Lt. General Torashiro Kawabe, Deputy Chief of the Army General Staff, would lead the delegation. He would lead a group of fourteen officers with two interpreters and translators sent by Emperor Hirohito by transport aircraft.

5th Fighter Command issued orders that the 421st NFS would play a part in the escort of the Japanese planes, in both their arrival and departure. Crews were quickly assembled and briefed. They were all eager for the chance to escort the planes that the eyes of the world would be watching.

At daybreak on the 19th the delegation met at Haneda Airport near Tokyo Bay. They boarded a Japanese version of the Douglas C-47, known to the Allies as a "Tabby." The aircraft was painted white and marked with green crosses as the Americans had directed. They took off at 6:11 that morning and landed at Kisarazu Airfield on the East Side of Tokyo Bay some 14 minutes later. The delegates were divided into two groups of eight each and loaded into two waiting "Betty" bombers, which were also painted white and marked with green crosses like the transport. Both bombers were airborne by 7:07 AM, heading for Ie Shima. As they approached the southern tip of Kyushu at 11:15, soon afterwards an escort of twelve P-38s from the 49th Fighter Group took over. This group was being somewhat honored, because they had more confirmed air victories than any other group in the southwest Pacific. While the P-38s provided top cover for the Bettys, B-25s from the 345th Bomb Group moved in as escorts for the bombers. Six planes, in groups of two, had been sent to escort the Bettys to Birch Airstrip, Ie Shima. At 12:40, the first of the two Bettys landed on the coral airstrip at Ie Shima.

As the door of the Betty opened, General Kawabe stepped out of the aircraft. His officers followed him out by rank. The second Betty was parked immediately behind the first, and its passengers also got out. The Japanese delegates were met by a small group of Americans led by General Smith, Commander of 5th Fighter Command, and his staff. The walkway was lined with the tallest MPs the Army had to offer; none of them were less than 6 feet tall, and they simply towered over the Japanese delegates. The Japanese were

First Japanese Betty bomber comes in for a landing at Ie Shima. *421st NFS*

The Betty has shut down its engines, and the Americans move out to meet the Japanese Peace Delegation. *421st NFS*

General Smith, 5th Fighter Command Commander, meets General Kawabe and the Japanese delegation by the C-54 that will take them to Manila. ***421st NFS***

led to a waiting C-54 transport aircraft that would be taking them all to Manila. The aircraft landed at Manila's Nichols Field at 6:00 that evening. The Japanese were received correctly, but coolly. To meet them MacArthur had picked Major General Charles A. Willoughby, his Chief of Intelligence. The Japanese were served a turkey dinner when they arrived at Rosario Manor in Manila. At 9:00 the Japanese delegates were taken to the city hall conference room to meet with the Americans. Plans were worked out for the American occupation of Japan starting on the 28th. The Americans had requested the harbor facilities at Yokohama and the airfield at Atsugi for the first staging bases of the occupation. Lt. General Richard Sutherland, MacArthur's Chief of Staff, led the American delegation at these talks. The talks continued until the 20th, and all the directives set down the demands concerning the arrival of the first Americans in Japan, as well as the formal surrender ceremony aboard the battleship U.S.S. *Missouri*, plus the subsequent reception of the occupation forces.

With the conferences over the Japanese were taken back to Nichols Field and boarded the waiting C-54, and then were taken back to Ie Shima by 1:00 that afternoon. At Ie Shima it was learned that one of the Bettys had mechanical problems and could not be repaired until the following morning. The whole delegation could not board a single Betty, so the group and the documents were divided up so that if one aircraft should have trouble, all would not be lost. The first Betty left Ie Shima at 6:40 that evening with a group headed by Lieutenant Takeuchi, in whose care was placed the conference documents. The P-38s and B-25s were again called upon to escort the Betty out from Ie Shima, but they discontinued their escort, as it was getting dark.

As it was nearing darkness two 421st NFS P-61s took over the escort from the P-38s and B-25s. One was piloted by Lt. Gerald Parker, with R/O Robert O'Lone and Sgt. Frank Hamilton as gunner. Lt. Robert Savaria and his R/O, Lt. George Freeman, and gunner Sgt. Davis flew the other plane. The 421st NFS P-61s had left Ie Shima at 6:40 in the evening, met up with the Bettys and B-25s, and took up their position. Two other P-61s were used as spares, but both were turned back 100 miles north of Ie Shima. Lt. Parker and Lt. Savaria stayed with the Japanese until they were approximately 15 miles off the southern tip of Kyushu, at which time they headed back to base, landing at 10:20 PM. After the mission had been completed, the men reported that it seemed strange flying over the Japanese waters with the knowledge that there would be no opposition.

Ironically enough, the first Betty did not make it back to Tokyo as planned. Just before midnight the Japanese delegation was given the command to prepare for a crash landing. The plane had ditched in the surf along a wide beach near Hamamatsu, about 130 miles short of Tokyo. The delegation made their way to nearby Hamamatsu Air Base to explain their situation. It was thought, due to the complication of language with the Americans at Ie Shima, that the fuel tanks in the plane were not completely filled. A transport was sent at 3:30 AM to pick them up and take them to Tokyo. The second Betty left Ie Shima the next day after repairs had been completed. They had an uneventful flight back to Kisarazu. The

The Japanese begin to board the C-54. ***421st NFS***

Japanese aircrew that were left on Ie Shima while delegation was in Manila. ***421st NFS***

Another view of the Japanese aircrew. ***421st NFS***

Japanese government accepted the surrender documents, and the terms would be carried out shortly thereafter.

The anxiety for further information appeared among the squadron members, who were ordered to resume patrols on the 22nd over Kyushu and Hanahu. Obviously, no one was taking any chances, since even after four years Pearl Harbor had not been forgotten by any of the Americans.

As the 421st waited for word from higher headquarters armed patrols were continued, but no bombs were dropped at this time. Squadron personnel found anything they could to keep themselves entertained. One way is remembered by Lt. Larry Lackey:

> One incident worthy of mention was at Ie Shima. One day we were fishing with hand grenades. We would toss the grenade into the water, and the concussion would stun the fish and they would float to the top. Not really the best sportsmanship, but a lot of fun. After one blast we were elated, as a good sized shark came floating to the top. Several of us jumped into the water to retrieve our prize. All went well until about halfway to the shore the shark came back to life. Needless to say, there was a mass evacuation. You have seen those cartoons, when someone in the water is frightened and swims to shore and keeps swimming up on the shore? That is not an exaggeration of how it happened.

The arrival of September 1945 marked the beginning of the 22nd month of overseas duty for the 421st NFS. Behind the organization was a record of nearly two years of hard fought war, disease, death, and discomfort from the hell that was New Guinea to the front door of Tokyo, Ie Shima. Ahead, peace and a subsequent return home loomed large and pleasantly. The formal signing of the surrender terms in Tokyo Bay on September 2nd wrote a finish to one of the most ghastly chapters in the history of the world, and brought into focus new vistas of peace and a world that was slowly turning the bloody toil of war to peaceful pursuits.

Even with the world approaching peace, death struck a savage blow to the squadron in the early morning hours of the 8th. Three of the squadron's officers met death as the left tire of their P-61 Black Widow blew out on take-off, and the plane crashed into an embankment at the end of Mocca Strip, Ie Shima. Lt. Neal E. Reinerd, pilot, and F/O David A Black, R/O, were killed instantly in the crash, and Lt. Preston Wilson, the Ordinance Officer, died a few hours later in the hospital from shock. This was caused by the loss of blood and severe injuries he sustained in the crash. The entire squadron attended the funeral services for the three victims on the 8th. Internment was at Island Cemetery, Ie Shima. Lt. Wilson, whose military career in the Army embraced service in both the enlisted and as a commissioned officer, joined the squadron back in the States in August 1943. He would be buried right next to Ernie Pyle, the famous war correspondent, who was killed on Ie Shima. Lt. Reinerd

Lt. Jerry Parker on left with his crew, Lt. Bob O'Lone and Sgt. Frank Hamilton, on the right. This is one of the crews that would take part in the escort mission of the Japanese. ***Hamilton***

A group photo of the personnel that took part in the escort mission. Standing on the far left is Major Kiick. In the front row from left to right are: Hamilton; Brown; Carter; Crawford; McDowell; Ferrari; Orcutt; Hollingsworth; Venderbeck; Males; Davis; and Hancher. The back row from left to right are: Parker; O'Lone; Zimmerman; Reed; Hebert; Faulstick; Reinerd; Block; Routtu; Dow; Savaria; and Freeman. They are standing next to P-61B #42-39581, one of the aircraft used on the mission. *421st NFS*

and F/O Block were relative newcomers to the squadron, having been assigned to it in May 1945.

There was some question about the cause of the accident, which would focus on the tires on the aircraft, as Richard Kiick explains:

> We had tire trouble starting on Ie Shima before the end of the war. Perhaps because of the coral or overloading due to hanging two 500-lb. bombs on the external shackles. We grossed out at about 34,000 lbs. with these bombs. Anyway, I went over to Okinawa and talked to the Commander of the 418th Night Fighter Squadron. The 418th was not having our problem. He had point defense missions (Okinawa) and also had a different tire. He had Goodyear tires, and we had Goodrich. I came home, and I called 5th Fighter Command and told him the 421st NFS was standing down for training. However, the 7th and 8th of September, operation orders came from 5th Fighter Command for some missions. I was not aware of this, and our Operations Officer sent them out. This is the time we lost Neil Reinerd. We also lost "Old Blue" Wilson, our Armament Officer, who was in the gunner's seat. Flight Officer David Block also died. "Blue" had bugged me all during the war to fly a mission in the gunner's seat, even though we had removed the turrets and the seat was empty. I would not take a chance on losing him and would not let him go. Later, when the war had ended he did go on a flight. On take-off Neal blew a tire and spun into the side of the runway.
>
> After the accident I stormed over to 5th Fighter Command and General Smith and asked for an investigation. He assured me the Inspector General would, however, despite follow ups I was never able to get any conclusions from 5th Fighter Command, and I do not think any action was ever taken. Incidentally, I landed a P-61, taxied in, and was making out a Form 1 when the tire blew with my foot on it.

Another view of the crews that took part on the escort mission. *421st NFS*

The 421st NFS in formation at Ie Shima. This was the formal announcement by Major Kiick that the war had ended. *Kiick*

With the cessation of all hostilities, aircraft of the squadron began routine patrol missions. In as much as it was no longer necessary to have gunners as crewmembers, seven gunners were returned to the States for "combat fatigue," including: T/Sgt. Danko; S/Sgt. Hawkins; S/Sgt. McDowell; Sgt. Davis; Sgt. Vanderbeck; Sgt. Cisarik; and Sgt. Mott. The remaining gunners were grounded and assigned to duties in various squadron departments.

Warnings of the approach of a severe typhoon were received on the 15th, and at 8:00 AM on the 16th the storm struck. At first it took the form of the usual heavy rains and strong gusts of wind, but as the hours passed the wind mounted in ever increasing ferocity, and the rain became a veritable deluge. Throughout the night and for almost thirty-three hours the typhoon continued unabated. The wind gauge recorded velocities of twenty to one hundred and fifty-five miles per hour, and there was no let up in the rain. Despite intensive preparations, including turning planes into the wind and running them, the squadron area was pretty much destroyed, and the sidewalls of headquarters were torn off.

The end of the typhoon saw much destruction done to the 421st NFS, but fortunately, no casualties were incurred. But most men, like Bill Gorman, still can remember what it was like:

> This one (typhoon) broke the airspeed indicator on the strip at 155 miles per hour. It rolled airplanes down the runway, turned them over, and destroyed many of them. B-24s were also turned upside down. It was a real bad one. My tent took off never to be seen again. I went into our mess hall, which was a Quonset hut, and it soon took off, too. I went into a cave, which began to fill up with water. Rats (big ones) also sought

Lt. Neal E. Reinerd standing by a squadron P-61. ***Lackey***

Lt. Preston Wilson on Ie Shima. ***Harding***

From left to right are Joe Heeb, Tito Peliconni, and Wade Mitchem of the Armaments Section, picking up after the first typhoon. ***421st NFS***

shelter in the cave, so it was an exciting time. All of a sudden, the wind stopped blowing and the stars came out. The eye of the storm was right over us. In about twenty minutes, the wind returned, but this time in the opposite direction, and it seemed to be stronger than before.

Almost immediately an all out effort was begun to restore the area to some semblance of order, and several new tents were secured to replace those which had to be salvaged after being buffeted by the typhoon. By the end of the month the squadron area was clean of its storm debris, and the entire area was in good order. Precautionary measures had been taken, including the installation of improvised locks, and in some cases 2 x 4 blocks were secured across the elevators of aircraft. Eight of the squadron's P-61s were damaged by the typhoon. Six of the P-61s were damaged beyond repair, necessitating their being salvaged, while two more were turned over to the 10th Service Squadron for intensive repairs.

With the coming of October, transfers, movement, and another typhoon would become the dominant factors for the month. The stream of transfers started in August and picked up speed from there. By the middle of October only three enlisted men that came overseas with the squadron on the *Sea Pike* in 1943 remained. All the original officers were long gone. Many of the former members left for the States on the U.S.S. *Hanover*. Approximately 1,983 Army personnel boarded the ship and began their trip back home. The *Hanover* arrived in Tacoma, Washington, on December 17, 1945, at 2:15 in the afternoon.

For the second time in less then a month, Ie Shima was again racked by a typhoon. On the 10th a storm of unprecedented intensity struck the Ryukyus Group, with maximum damage being sustained by Army and Navy units at Ie Shima and Okinawa. The typhoon that had devastated the squadron in mid-September was eclipsed in all respects by this typhoon, which struck in mid-afternoon, and continued in increasing ferocity for more than four hours. Again, damage to the squadron tents and buildings was extensive. The weather appeared to be doing more damage to the squadron then the Japanese ever did.

Early in the month word came down from 5th Fighter Command that they would move the 421st NFS to Itazuke, Japan, within a few weeks. Accordingly, a contingent of squadron personnel headed by Major Richard Kiick flew to Itazuke to inspect the site that would be the squadron's future home. Making the trip to Japan with Major Kiick were: Captain Robert Rothen, squadron Medical Officer; Lt. Mack Ballard; Lt. Allen Dale; Lt. Barnard Faulstick; Lt. Francis Gilmartin; Lt. Robert Schoonover; and Sgt. Teddy Anderson. All personnel returned to Ie Shima within 48 hours, except Captain Rothen, who remained at Fukuoka to supervise sanitation of the area the squadron was slated to occupy. The imminence of the squadron's move to Japan became more apparent when seven enlisted men were sent to assist in the construction of a new camp. Included in this group of men were carpenters, plumbers, and electricians.

U.S.S. *Hanover* arriving at Tacoma, Washington. ***421st NFS***

421st NFS members and other service members on the deck of the U.S.S. *Hanover*. ***421st NFS***

George E. Humphries, a medic in the squadron, at the Ernie Pyle Monument. ***421st NFS***

Left to right are P-38 pilots Lt. Robert Sims, Lt. Goodwin, and Lt. Jean Pierre "Pete" LaBorde of the 8th Fighter Group. *Sims*

The detachment that went to Itazuke found the field was bombed out and in pretty bad condition. Because of this, when the move came the aircraft of the 421st NFS were sent to Ashiya, Japan, under Lt. Lawrence Lackey until repairs could be made to the landing strip at Itazuke sometime in November.

Anticipation for the move to Japan keynoted the activities of the 421st NFS throughout the month of October. Uncertainty as to the actual time for loading the ship which would take them to Japan made it necessary for the squadron to be ready to "pull up stakes" on a 12 hour notice. Accordingly, all departments packed the major portion of their supplies and equipment and proceeded to operate on a skeleton basis. Word finally came that the 8th would be loading day for the squadron. Under the direction of Lt. Donald Johnson, loading of bulk and mobile load equipment was begun at 3:00 that afternoon. Although shorthanded from all the transfers, loading the ship proceeded at considerable speed, and by 5:00 the next morning all equipment was loaded and lashed down for the trip to Japan. The ship sailed for Buckner Bay, Okinawa, and anchored there at 5:00 on the 10th where it remained there for the next ten days.

For the forty officers and ninety enlisted men aboard LST #828 life definitely resembled "stateside" living. During their ten days at anchor in Buchner Bay, while standing by for the convoy to assemble they ate steaks, chops, chicken, and other delicacies that had not been on the menu for a long time. To vary the monotony aboard ship, arrangements were made for the Army personnel to go ashore at Okinawa for part of each day. The Navy motor pool located near Brown Beach furnished drivers and buses to several shore parties and sightseeing trips. The flight echelon still in operation at Ie Shima brought mail to those who were aboard the ship. One of these mail drops became one of the most famous in 421st NFS history. Lt. Lawrence Lackey had the following memory of this event:

> The place: Ie Shima, a small island in the Ryuku chain of the West Coast of Okinawa. At one point during the war it was a highly contested piece of real estate. Possibly the only re-

Lt. Al Hebert in the cockpit of his P-61. ***Moe***

The 421st Night Fighter Squadron's first home in Japan. ***Moe***

minder that a great war even passed that way is a lone monument with a plaque inscribed as follows, "AT THIS SPOT THE 77TH INFANTRY DIVISION LOST A BUDDY, ERNIE PYLE, 8 APRIL, 1945.

My unit, the 421st Night Fighter Squadron, equipped with the P-61 "Black Widow," had started its move to Ashiya, on the island of Kyushu, Japan. All the squadron assets and personnel, except the aircraft and flight crews, had been loaded aboard an LST and anchored on the far side of Okinawa with many other surface vessels. Our aircraft and flight crews had moved in with the 8th Fighter Group, at the time a P-38 outfit, where we would stay until we all flew to Japan together.

Our detachment commander was a young officer, whom we will refer to as Al. In the 8th Fighter Group is a jockey named Pete. Pete was known to us in the 421st from our cadet days, and now Pete and Al become the main characters in our story.

One of our chores while awaiting the flight north was to go to the Army Post Office, pick up the mail for the entire squadron, and then load it into one of our P-61s and deliver it to the LST. This was accomplished by flying over Okinawa, making a low pass over the LST, and then landing at a nearby strip. A ship would send a boat to the nearest dock, pick up the mail, and return to the ship.

Major Kiick and Gizmo. ***421st NFS***

Pete and Al, being young and handsome officers, became acquainted with two nurses from one of the nearby medical units. In the course of the friendship the nurses decided they would like to have a ride in a P-61. This was agreed on, and Al decided to use the daily mail run to give the cuties a ride. This brought about one problem; there were Pete and Al, and the two nurses for a total of four, and the P-61 had only three seats.

The flight proceeded without incident. Everyone was enjoying themselves, and the girls were getting a grand tour of the local flying area. Then Al decided it was time to deliver the mail. After identifying the proper ship, Al prepared for his low pass to give the signal that the mail would be delivered to the pickup point. But instead of a simple, low pass over the ship as was pre-arranged. Al, no doubt to show off a bit, made a pass out of a screaming high-speed dive with a high "G" pullout. For those occupying the seats the high "G" pullout was no problem, but for Pete, in a standing position and with no hand holds and only the rear of the Radar Operator's seat, it was quite a different situation.

As the "G" load increased, Pete found it harder and harder to stand in an upright position, and when his hands slipped from their hold on the seat, he sat down, with great force, on the entrance hatch. The latch was closed, but it was not built to sustain that much force, so the latch failed. The hatch came open, and according to Pete, "the airplane was simply gone."

Meanwhile, back at the LST, the Black Widow was sighted and a shout went up, "time for the mail." Then someone remarked, "look at that fool Al. He's tossing the mail out right here." The so-called "mail bag" sprouted arms and legs, then a parachute. Before the chute could make one swing, Pete was in the water. The Navy, being near at hand and always alert and efficient, had a launch on the scene in a matter of minutes. Hardly before he could comprehend what happened, Pete was safely aboard the launch, and except for a few upchucks due to

Captain William C. Behnke on the flightline. *Behnke*

swallowing sea water, Pete was just a little worse for the experience.

After Pete's rapid departure from the P-61, the nurse in the R/O's seat did not know how to operate the interphone system, so Al up in the pilot's seat knew nothing was amiss until he landed back at the home base. They had a few anxious hours until Pete was able to communicate that he was OK.

I don't know if this story has a moral, or if anything was learned from it. I did hear rumors, however, that Pete never again got close to a P-61. In fact, he did not even like to see pictures of them.

Lt. Fred Kohl was a little more clear on the actual names of the persons involved:

The most interesting story of the entire war is Al Hebert's dumping of Lt. Pete Laborde (a P-38 pilot) out of the R/O's compartment into Buckner Bay. Hebert had taken up two Army nurses. They were strapped into the gunner's and R/O's seats, and "Pete" (Jean Pierre) was standing behind one of the nurses in the rear, directly over the entrance hatch. Al buzzed an LST and did a screaming chandelle right off the ship. Pete fell over and busted the back door. He barely got his chute open before he hit the water. Hebert made a great impression on the nurses, and a few others, also!

Lt. Colonel Emmet "Cyclone" Davis, the 8th Fighter Group Commander, viewed this a little differently:

When I heard about this incident I requested Lt. Al Hebert to come talk to me so I could get the full story. I was the Commander of the 8th Fighter Wing, and Lt. Leborde was under my command. He told me that they had gone out on a flight to deliver the mail, and when he got back, Leborde was gone. He left out the part about the nurses and the stunt that caused the accident. Leborde had managed to get his chute open just before he hit the water, and he came to suffer no injuries. The Navy had picked him up, and he was flown back to the unit in a Navy SNJ(T-6) the next day. I was visiting the hospital a few days later, and I happened to overhear a couple of nurses talk-

A Christmas Tree set up for the squadron. *Lackey*

Another view of the Christmas Tree and Japanese "House Girls." *Lackey*

ing about the incident. They were, in fact, the two nurses who had been flying with Hebert and Leborde that day. I made them tell me the full story, and I was pretty upset that Lt. Hebert had not told me the truth. I wanted him to face a court-martial over the matter, but Richard Kiick, the 421st Night Fighter Squadron Commander, was a friend of mine, and I called him. He assured me he would take care of it. Lt. Hebert never faced any charges, but I guess Kiick gave him some kind of administrative punishment.

After the ten days had passed and a few more "uneventful" mail deliveries were completed, the convoy got underway for Kyushu, Japan, at 7:00 in the morning on November 20th. The weather was good for the two-day trip, and the only incident along the way occurred the first afternoon out when some drifting mines were spotted. They were immediately destroyed by one of the destroyers that accompanied the convoy. The weather was warm and sunny throughout the trip. The convoy anchored in the outer harbor of Saneha, Japan, at 10:00 on the 22nd and remained at anchor until 2:00 on the 24th. Then, LST #828 moved to the unloading area in the inner harbor. Just as soon as they docked unloading of the LST was hampered by orders from headquarters to furnish 29 enlisted men to the 388th Service Squadron to drive that organization's vehicles to the Fukouka area. Despite the shortage of manpower the unloading was completed by 10:00 that night. The following day the squadron's motor convoy drove 90 treacherous miles to its new area at Kasugabaru, Ohukushisun, Fukuoka-ken, Japan, arriving without any problem.

When the squadron personnel arrived at their new home they found ample evidence of hard work on the part of the advanced echelon. A small Japanese Army factory had been set aside for the 421st NFS. In this building were to be located departmental offices, including headquarters, and quarters for the enlisted component. The advanced echelon, in the short time they were there, had laid a wood floor over a concrete floor, had managed to partition off seven living compartments, and had constructed some of the squadron's offices. The mess hall and kitchen were nearly completed and were already in use.

Richard Kiick remembers the first sight of the squadron's new home:

> When the 5th Fighter Command gave us our new location in Southern Japan after the war I took a B-25 up to take a look. I can't remember who went with me, except for Doc. They had given us an old factory site complete with oily floors. Later, with Captain Govoni, some booze, and the Doc's help, I was able to "buy" Navy plywood to cover the floors and a few walls. But the thing I remember most about this trip was the take-off to go home. The runway was in poor shape, and I was interested in getting airborne as soon as possible. The nose wheel came up easily, but the main gear rolled and rolled. Finally airborne, I rolled in a lot of trim to counter a tail-heavy condition. Upon landing, I discovered that two of the men had also loaded beer in the tail. A beer factory was apparently adjacent to our new campsite.
>
> Liquor was the medium of exchange during these days. Each pilot was authorized 2 oz. of liquor after completion of each combat mission. Doc was the "bonded" custodian of the liquor inventory. Whenever I had the opportunity to "buy" something the squadron could use, I went to Doc, and we would both sit down and solemnly sign the distribution certification for booze "broken during the last move." The squadron acquired plywood, a small grader (for volleyball courts), and even a Navy landing craft.

Not only did Kiick have to worry about getting the new home for the squadron set up, but also some of the personnel problems that were sure to come about in the post-war squadron:

> Once the squadron was entrenched in Japan, the war over, of course, everyone looked forward to going home. We had solid leadership from Captain Govoni on down, and no discipline problems to speak of. That was fortunate, because General Smith had issued strict orders that the occupational forces

Squadron P-61 landing at Itazuke after day mission. *421st NFS*

P-61B #43-8239 on the flightline at Itazuke. *Cox*

would bend over backwards to get along with the conquered Japanese. Until one night, I got a call from the local Army Provost Marshall to the effect that he was holding two officers on numerous charges and suggested I come down there immediately. Upon arrival, I found out these two officers had been drinking and had driven a jeep (my jeep) into the back of a honey wagon, seriously injuring the owner. Furthermore, the Provost Marshall showed me two sworn statements to the effect that each claimed he was the driver. After much discussion, the Provost Marshall finally released the two officers to my custody after I promised to meter out punishment. Subsequently, after I made my own discussion as to who the driver was I quickly gave him an Article 104, severe lecturing, and denial of certain privileges. The two officers were Captain Bill Bowers, our Operations Officer, and Captain Al Hebert, who had previously been involved in the P-61 "buzzing" incident.

In December, once again the steady flow of transfers took its toll on the squadron. Most significant of all the transfers was that which terminated Major Richard Kiick's tenure as Commanding Officer of the 421st NFS. Major Kiick was transferred to the 11th Replacement Depot for redeployment. Succeeding him as the commander was Captain William C. Behnke, who was assigned to the 421st NFS by the same orders which ordered Major Kiick's departure for the United States. Behnke had been asked by General Hugh A. Parker, the Commander of the 315th Bombardment Wing, to go over to the 421st NFS to check out the position, a position he gladly accepted.

Captain Behnke, formerly Commanding Officer of the 547th Night Fighter Squadron, who had flown P-61s out of Atsugi, Japan, brought with him eight years of Army experience, including four years of National Guard duty. Graduating as a Second Lieutenant from Yuma Army Air Field, Arizona, in June 1943, he took B-25 transitional training at La Junta AAF, Colorado, and went on to night fighter training at Orlando, Florida, before coming overseas in August 1944 to join the 547th NFS. He had flown a total of 99 combat missions and amassed a total of 243 hours in the Pacific, most of which were in the P-61.

Despite the numerous transfers of personnel the squadron continued to function efficiently. By mid-December the enlisted men had improved their living quarters to such a degree that they were commended following an inspection by higher headquarters. Lacking the necessary lumber to construct ceilings over their sleeping quarters, the men ingeniously made use of squad tents earmarked for salvage as temporary ceilings. They also constructed efficient improvised stoves for heating their quarters. Japanese labor hired in quantity was utilized for many of the odd jobs that the squadron had in order to help out.

The activities of the Japanese were naturally under observation of all personnel with many mixed emotions since the end of the war. Many members of the squadron had only a few months before been involved in aerial conflict against Japanese fighters and bombers, not to mention being bombed and strafed by the same. They had all kinds of reasons to be untrusting and maybe a little paranoid. But there were no incidents or difficulties at all with the Japanese help. Several Japanese were brought in as houseboys, cooks, and translators, and proved to be honest and hard working.

Highlighting the month from the standpoint of extracurricular activities was the Christmas party staged for the enlisted personnel in the squadron mess hall on Christmas Eve. The mess personnel furnished copious quantities of sandwiches and cold cuts, and squadron officers graciously donated several cases of beer for the party. The officers knew all too well how much they depended on these men to keep the squadron in operation.

As time went on the squadron was making commendable progress in all departments. The operations section was functioning in full force with the addition of eight more P-61s that had been procured for the squadron's use. Flying missions for December consisted of a series of calibration missions with the 35th Fighter Control Center. For the remainder of the month squadron aircraft were released for maintenance and limited training flights, except for one search mission on the 27th. Two aircraft searched a twenty-five mile strip either side of a direct line between Ashiya Air Base and Kanoya for a B-25 believed lost in that area. No sightings of the B-25 were reported.

10

Into the Sunset: The Post War 421st

The new year, 1946, found the squadron striving to become more comfortably settled in its new life and occupational home in Japan. Improvements in living conditions were one of the chief concerns of everyone at the time, especially those individuals who were faced with the prospect of remaining with the occupational forces for any length of time. To this end Lt. Bruce LeFord was appointed the unofficial Construction Officer in an effort to coordinate construction projects and requisitioning. Working with LeFord were Lt. Harold Hopkins and Sgt. Raymond Passler. The results were improvements of the existing showers, living quarters, officer and enlisted mess, dayrooms, and other building projects being completed. On the 25th they did not find it too promising that the point system used by the military had been lowered again, opening the door for more transfers and in turn leaving the 421st NFS with pretty slim pickens. As a result, many officers in the squadron found themselves doing jobs that they were unaccustomed to or not trained to do. Some were put in charge of supervising Japanese work crews doing construction and clean up. Some officers were driving trucks, some doing guard duty, and still other officers were on the flight line servicing the P-61s. The end result of this was the hiring of more Japanese labor. In most cases, however, they were restricted from the flightline and aircraft. The squadron was fortunate enough to find a Japanese mechanic for the motor pool that proved to be a great asset. The squadron also managed to find a Japanese cook who had cooked in a New York restaurant before the war, so everyone ate pretty well. Other areas, as well, were soon taken over by the Japanese, who were screened by Headquarters and given squadron passes to return each day. The workers all proved their worth a couple times over and made life a little easier for the squadron.

Flight training through January once again consisted of practice interception flights, again under the control of the 35th Fighter Control Squadron. These were all scheduled as daytime missions, as no nighttime activity was going on at this time. Throughout the month the squadron had a total of ten air-worthy P-61s for their use; the main problem still remained, however, a lack of qualified personnel to crew them.

By the start of February the squadron consisted of thirty-two enlisted men and thirty-two officers. To help on the line and around the squadron it was decided to "acquire" some GIs from the 32nd and 97th Divisions. Basically, regular infantrymen were recruited

421st NFS Headquarters building at Itazuke, Japan. ***Timmons***

Squadron P-61 taking off from Itazuke. ***Cox***

421st P-61s lined up on bottom right of photo at Itazuke. *Moe*

for the new duty. Working on the line turned out to be the most popular assignment, because many of the men wanted to be trained as mechanics and many others just wanted to get a close look at the Black Widow. They found that life in the squadron was quite a change from what they had experienced in the infantry. Their gun was no longer their best friend, and in the Air Corps the relationship between enlisted and the officers was not as strict as it had been.

The guys that turned out to be the most unhappy were, of course, the gunners. Until they were grounded they had been viewed as the "fair haired boys" of the organization in the eyes of the enlisted. As aircrew they drew fewer details and received more money with their flight pay. They became more or less misfits until the old men began going home and vacancies had to be filled by the gunners. All of them soon proved to be responsible in all the squadron positions they filled. In fact, one gunner, S/Sgt. Frank Hamilton, was appointed acting First Sergeant for a period of time. Other gunners also got involved with key positions, including: S/Sgt. George Harry became the Sergeant Major; S/Sgt. William Young became Chief Supply NCO; S/Sgt. Robert Binns became NCO Chief of Personal Equipment; S/Sgt. Robert Young became Communication NCO; S/Sgt. Donald Lacy was in charge of Special Services; S/Sgt. John Slocum became Chief Operations Clerk; S/Sgt. Robert Bonbrake the Personnel Clerk; and Sgt. Nicholas Natiello became the Engineering Clerk. With the gunners grounded, many of the squadron's P-61s had their turrets removed. In fact, there had been a shortage of these turrets during the war because the Boeing B-29 "Superfortress" used the same turret assembly.

During the first few weeks of the month a new night fighter project was introduced. During the course of the war there was a lot of information gained through actual night fighter experience leading to new technology, and of course new designs in aircraft. One

P-61B #42-39585 on the ramp at Itazuke. *Moe*

of the results turned out to be a modified P-38 Lightning, designated the P-38M. This particular P-38 model had a radar pod attached to the nose of the plane and an extra bubble canopy in the rear behind the pilot to house a Radar Observer. Four of these aircraft made it to the Pacific at the end of the war and were reassembled in the Philippines. All four were assigned to the 418th Night Fighter Squadron stationed at Atsugi, Japan, for flight testing. After a short period with the 418th three of the aircraft and crews were sent to the 421st NFS for further evaluation. The crews that came with the P-38M included: Lt. Gerald Bliss and his R/O Lt. John Brewer; and Lt. David Hopwood and his R/O Lt. George O. Wagner. One of the P-38s had been lost with the 418th when Lt. Gerald Bliss ran out of fuel. This happened while he was on a practice flight over Japan. In the R/O position with Bliss was Lt. Leo Pervinko. When they were flying over Makoya Bay, just south of Tokyo, Bliss experienced fuel problems and had to set the plane down. Both crewmen climbed out on the wing and were shortly picked up by a Japanese boat. The P-38 sank, and within another day a party was sent down to salvage the plane and remove any secret equipment. The other three were flown by the 421st NFS up until March 7th. Then these remaining aircraft were sent on to the 45th Service Group at Manila, where the project and the planes were scrapped. Feelings about the P-38M were mixed among the pilots. Some liked it because it was a little faster, while others still preferred the P-61 as the night fighter of choice. The Radar Operator's cockpit was very cramped, and if anyone had a complaint, it surely would have been the man in back.

Lt. Larry Lackey recounts one of his flights in the new P-38M:

> We had a crew chief, Artie Anos. We had recently acquired three P-38M aircraft, which Artie worked on and became pretty attached to. The M model was unique in that it had a back seat and a radar set, but not a very good one. One of the P-38s had maintenance and required a test hop. As it was my job, I was preparing for the flight. Artie asked if he could go along. It was fine with me, so the flight proceeded without incident. When it was completed, Artie asked me how I liked the P-38M in comparison with other aircraft I had flown. I really had to confess that I could not make much comparison, as it was the first time I had flown the P-38. Needles to say, he was not happy about this. For 50 years afterward he was still upset about it.

Frank Hamilton on left with Bob Bonbrake. ***Hamilton***

Lt. Gerald Bliss by his P-61. ***Bliss***

By the end of the month the squadron was down to nine P-61 aircraft. One had been transferred out of the squadron to 45th Service Group in Manila on the 15th as "war weary." Flying continued to be practice intercept missions, as well as one search mission over the Inland Sea, which was an arm of the Pacific Ocean in southern Japan between Honshu, Shikoku, and Kyushu. One P-61 and one B-25 participated in the search for a missing plane. No sightings were made. There was also a limited amount of flights to check on the Russians, who had moved into the area at the end of the war.

With the coming of March the 421st NFS began a regular "on the job training" of men to fill in the manpower needs of the squadron. Classes were begun in the Radar, Communication, and Engineering Sections. Also planned were classes for the Supply, Personal Equipment, Armament, and Administrative departments. Lt. Francis Ingalsbe and Lt. Winston Puttick began to lecture and teach classes for radar repair. Lt. William Miller began to teach a flight line course for airplane engine mechanics.

Lt. George Wagner on left with Lt. David Hopwood by P-38M Night Fighter. ***Hopwood***

Also at the beginning of March Captain Behnke, Lt. Lackey, Lt. LeBuef, Lt. Jarchow, and Lt. Mash all reported to the 118th General Hospital in Fukouka. These officers, plus three others had all come into the military as members of the AUS (Army of the United States), which at that time was the forerunner of today's Reserves. Under the terms of the AUS these men were in the military for the duration of the war and no more. In applying for "regular" Army commissions each had to take a physical, then travel by rail to I Corps Headquarters at Kyoto to take a written examination. From there they were required to appear before an interviewing board. These five officers all passed and were accepted, while the other three officers were rejected during their physical examinations.

While in transit after his exam and trying to get back to base Captain Behnke remembers the following troubles:

> I was in a hurry to get back to the base, and I got nabbed by a couple of Marine MPs for speeding and I got a ticket. Colonel Van Auken, 5th Fighter Command Chief of Staff, decided to make an example of me. He gave me an Article 104, plus a fine of about seventy-five dollars. General Parker turned around and recommended me for promotion about the same time. There were about seven of us promoted shortly thereafter. I got it in spite of the 104 and ticket.

Another incident involving Captain Behnke was his involvement in an "unofficial" airplane race that took place in Japan that March. Behnke still remembers it well:

> This began up at Ashyia, Japan, where Lt. Larry Lackey and our P-61s were located at that time. Larry was drinking with members of the various other squadrons stationed there and bragging to them just how great the P-61 Black Widow was. Naturally, the other units were not impressed with the wonder machine; to them their own aircraft were much better. By the end of the evening a "race" was organized between all parties. The race would include a P-51, a P-38, an A-20, an A-26, and of course the P-61. The date, time, and course were soon set up, and as far as I remember there was a lot of betting all around. There were more or less a lot of people involved. All this without a word to higher headquarters, who most likely would have killed the plan. The course would start on the southern end of Kyushu, where all the aircraft would line up abreast to start, and the course would end on the deck at Ashyia. All participants stripped down their airplanes; in fact, if I remember right, the P-51 was a reconnaissance version and already pretty light and fast. I was the only one in the P-61 that day, and Larry had stripped it down so much that it would not even start. After getting it going we all went to the starting point. After getting all lined up in flight, somebody on the ground yelled go, at which time we firewalled the planes all the way back. The results of the race put the P-51 first, the A-26 second, the P-38 took third, my P-61 was fourth, and the A-20 came in last and very far behind. Bragging rights were established, and some people made money I am sure. I remember the P-51 pilot kept trying to stall me before the race. I think he was really worried that the P-61 was going to beat him. After all was said and done, Headquarters never did know a thing about it.

P-38M setting on the ramp at Itazuke. ***Hopwood***

As far as the routine business the Fifth Air Force Commander, General Kenneth B. Wolf, inspected the squadron on the 21st with favorable comments from the General. On the 23rd Colonel Van Auken, Command Chief of Staff, also paid the squadron a visit and was impressed by the training program that had been initiated by the 421st NFS.

Flying was limited this month to nine surveillance flights covering the area in western Kyushu from Kanoya north to the Moji area. Also, three more search missions for two aircraft were conducted over western Shikoku and eastern Kyushu with no sightings were reported.

April became the point in time for the 421st NFS that, for the first time in several months, flying again became the chief activity. Lt. Larry Lackey had done a creditable job getting the outfit's nine P-61s to a combat capable status. The squadron furnished two aircraft per day on most flying days of the month for Ground Controlled Approach practice at Kanoya Air base. The pilots reported a steady improvement in the techniques of the controllers, so their efforts were for a good cause. To date each pilot had 15 to 20 approaches. Surveillance flights continued through the month. Some large Japanese coastal defense guns under camouflage were discovered on one such flight. A large forest fire on the north side of Iwakure Mountain on western Shikoku was also reported, so some benefits from the flights were finally coming through.

For some reason there was a severe outbreak of delinquencies occurring among the enlisted men which lasted about two weeks during April. It became a daily occurrence to sign for the release of one or several men from the Sixth Marine Military Police. A good share of the squadron officers were kept busy conducting investigation reports. The plaguing and alarming frequency of the delinquencies turned out to be, for the most part, only minor offenses that might never have been reported if the Marines had not seemingly missed their cue as Military police, "to help keep a soldier out of trouble." However, sharp disciplinary action and a rehash of the squadron's direct responsibility for morale of the men halted the reports completely.

Two 421st NFS P-38Ms in flight over Japan. ***Hopwood***

Another view of P-38M on the ramp. ***Hopwood***

Along with the problems with the enlisted there was also a rash of petty thievery being carried out by some of the Japanese help. Japanese workers were caught at the gate with a variety of items ranging from eight pounds of sugar to a few quarts of liquor. The squadron had no choice but to also crack down hard on these individuals and bring the "walking PX" to a halt.

In May the flying once again was focused on ground controlled approaches at Kanoya, surveillance flights, and routine training. However, plans were set in motion to once again start bombing and gunnery practice, which had not been done since the end of the war. Also, the reinstatement of night flying was again scheduled, however, this only included a few check-out rides, since most of the pilots have had very little night flying in about eight months. The squadron was still carrying nine P-61s, and throughout the month kept an average of five operational aircraft ready for flight. The program of training infantrymen to be flightline mechanics through specialized training was finally getting results.

This flying and training schedule would continue into June, but the squadron would soon be losing a couple of its already limited P-61s. The occupation of Japan was to be shared by another night fighter unit. The 6th Night Fighter Squadron had just come in from Hawaii and was assigned to Atsugi, Japan. The 421st NFS was directed to furnish the new Black Widow unit with two 421st NFS aircraft. Lt. Larry Lackey and Lt. David Hopwood ferried the

Captain Behnke standing by the squadron sign. ***Behnke***

Lt. Lackey in P-61 cockpit. ***Lackey***

two P-61s to Atsugi Air Drome later that month, leaving the 421st NFS with only seven aircraft.

It was not until July that night fighter pilots of the 421st NFS were looking forward to the moonlit skies as they again took off into the night. They logged over 40 hours of night flight time, a considerable accomplishment taking into account the 421st NFS consisted of seven P-61s, eight pilots, and one Radar Operator. Probably of more significance is the negative accident rate they had been holding for a long period of time. Soon things would improve for the squadron with the addition of another pilot, Captain Robert A. McMaster, and two R/Os, Lt. Michael Hill and Lt. Gordon J. James. Flight training for the 421st NFS would also be continued in all areas.

One of the primary duties that came up was training for upcoming maneuvers in Japan in the next couple months. This would be the first of its kind in Japan since the war, and all the services would be involved. The 421st NFS P-61s and their crews were airborne nightly from dusk to dawn working ground control interception, ground control approach, and practicing cross-country navigation. Even with their limited resources the squadron wanted to have a good showing when they would be in the spotlight during this planned exercise.

On August 12th Major Behnke received a letter delivered to the 421st NFS from a Major John J. Ruettgers at Atsugi Army Air Base outlining the following:

1. On 31 July 1946 a flight of six (6) P-61s and one (1) B-25 aircraft, belonging to the 421st Night Fighter Squadron, departing Atsugi AAB at 1044/I. After using only an estimated 2,000 feet of runway four (4) of the P-61 aircraft made extremely low sharp climbing turns over the hangar line and living quarters of the Third Bomb Group. Each pilot seemed to be intent on outdoing the performance of the preceeding pilot.

2. In no way or manner did these take-off patterns conform to established traffic patterns for this base. These take-offs were extremely dangerous and showed a complete lack of air discipline and good judgment.

3. In as much as this type of flying has been condemned in policies established by higher headquarters, it is recommended that this discrepancy be brought to the attention of the Commanding Officer of the 421st Night Fighter Squadron for disciplinary action.

Squadron B-25 "Two Bits." ***Cox***

Flight Sergeant Bryan Cox in the cockpit of a P-61. ***Cox***

The decision of what to do with the "bad boy" pilots was now firmly in the hands of Major Behnke to take any course of action he pleased. The problem was, however, that Major Behnke had been the pilot leading the flight, which had upset Major Ruettgers at Atsugi. Needless to say, the punishment dealt out to all involved was not too severe.

The squadron tragically lost one of its enlisted men in August when Private Andreas Alvarado was accidentally shot and killed by Military Police of the 24th Artillery. The circumstances in the shooting have never been disclosed in any way. A memorial service was held by the squadron at the Chapel of Itazuke, where officers and enlisted men all paid their last respects.

Just when things had started to look good for the squadron, the situation for the 421st NFS as far as manpower was suddenly becoming worse. They were directed to furnish seven men to the 808th Engineering Battalion and four more to the 610th Aircraft Warning Squadron. Once again, many of the officers found themselves out on the flight line and other areas just trying to keep operations going.

From the 4th through the 10th of September, with the completion of repairs to the runway, the 421st NFS was kept busy moving the detachment from Ashiya down to Itazuke Army airstrip. Quonset huts were quickly set up and painted for Flight Operations, Engineering, Communications, and Radar. The strip was immediately put to use by the P-61s for more strenuous training for the forthcoming maneuvers. Every night the P-61s would take off and practice until dawn, at which time the training would cease and begin again at sunset.

The 421st NFS would play host to a group of New Zealand Air Force officers and enlisted men on the 20th. Flight Sergeant Bryan Cox, one of the New Zealand pilots, wrote about his meeting with the night fighters:

> One day in August, taxiing in after a patrol, I was greeted by the sight of two ominous looking, completely black twin-

New Zealand aircrew and 421st NFS personnel by P-61 "Dirty Delmar." ***Cox***

engine aircraft parked on our tarmac, and immediately recognized them as P-61 Northrop Black Widow night fighters.

Parked side by side, they sat slightly tail low with their twin-boom tail sections protruding well aft of their large tricycle undercarriage, to balance their rather bulbous nose section which housed a variety of electronic and radar equipment. Their deadly appearance was enhanced by a total of eight weapons firing forward, consisting of four 20 mm cannon and four .50 caliber machine guns mounted above and below the fuselage, with 2,000 hp Pratt & Whitney R2800 engines mounted at the front of each boom. The center section housed the pilot, in his small single seat cockpit, the gunner in a raised compartment just behind and above the pilot, and isolated in a plexiglass bubble at the rear, between the two booms, the radar navigator.

We were soon conversing with the two lanky American pilots, who seemed delighted to find that we were New Zealanders, and before long were inviting us to come and visit their unit in Itazuke for a weekend. Lieutenants Al Hebert and Larry Lackey told us they were from the 421st Night Fighter Squadron based at Itazuke near the city of Fukuoka, about 100 miles southwest of Iwakuni on the island of Kyushu. They said that transportation would be no problem. They would merely come up in their P-61s or bring their old B-25 Mitchell, also painted black, pick us up on a Friday afternoon, and deliver us back to Iwakuni on Monday morning. They operated the B-25 Mitchell as a squadron bus, or hack; it had been stripped bare of all its armaments, and they fondly referred to it as "Two Bits," which is American Jargon for 25 cents.

Another view of crews meeting around "Dirty Delmar." ***Cox***

True to their word, a few weeks later a dozen members of No. 14 Squadron, including myself, were picked up from Iwakuni in "Two Bits" on Friday afternoon, and after a 45 minute flight landed at Itazuke Airbase, Fukuoka. Although Keith Wakeman and I were warrant officers, we were treated as commissioned officers by the Americans and were guests in their mess for the weekend and on a number of subsequent occasions. Their aircrew were very friendly, and a cosmopolitan group of Americans with a few Canadians thrown in, and obvious traces of English, German, Italian, and French decent. We soon found that we could not banter about racial backgrounds as Kiwis and Aussies can! One of their pilots named Herman was very upset when one of our boys facetiously called him "Herman the German."

As an "all weather" and night fighter squadron they kept their mess appropriately dimmed and had a large model of a Black Widow hanging from the ceiling. Around a circular bar they had safety harnesses installed so that one could drink without risk of falling over. They drank what they called "bloopers," which consisted of spirits poured into a glass of beer. Behind the bar was a perpetually smiling barman appropriately called "O'Reilly's Bar." In both their drinking mess and their accommodation quarters they employed an impressive array of the most beautiful kimono'd Japanese girls, obviously hand-picked.

The casualness of their approach to flying never ceased to amaze us. At any hour of the day or night in their mess, a P-61 pilot would stroll up to Major Behnke and ask to take "Two Bits" to Tokyo or some other destination on a private errand.

Apart from their mess gimmickry they were not a hard-drinking outfit, and under the command of their rather serious-minded CO, their crews were flying fifty hours a month at night as against our total one hundred fifty hours by day for the whole year of occupation. They were safety-conscious, and once a week their aircrews had a flight safety meeting chaired by a different pilot each week in rotation.

On Sunday Keith Wakeman and I both rode in the gunner's seats behind the pilots in a formation of three Black Widows. My pilot was "Lacky-san," as the house girls called him, and as I clambered into the gunner's seat attired in a borrowed parachute, he diligently explained in detail how to accomplish an emergency exit from the P-61 should the occasion arise. On taxiing out I was surprised to find that with no apparent pre-take-off checks or engine run-ups the three P-61s opened their throttle wide as we entered the runway, and within seconds the formation was in a steep climbing turn to the right, apparently being propelled by every one of their 12,000 horsepower. The plane was maneuverable, and despite its bulk, the pilot could throw the P-61 around like a smaller fighter with use of a control wheel only.

The New Zealanders were also treated to an American baseball and basketball game. On their last evening at Itazuke they were given a party in their honor. The squadron personnel were also given a standing invitation to visit the New Zealanders at their base sometime in the future.

By the end of the month the squadron finally received two new P-61 aircraft. Four 421st NFS officers were put on TDY to Florida Blanca to fly the new aircraft back to Japan, where they would undergo acceptance checks.

On the 14th of October the long awaited day arrived. The flight echelon, consisting of fourteen officers and nine enlisted men, was placed on Temporary Duty assignment at Yokota Army Air Base for participation in practice maneuvers. In conjunction with other squadrons and regular military units the exercise went off without a hitch, and the 421st NFS received a good commendation for their participation.

The squadron would still fly with seven aircraft and would not receive any more until November 16th, when four officers and one enlisted man departed TDY to the Hawaiian Air Material Area for the purpose of picking up three aircraft for the squadron. These aircraft were a welcome addition, even though they were older models and had to be modified for squadron usage.

P-61 #42-39574 "Dirty Delmar" on Itazuke flightline. *Cox*

On December 10th the squadron again lost a man. Lt. Charles W. Moss, a Radar Observer was killed in an aircraft accident at Itami Air Base while riding in a 317th Troop Carrier Plane. A memorial service was again held at Itazuke for the squadron members.

Things slowly got more organized in flying and training as time went on. An airplane mechanic school was set up at Yokota Army Air Base, and a sixteen-week course was initiated. More classes were also set up for the other areas of aircraft technology that would help bring in more qualified people to the squadron. Two civilian mechanics that had been working with the squadron, Mr. Cole and Mr. Kwiatkowski, both transferred to the school to help educate the future flightline personnel.

With the coming of the New Year the three expected aircraft arrived at Itazuke. With new planes came a new commander to the 421st NFS. Lt. Col. Gordon Timmons relieved Major Behnke on January 1st. Major Behnke received orders returning him back to the United States, having served thirty months overseas. But other changes were also ahead.

With the coming of February the 421st had performed its sixteenth month of occupation, and its time in history was quickly coming to an end. On February 20, 1947, the 421st Night Fighter Squadron became the 68th Fighter Squadron (All Weather). The personnel and the aircraft that had been the 421st NFS did not change, just the squadron designation.

Most of the former members of the unit would go on serving in the 68th FS (AW) and later to other units in the newly formed Air Force. There would be three tragic losses of former 421st pilots down the road that would still impact the people who had served with them.

On July 3rd, 1947, Captain Robert A. McMaster and his crew, Lt. Francis L. Burrell the Radar Observer and Corporal Ralph Gilmaier their crew chief, would be involved in an accident. They were en-route to Yokota Army Air Base for an Air Show over Tokyo on the 4th. Getting caught in some low lying clouds the plane crashed into the mountains west of Odawara, which is a few miles from Mt. Fuji. All on board were killed.

Lt. Colonel Gordon Timmons. ***Timmons***

Lt. Col. Timmons leaving the operations building. ***Timmons***

In April 1949, Captain Owen M. Wolf, who had shot down four Japanese aircraft and damaged a couple more, would lose his life in an F-82 during a bomb run near Moses Lake, Washington. The cause of the crash had not been determined. His R/O was also killed.

On August 23rd, 1963, a forest fire broke out on the Tule River Indian reservation southeast of Porterville, California. Flying the P-61 was former 421st NFS pilot Robert E. Savaria. Savaria dropped his first load of benetonite at 2:30 that afternoon. By around 4:30 the fifth run of the day was being made. His right wing tip struck three oak trees about twelve feet above the ground. The P-61 cartwheeled and burst into flames, killing Savaria and destroying the world's last flyable P-61 Black Widow.

With the end of the 421st NFS, perhaps the best epithet was written by the Squadron Historian at that time:

> As of the date of this writing, the relatively short, albeit fast moving tale of the 421st Night Fighter Squadron comes to an abrupt halt. Having served its time in the Army, it received its honorable discharge from service effective 20th February 1947. The Night Fighters as such are no longer. Beginning in May 1943, the squadron traced its path through the Pacific war from Australia to New Guinea, and through to the Philippines, finally ending up in Ie Shima to see the landing of the "surrender envoys." From there to Japan, it took its place among the tactical organizations assigned to the occupation force, where from November of 1945 until inactivation this date it has held an enviable record of maintenance and fulfillment of all duty assignments, in a manner to bring credit upon itself and its personnel. Rated as one of the best Night Fighter Squadrons in the Pacific during the war, it closed its chapter in the history of Army Air Forces as one of the best tactical organizations in the Occupation forces. The Night Fighters are gone, and in their place we start a new chapter as "All Weather Fighters" carrying on the tradition of the Air Forces in the manner of the "421st."

The 421st Night Fighter Squadron was inactivated per section III, paragraph 1, General Order 16, Headquarters Fifth Air Force dated 12 February 1947, effective 20 February 1947.

At the time of inactivation the 421st NFS had tallied up an impressive record in their three plus year span. Among the decorations received by the squadron were: one Legion of Merit; four Silver Stars; eight Distinguished Flying Crosses and Oak Leaf Clusters; one Bronze Star; eighty-six Air Medals and forty-five Oak Leaf Clusters; one Soldiers Medal; and thirty Purple Hearts and one Oak Leaf Cluster. They had shot down thirteen Japanese aircraft, three more listed as damaged, and one listed as probable. This was not including one victory that had been taken away and a couple more never given credit.

Another total that came out of the war was the amount of weapons that were used. Throughout operations the squadron used 28,205 rounds of 20 mm and over 100,000 rounds of .50 cal. The squadron also used a lot of bombs throughout the war. Included in the total were: thirty 20 lb. fragmentation bombs; one hundred sixty 250 lb. general purpose bombs; eighteen 300 lb. general purpose bombs; four 200 lb. incendiaries; four 120 lb. fragmentation bombs; twenty-four 150 lb. fragmentation bombs; seventy 500 lb. general purpose bombs; and one hundred sixty-five 165 lb. fragmentation bombs.

The 421st Night Fighter Squadron's journey had finally come to end. With each passing year, fewer signs of the squadron would be left across the Pacific at places such as Nadzab, Tacloban, and Ie Shima. Sadly, many of the members that served with the squadron from 1943 through 1947 are also gone. But in their memory and those still talking about "The old days," the men of the 421st NFS and their accomplishments will never be forgotten.

This tribute to the 421st NFS currently resides in the USAF Academy in Colorado Springs, Colorado. *421st NFS*

11

Aircraft and Crew

"Nocturnal Nuisance" was flown by Lt. Tom Malone with his R/O Lt. Tom Glynn. ***421st NFS***

Another view of "Nocturnal Nuisance." ***421st NFS***

Crew Chief Harold Burdue was the crew chief on "Nocturnal Nuisance." ***Burdue***

A squadron P-61 going through overhaul. ***421st NFS***

Sgt. Loda Rogers overhauling a P-61 after 100 hours flight time. ***421st NFS***

Another new P-61 for the squadron. Left to right are: Douglas Ponsford; Lynn Ballard; Louis Paulo; Raymond Ferrari; Rolland Forrester; Pew; Thomas Glynn; John Jones; and James Brown. ***421st NFS***

Squadron personnel stand around one of the new P-61s that just arrived. The radomes on these early planes were painted white, but were later changed to black. ***421st NFS***

Sgt. Jake Loran beside Major Richard Bong's P-38. ***421st NFS***

Japanese aircraft wreckage being looked over by squadron personnel. ***Harding***

More of the Japanese wreckage. ***Harding***

421st NFS P-61 setting on ramp. ***421st NFS***

Crew Chief Corporal Joe A. Bradford stands next to Captain Bill Bradley's P-61. The owner of the "kill" marking above the nose art was Lt. Owen Wolf. It was common practice for pilots to fly a number of planes, especially if the serviceable aircraft were limited. *421st NFS*

Another view of Bradley's aircraft later in the war. At this time three "kill" flags can be seen, and again the owner of each is Lt. Owen Wolf. *421st NFS*

Sgt. Ben Hardin next to "Midnight Mama." *421st NFS*

Sgt. Dick Heldt on top of "Midnight Mama." *421st NFS*

Sgt. Harold Burdue next to "Old Forrester." ***Burdue***

Crewmen prepare to use tripod jacks on "Chris Couldn't Wait." ***421st NFS***

Sgt. Curtis Burgess next to "Old Forrester." ***421st NFS***

Sgt. Archie Picard in front of "Janie." ***Burdue***

Lt. Howard Blanchard setting in "Janie." *Blanchard*

Lt. Neal Reinerd's aircraft, in which he had to belly in on August 9, 1945. *421st NFS*

Lt. Robert C. Pew at the controls of a P-61. *421st NFS*

Lt. Neal Reinerd on left with Lt. Fred Kohl at Ie Shima. *Kohl*

Sgt. Harry Barrick works on the 20 mm cannons, with Sgt. Louis Paulo assisting at Clark Field. *421st NFS*

Sgt. Harry Kniss beside P-61A #42-5511. *421st NFS*

P-61 maintenance at Clark Field. *Harding*

Lt. Carl Bjorum on left being helped by Sgt. Harold Burdue into a P-70. *421st NFS*

Sgt. Bill Gorman setting in front of a P-61. *421st NFS*

Lt. Pahlka's P-61 "Bright Eyes." ***421st NFS***

Sgt. Harold Burdue standing in front of his P-61 at Clark Field. ***Burdue***

Lt. David Hopwood flying in his P-61 over Japan. ***Hopwood***

Lt. David Zimmerman at the controls of his P-61. ***421st NFS***

Lt. David Hopwood flying over Japan, minus mustache. ***Hopwood***

Lt. John T. Holmes on left with Sgt. Frank Hamilton. *Hamilton*

Lt. Dave Corts' P-61 "Nocturnal Nemisis." ***421st NFS***

P-61A #42-5500 after being hit by a B-24. ***Burdue***

Lt. Larry Lackey starting his P-61 at Itazuke. ***Cox***

Well worn 421st NFS P-61 setting at Itazuke. ***Hopwood***

Lt. Virgil Moe on left with his gunner Sgt. Truman Kojosa. ***Hamilton***

Lt. Gerald Bliss in a squadron P-61 at Itazuke. ***Hopwood***

Lt. Virgil Moe on left with Sgt. Frank Hamilton and Sgt. Truman Kojosa kneeling. ***Hamilton***

Squadron P-61 setting at Itazuke. *Cox*

Lt. John Brewer on left with unknown. ***Hopwood***

Lt. George Wagner on left with Lt. David Hopwood near one of the squadron's P-38Ms. ***Hopwood***

Sgt. Frank Allen in front of a P-61. *421st NFS*

Lt. Larry Lackey on left with Lt. Keith Lawrence under wing of P-61 at Ashiya, Japan. *Lackey*

Lt. Melvin Jarchow hit soft sand with his P-61, collapsing the nose gear at Itazuke. *421st NFS*

Lt. Jarchow's plane a day later sitting on a fuel drum. New nose art "Jarchow Slept Here!," obviously poking fun at Jarchow's taxi skills. *Moe*

A squadron P-61 comes in for a landing at Itazuke. *421st NFS*

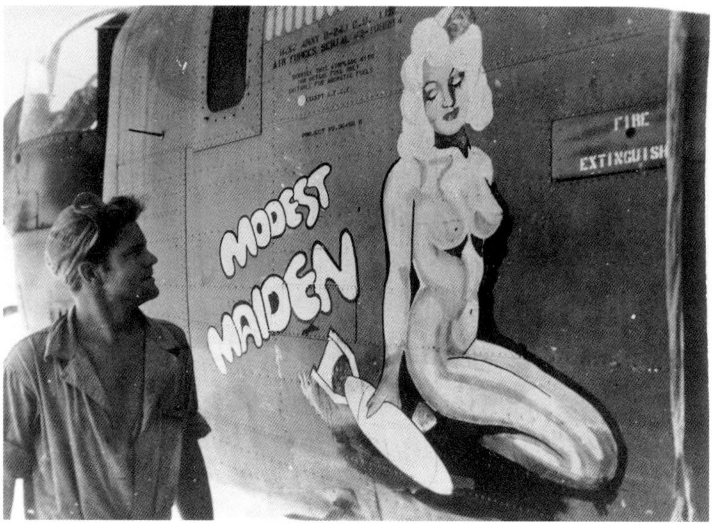

Sgt. Richard Mulligan beside a B-24 bomber. *421st NFS*

Sgt. Mike Hancher beside P-61 at Ie Shima. *421st NFS*

Harold Burdue on left, with Loda Rogers and Archie Picard on right holding a cylinder that they just removed from a P-61. *Burdue*

P-61B #42-39439 crewed by Harold Burdue. On May 3, 1945, a new crew took it up and had landing problems. On the third try they overshot the runway and ended beyond the runway, damaging the aircraft, though all personnel were unharmed. ***Burdue***

Another view of Burdue's plane. ***Burdue***

Squadron P-61 on flightline at Itazuke. ***Hopwood***

Sgt. Mende on left with Sgt. Hall, and Sgt. Winter on right standing by a B-24 "Lucky Strike." ***421st NFS***

Lt. David Hopwood on left with Lt. John Nash by a squadron P-61. ***Hopwood***

Squadron personnel are hanging external fuel tanks on P-61B #42-39466. ***Burdue***

M/Sgt. Jake Loran standing by B-24 "Million $ Baby." ***421st NFS***

Sgt. Louis Theide standing by B-24 "Barbara Jean." ***421st NFS***

Lt. Mack Ballard on left with Lt. Al Routtu by a squadron P-61. ***421st NFS***

Harry Popovich watches Robert Bittenbender work on the radar of "Skippy" *421st NFS*

John Russo left with John Efstathiou, right, unknown in cockpit. *421st NFS*

Nick Blodis on top of P-61 turret. *421st NFS*

Tire change crew left to right are: Hollingsworth; Ponsford; Farrari; Burgess; and Swedgler. *421st NFS*

Joe Powell on left with Bill Gorman on P-61. *421st NFS*

Bill Mercer beside an 8th Reconnaissance Squadron P-38 in New Guinea. *Hagen*

Unknown squadron member by P-61. *421st NFS*

12

Men and Places

Bob Bonbrake at Ie Shima. *Hamilton*

Dispensary at Nadzab. *421st NFS*

William Behnke in his work clothes. *Behnke*

R/O Lt. Tom Holmes. *Hamilton*

A strong statement against mess hall food. ***421st NFS***

Isadore Nachman on left with Daniel McQuire. ***Stevens***

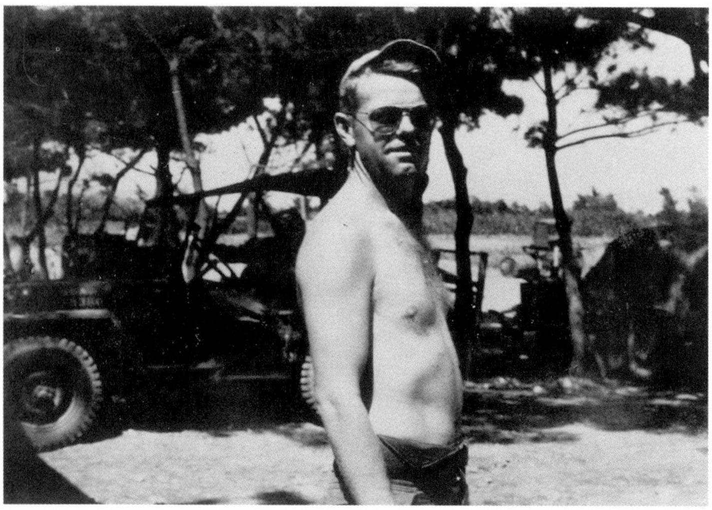

Richard Mulligan at Tacloban. ***421st NFS***

William Behnke at Itazuke. ***Behnke***

Joe A. Bradford at Nadzab. *421st NFS*

Bob LeBeuf at Ashiya, Japan. *Lackey*

Bob Schoonover on left with Larry Lackey. *Lackey*

Walter Pharr on left with Charles Townsend. *421st NFS*

Ralph Dodge on Ie Shima. *421st NFS*

Left to right at Kissimmee, Florida, are: Glen Meeks; Richard Mulligan; Adolph LeGrand; Edwin Pokorski; and Sidney Smolowitz. *421st NFS*

Isadore Nachman on left with Lawrence Carr on Wakde. *Stevens*

Francis D. Harris at Tacloban. *Harding*

From left to right standing are: Loran; Townsend; and Goldstein. Setting are Moore; Barker; and Rife. *421st NFS*

Dave Corts between missions. *421st NFS*

421st NFS personnel on LST on the way to Leyte. *Burdue*

From left to right at Leyte are: Weller; Stevens; Buchanan; and Shepard. *421st NFS*

From left to right at Ie Shima are: Neville; Lopez; and Goldstein. *421st NFS*

From left to right on Wakde are: Gill; Reese; Barrick; Lockman; Snyder; Harding; Lopez; and Cox. *Stevens*

From the left to right at Leyte are: Turse (418th NFS); Noyes; and Snyder. *421st NFS*

Herb Goldstein on left with the medical crew, Stancik, Allen, and Reese. *421st NFS*

Lynn Ballard at Tacloban. *421st NFS*

Art Munn at Tacloban. *Burdue*

Harold Burdue on left with Harold Mercer on LST to Leyte. *Burdue*

William Behnke with squadron sign. *Behnke*

Hubert Welder left and Bob Buchanan erecting the Intelligence hut. *Stevens*

Wes Harding at Tacloban. *Harding*

From left to right at Nadzab are: Pharr; Bradley; and Townsend. *421st NFS*

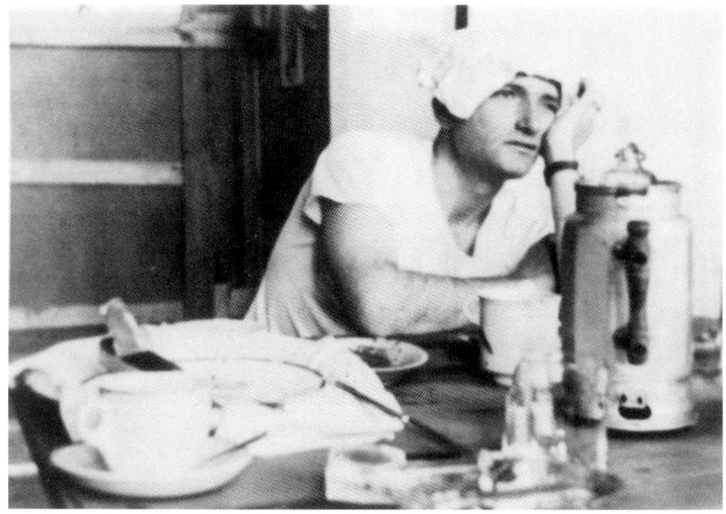

Warren Lewis fighting a long night. *Lackey*

Bill McWhirt (427th NFS) on left with John Leckie. *Lackey*

Joseph Govoni at Ie Shima. *421st NFS*

Squadron personnel around first 421st NFS sign. ***421st NFS***

Relaxing at Wakde from left to right are: Carr; McGuire; Alcure; Barresi; and Swinney in front. ***Stevens***

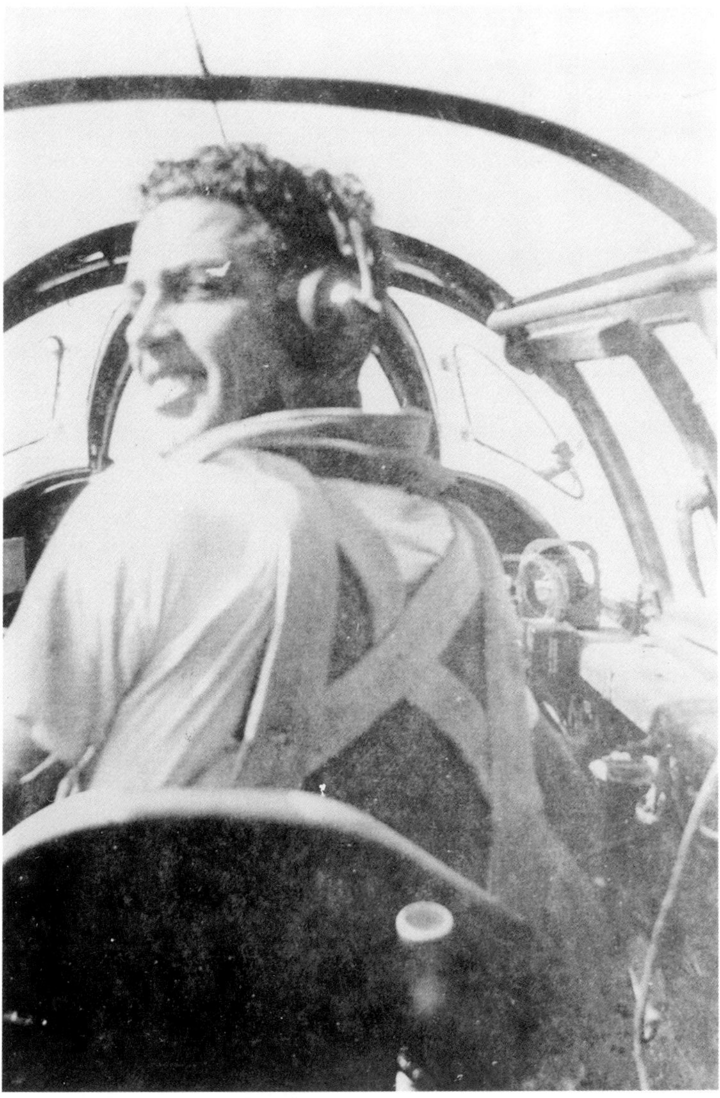

William Gill at the controls of a P-61. ***421st NFS***

Glen Meeks in front of 46th Engineers repair shop. ***421st NFS***

Philip Gabriel on left with William Beard holding Adolph LeGrand, Bob Wressig is on the right. ***421st NFS***

Herbert Dietel at Nadzab. ***421st NFS***

421st NFS at the rifle range at Kissimmee. ***421st NFS***

Dove on left and Ferrari enjoy mail call on the Kissimmee rifle range. ***421st NFS***

Howard Voland on left with Harry Barrick. ***421st NFS***

Joe Heeb taken at Tacloban. ***421st NFS***

Warren Stevens at Nadzab. ***Stevens***

From left to right at Wakde are: Nachman; McGuire; Carr; and Collins. ***Stevens***

Mike Grasso at Ie Shima. *421st NFS*

Ralph Hulsey on left with Robert Clodfelter at Tacloban. ***Stevens***

Dorrie Jones on left with Owen Wolf relaxing between missions. ***421st NFS***

Natives at Nadzab with fresh lizard. ***Goldstein***

Bill Bradley out on the Wakde flightline. ***421st NFS***

Borgeron Norris on left with Bob Smith near their hut at Tacloban. ***421st NFS***

Lindsey Cashion on left with Orien Cown. ***421st NFS***

Left to right are: Calvin McGuire; Preston Wilson; and Robert Wimberley at Tacloban. *421st NFS*

Richard Sheppard operating the radio at Wakde. *421st NFS*

William B. Robbins at Tacloban. *421st NFS*

Charlie Betchtold on Owi island. *421st NFS*

Richard Mulligan and his "Line Chief" jeep. 421st NFS

Larry Lackey on left with Bob McDonald. ***Lackey***

Squadron sign at Ie Shima. ***421st NFS***

From left to right on Ie Shima are: Albert LePage; Ralph Tourso; John Miotpher; Edward Gay; and Mack Ballard. ***421st NFS***

From Left to right on Wakde are: Dick Sheppard; Mitchell Foster; Larry Neville; Ben Hardin; and Glen Meeks. ***Stevens***

Herbert Goldstein on left with Cliff Grider at Nadzab. ***Stevens***

The 421st NFS camp at Owi. ***421st NFS***

Thanksgiving 1946 at Itazuke. From left to right at the front table are: Lewis; Mathews; unknown; Weisman; LeBeuf; and Ingalsbe. On the second table are: Hill; Bliss; James; Lackey; and unknowns. Hebert and Mash are on the back right table in front. ***Behnke***

From left to right in the back row are: Gresset; Loran; Noyes; Paula. In front are Rogers, Stout, and Gold. ***421st NFS***

William Beard on left holding a Japanese rifle with Donald Brannon. ***421st NFS***

Another view of Thanksgiving 1946. *Behnke*

LST #663 being loaded for trip to Leyte. *Stevens*

Ben Hardin on left with Joe Demyanchik digging a new latrine for the unit. *421st NFS*

Joe Bouchard on LST on the way to Leyte. *Burdue*

Leon Ward near squadron barracks at Kissimmee. *421st NFS*

Robert Grossman at Tacloban. ***Neville***

Daniel McGuire at Wakde. ***421st NFS***

Squadron members on the local transport at Tacloban. ***Stevens***

Roy Stancik on left doing laundry with Frank Allen at Nadzab. ***421st NFS***

From left to right are: Dobrovolsky; Beard; Hitchcock; Nachman; and LeGrand on the ground demonstrating the effects of hard liquor. *421st NFS*

Beard with hands up explaining to Nachman on right and squadron members what was going on. *421st NFS*

From left to right are: Adolph Le Grand; Harry Kniss; Albert Cereo; and Stephen Podibinski at Signal Hill; Florida. *421st NFS*

From left to right are: John Russo; Stephen Podibinski; and James Brown. *421st NFS*

Clifford Nelson at Tacloban. *421st NFS*

Right: Walter Hitchcock in a fox hole on Owi. *421st NFS*

William Cunningham on left with Joe Cox and their pet kangaroo. *421st NFS*

Left to right are: Bud Farnum; Ed Flickner; and Charles Townsend. *421st NFS*

Lt. Virgil Moe beside his P-61 at Ie Shima. *Moe*

Tito Pellicone on left with James Snyder at Tacloban. *421st NFS*

Major Richard Kiick receiving the Distinguished Flying Cross from General Fredric H. Smith. *Kiick*

Left to right are: Alexander Kuzmack; Lt. Robbins; and unknown. ***421st NFS***

Left to right are: Woodring; Mott and McGuire. ***421st NFS***

Squadron personnel around supply jeep at Kissimmee. From left to right are: Behm; Stout; Scoles; unknown; unknown; unknown; unknown; Radisich (hand on hip); Poyner (leaning on jeep hood); Blanchard (on left bumper); and Noyes (on ground). ***421st NFS***

Left to right are: unknown; Radisich; Barker; Bechtold; and Goldstein. ***421st NFS***

Left to right are: Bogart; unknown; Dew; Barrick; Wilson; unknown; Bittenbender; and Keener sitting. ***421st NFS***

From left to right on Ie Shima in 1945 are: Boger; Dow; Hoehn (standing) and Ballard; Routtu; Youker; and Chew (kneeling). ***Kiick***

Squadron personnel with local transportation on Owi island. ***421st NFS***

The 421st NFS' own version of a washing machine on Ie Shima. ***Moe***

Hurshell Pattison with a native girl at Tacloban. ***421st NFS***

Sgt. Richard Sheppard at Nadzab. ***421st NFS***

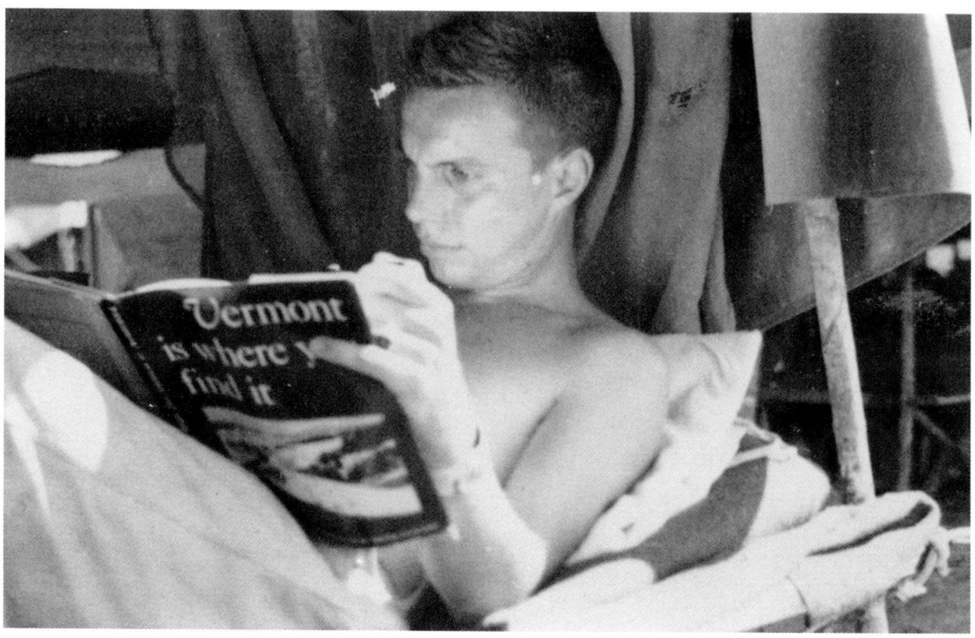

Sgt. Warren Stevens. ***Stevens***

Results of the rain in the Pacific Islands. ***421st NFS***

Above Right: Lt. Hopwood at Itazuke, Japan. ***Hopwood***

Picard and Gresett. ***421st NFS***

Color Gallery

Flightline mess kitchen at Nadzab, New Guinea. *421st NFS*

Headquarters building at Nadzab. *421st NFS*

Squadron P-61 flying through the clouds near Owi, Island. *421st NFS*

Another squadron P-61 over Owi. ***421st NFS***

Squadron P-61 on patrol over the Pacific. ***421st NFS***

Left to right are: Paul Zimmer; Captain Ball (GCI Officer); and Bill Bradley on Owi. ***421st NFS***

Clockwise from top left:
Captain Bill Bradley by his P-61A #42-5521. ***421st NFS***

Lt. Ed Crawford (R/O) by a squadron P-61. ***421st NFS***

Lt. Ray Eynon at Tacloban. ***421st NFS***

Captain Bill Bradley flying his P-61. ***421st NFS***

Lt. John Olley on left talking to Lt. Bjorum at Nadzab. ***421st NFS***

The Flight Surgeon, Doctor Collins, at Nadzab. ***Bjorum***

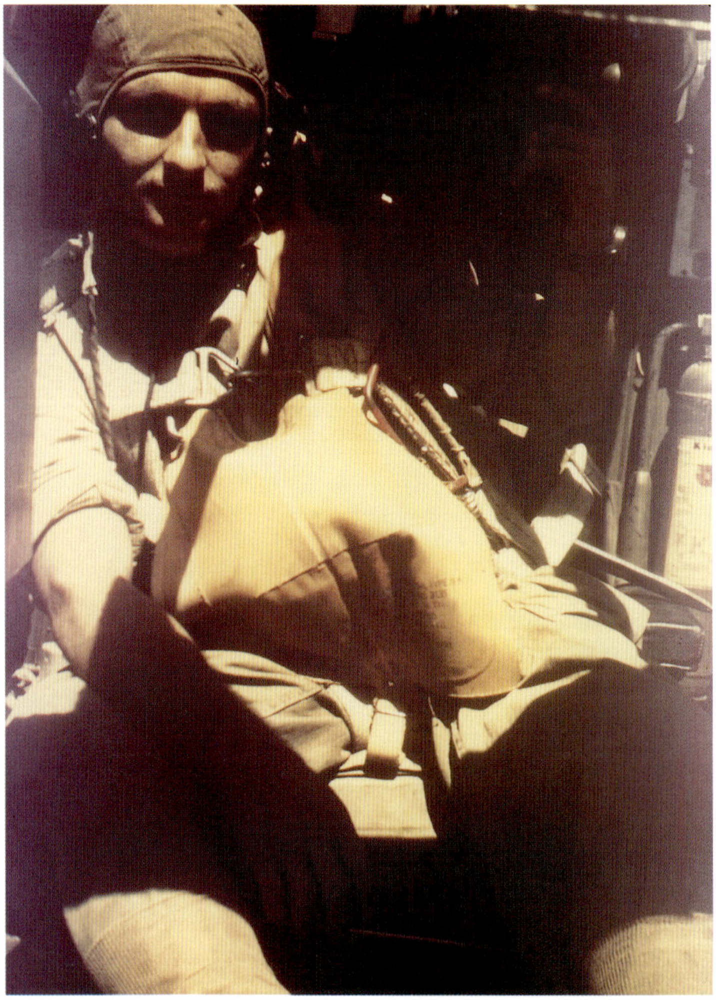

Clockwise from top left:
Sgt. Joe Mazur sitting in his gunner's position in a P-61. *421st NFS*

Lt. Isadore Nachman (Intelligence Officer) standing by a squadron P-61. *421st NFS*

Carl Bjorum on left with Bob Williams at Nadzab. *421st NFS*

"Nocturnal Nemisis," also known as "Skippy," at Tacloban. *421st NFS*

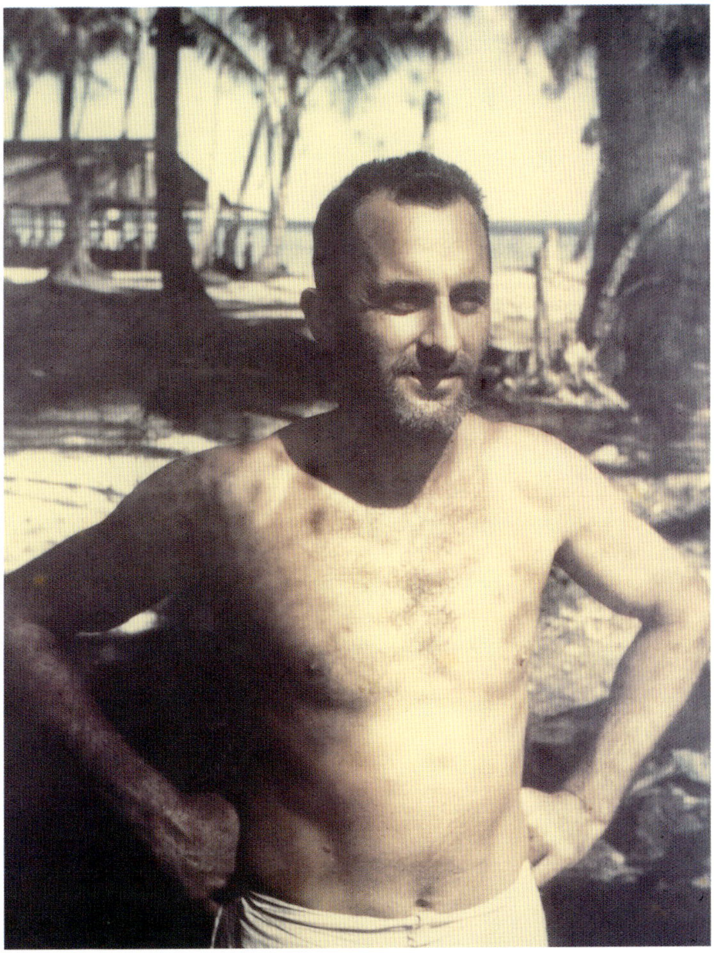

Lt. Joseph Govoni on Owi island. *421st NFS*

Lt. Bob Savaria's P-61B "Which Way'd They Go George." The name was based on his R/O George Freeman and asking him directions to the Japanese aircraft. *Chew*

Lt. Mack Ballard on the left with his R/O, Lt. Paul Boger, in front of their P-61 on Ie Shima. ***Chew***

Officers cleaning up their area after the typhoon on Ie Shima. ***Chew***

Lt. Virgil Moe in uniform observing some of the clean up after the typhoon hit Ie Shima. ***Chew***

Lt. John Owen on Ie Shima. *Chew*

Lt. Al. Routtu, known to the squadron as "Baby Face," which he hated. *Chew*

Left: Lt. John Chew on Ie Shima. The band-aid on his nose is the result of a bad fitting oxygen mask. *Chew*

Paul Boger on left with Al Routtu and Mack Ballard on the right. ***Chew***

Squadron P-61s on the flightline at Ie Shima. Chew

Another view of the 421st NFS flightline. ***Chew***

The squadron camp on Ie Shima. *Chew*

Another view of the squadron camp on Ie Shima. *Chew*

Gizmo the monkey. *Chew*

Mack Ballard and Paul Boger standing in front of their P-61. *Chew*

Squadron personnel working on their tents. *Chew*

The military cemetery on Ie Shima. *Chew*

Another view of the cemetery. *Chew*

Lt. Preston Wilson on left with unknown on Ie Shima. ***Chew***

Herbert Goldstein on left with unknown at Ie Shima. ***Goldstein***

Squadron P-61s in flight over Japan. ***McLaren***

Squadron P-61s on flightline at Ashiya. *McLaren*

The squadron's B-25 "Two Bits" on the flightline at Ashiya. *Lackey*

The cockpit of one of the squadron's P-61s. *Behnke*

Lt. Gerald Bliss and his P-61B #42-39575 at Itazuke. ***Bliss***

Japanese "House Girls" who did all the housekeeping in the officer's quarters. ***Behnke***

P-61B #42-39410 lined up with other 421st NFS aircraft at Itazuke. ***Behnke***

Lt. Col. Behnke buzzes the field at Itazuke. ***Behnke***

Patches of the 421st Night Fighter Squadron. In June 1943, Captain Pharr requested that a competition be held to design a squadron insignia. The original design was done by the wife of Lt. John Olley the Engineering Officer. The prize was a dinner for two at the Orange Court Hotel in Orlando, Florida. The original shows "Bugs Bunny" on a P-70 aircraft. The second style of "Bugs" on a P-61 was adopted about the time the squadron arrived at Ie Shima in 1945. ***421st NFS***

The other patch worn by the 421st Night Fighter Squadron was the 5th Air Force. Two versions of this patch are shown here. ***421st NFS***

Appendix A: 421st Night Fighter Members 1943-1947

A	
Milton R. Albrecht	Communications
Vincent J. Alcure	Gunner
Byron H. Allain	R/O
Frank J. Allen	Medical
Andreas Alvarado	
Authur T. Amos	
Chris Anderson	Transportation
Robert F. Anderson	Communications
Teddy L. Anderson	Aircraft Maintenance
Lester O. Andre	Transportation
Artie Anos	Aircraft Maintenance
Curtis A. Archibald	
Olynn W. Archibold	Aircraft Maintenance
Elmer L. Arnold	
Owen B. Arnold	
Charles E. Atwell	Communications
B	
Edward G. Babb	Ordinance
Raymond C. Bailey	
Albert W. Baker	Armaments
Arnold "Mack" Ballard	Pilot
Lynn L. Ballard	Aircraft Maintenance
Billy H. Battershell	Headquarters Staff
Maxwell G. Barber	
Richard D. Barker	Headquarters Staff
Donald L. Barlow	Pilot
Nelson L. Barth	Communications
Joseph V. Barresi	Gunner
Harry R. Barrick	Armament
Nelson L. Barth	
Norman Bartlett	Gunner
Robert R. Basere	
Woodrow W. Baucom	Engineering
William E. Beard	Ordinance
Robert W. Bechtold	Supply
Lawrence E. Behm	Technical Supply
William C. Behnke	Pilot/Commander
Michael Behurjak	
Charles H. Belcher	Communications
Kenneth E. Bennett	Flight Surgeon
Robert R. Basere	Armaments
Alexander Berg	R/O
Robert G. Binns	Gunner
Robert A. Bittenbender	Radar
Arther E. Bittner	Engineering
Carl M. Bjorum	Pilot
Howard J. Blanchard	Communications Officer
Gerald B. Bliss	Pilot
David A. Block	R/O
Nicholas J. Blodis	Aircraft Maintenance
Albert T. Bloomgren	Engineering
Leon C. Blose	
Glenn M. Bloyd	Operations
Henry E. Bobo	Gunner
Charles R. Bobst	Gunner
Henry F. Bockstege	Pilot
Robert Boehmer	
Earl W. Bogart	Transpertation
Paul L. Boger	R/O
Robert C. Bonbrake	Gunner
Marion L. Booth	Gunner
Alexander Borg	R/O
Fred Bosworth	Radar
Frank A. Bosch	Pilot
Joseph Bossman	Communications
Fred W. Bosworth	Radar
Joseph W. Bouchard	Aircraft Maintenance
Beverly S. Bowers	Pilot
Leonard O. Box	Tech. Supply
William T. Boze	R/O
Joe A. Bradford	Aircraft Maintenance
William T. Bradley	Pilot/Commander
John P. Brady	Aircraft Maintenance
Gerald W. Bragg	

Donald A. Brannon	Engineering
Donald G. Branstine	Armament
Neil E. Braun	Communications
Millard E. Braxton	Gunner
Robert K. Bremer	R/O
John W. Brewer	Pilot
Ralph K. Brockman	
James H. Brown	Armament
James L. Brown	Operations
Leonard Brown	Operations
James O. Brown	Aircraft Maintenance
Dale Bruton	
George R. Bryan	Engineering
Wayne F. Bryers	
James L. Buchanan	Radar
Robert E. Buchanan	Intelligence Officer
William C. Bundrick	Tech. Supply
George Burdis	R/O
Harold W. Burdue	Aircraft Maintenance
Curtis A. Burgess	Aircraft Maintenance
Gerald V. Burns	Transportation
Francis L. Burrell	R/O
Buford E. Bush	Transportation

C

Preston H. Callison	Communications
Edward Cambrel	Aircraft Maintenance
Lawrence R. Carr	R/O
Lindsey N. Cashion	Ordinance
Albert P. Cereo	Aircraft Maintenance
John H. Chancey	
Paul I. Chappell	Aircraft Maintenance
John F. Ciesialski	Mess
Andrew W. Cisarik	Gunner
John F. Cleary	1st Sgt.
Robert W. Clyde	R/O
Robert R. Clodfelter	R/O
Robert W. Coates	Pilot
Harold L. Cobb	Gunner
Harold C. Cole	Civilian Maintenance Technician
Joseph E. Cole	
Frank R. Coleman	Aircraft Maintenance
Vincent P. Collins	Flight Surgeon
Elmer H. Cooper	Radar
Philip L. Corbin	Radar
Paul W. Cornette	
Albert P. Corso	
David T. Corts	Pilot
Ralph P. Courso	
Orien S. Cown	Ordinance
Joe F. Cox	Armament
Chester C. Craft	Pilot
Joseph B. Crain	
Edgar Crawford	R/O
James M. Crawford	Aircraft Maintenance
Howard R. Crimmel	R/O
Ken Cryson	
Roy B. Cude	Medical
William J. Cunningham	Ordinance
Raymond F. Curren	
John B. Cutshall	Pilot
Raymond F. Curren	Gunner

D

Raymond Daniels	Pilot
Allen C. Dale	Intelligence Officer
John Danko	Armament
George C. Darrah	Aircraft Maintenance
Kenneth S. Daugherty	
Lloyd A. Davey	Headquarters Staff
Dewell C. Davis	Armament
Harlan Davis	Gunner
James W. Davis	Pilot
George L. DeHaven	
Vincent M. DelaGardelle	Communications
Andrew D. Della	Radar
Joseph Demyanchik	Aircraft Maintenance
Thomas L. Denning	
John Dew	Radar
Herbert A. Dietol	Engineering
Harvey Dittle	
Gaza Dobrovolsky	Communications
Ralph Dodge	
James V. Doke	Armament
Fredrick S. Doll	R/O
Robert Doolittle	Aircraft Maintenance
Charles E. Domke	Armament
Vincent J. Dornoff	Radar
Alexander Dove	Engineering
John M. Dew	Radar
George L. Drain	
Willard P. Durgin	

E

James R. Eckerle	Personal Equipment Officer
Peter Economy	
John Efstathiou	Aircraft Maintenance
Alexander C. Efthim	Intelligence
Thomas J. Elder	Headquarters Staff
Harry J. Ellwanger	Communications
Chester L. Ende	Radar
Carl D. Ernst	Headquarters Staff
Harold G. Ernst	Transportation
Ray A. Eynon	R/O

F

Philip V. Fabel	
Joe J. Fanelli	Radar
Maxwell G. Farber	Radar

Eldon Farmer	Engineering
Herman H. Farr	Communications
Bernard C. Faulstick	R/O
Charles Faust	R/O
Henry J. Fehrman	Armament
Samual Feldman	R/O
Frank A. Felix	
Raymond E. Ferrari	Aircraft Maintenance
William J. Filardi	Gunner
Raymond Finchum	Mess
Bernard B. Fischer	
Edward A. Flickner	Weather Officer
Rolland L. Forrester	Pilot
Mitchel W. Foster	Radar
Paul L. Foster	
William E. Foster	Ordinance
William H. Foster	Mess
John E. Franz	
Alfredo M. Fraser	
Joseph W. Frazier	Mess
George A. Freeman	R/O
Harold O. Freeman	R/O
John G. Freise	Armaments
Joseph W. French	Mess
Raymond T. French	
Eddie Friday	

G

Philip F. Gabriel	Communications
John C. Gamble	Aircraft Maintenance
Edward Gambrel	
Albert R. Gann	Pilot
George Garenger	R/O
Charlie Garrison	Mess
John W. Gaskins	Armament
Martin J. Gassner	
Clinton C. Gaston	Pilot
William T. Gattis	Pilot
Edward Gay	Mess
Russell C. Gebler	Pilot
Francis S. Geigen	Communications
Armand Giarruso	
William H. Gill	Pilot
James C. Gillet	
Jim Gilliam	Radar
Michael J. Gillian	Radar
James C. Gillot	
Francis E. Gilmartin	R/O
Ralph Gilmaier	Aircraft Maintenance
Armand Giorruso	Engineering & Operations Clerk
Thomas J. Glynn	R/O
Walter Gold	Aircraft Maintenance
Reuben Golden	
Herbert C. Goldstein	1st Sergeant
Raymond S. Gomez	Mess
Ricardo Gonzales	
William H. Gorman	Aircraft Maintenance
Clint E. Gosnell	
Joseph F. Govoni	Adjutant
Francis H. Gower	
Michael J. Grasso	Ordinance
Kenneth G. Grayson	Armament
James S. Green	Communications
Louis H. Greenberg	Mess
Earl J. Greer	Ordinance
Roy C. Gressett	Aircraft Maintenance
Cliff Grider	HQ/ Mail
Robert M. Grossman	Armament
Robert B. Gunter	R/O

H

Arthur E. Hagan	Radar
Albert B. Hall	Ordinance
John L. Halleran	Radar
Frank A. Hamilton	Gunner
Mike Hancher	Aircraft Maintenance
Hayden H. Hankins	Communications
Harry H. Haproff	Engineering
Earl V. Hardee	
Benjamin F. Harden	Engineering
Wesley A. Harding	Armament
Howard Hargrave	Communications
Carl K. Harper	Engineering
Gordon R. Harper	Communications
Herman C. Harper	Communications
Francis D. Harris	Armament
Victor Harris	Gunner
George Harry	Gunner
William R. Hartsock	R/O
James L. Hawkins	Gunner
Wilbur Hawkins	
Ervin D. Hayes	Radar
Erwin D. Hays	Radar
Albert N. Hebert	Pilot
Joseph F. Heeb	Armament
Ted Heinz	
Richard W. Heldt	Aircraft Maintenance
James S. Herman	
Andrew R. Hernandez	Communications
Eugene V. Higgens	Supply Officer
Gordon L. Higley	
Michael J. Hill	R/O
Ployer P. Hill	R/O
Walter D. Hitchcock	Communications
Frank C. Hixenbaugh	Mess
James R. Hoak	
William W. Hodgson	Armament
Bernard R. Hoehn	R/O
Paul Hoko	Radar

Milton R. Holbert	Pilot
John H. Hole	
Louis p. Hollandsworth	Aircraft Maintenance
John Holloran	Radar
John H. Holmes	
Harold R. Hopkins	
David Hopwood	Pilot
Harold M. Howe	Pilot
William I. Hudson	Headquarters Staff
Ralph V. Hulsey	R/O
George E. Humphreys	Medical
Harry H. Hutchinson	Gunner

I

Anthony F. Incovitti	R/O
Francis M. Ingalsbe	Communications

J

Ralph A. Jackson	
Gordon J. James	R/O
Theron O. Jaquish	Armament
Melvin H. Jarchow	Pilot
Billy R. Jarvis	Mess
William H. Jennings	
George E. Jennison	Gunner
Charles M. Johnson	
Donald H. Johnson	Radar
Donald L. Johnson	Aircraft Maintenance
John B. Johnson	
Dorrie E. Jones	Pilot
John Jones	Armament Officer

K

Leroy M. Kaegi	Pilot
George W. Kantzler	
Rubin J. Kaplan	Engineering
Geroge J. Karwowski	Armament
Allen L. Kay	
Homer D. Keener	Engineering
John A. Kelly	Aircraft Maintenance
Homer W. Kilge	Mess
Joseph W. King	Mess
Endrick J. Kinslow	
Ernest J. Kison	
Truman A. Kjosa	Gunner
John V. Knapp	Radar
James L. Knight	Aircraft Maintenance
Harry S. Kniss	Aircraft Maintenance
Steve Kobesak	
Fred E. Kohl	Pilot
Max Korman	
Herbert F. Krueger	Engineering
Robert L. Kunzman	R/O
Stephen P. Kutz	
Alexander A. Kuzmack	Pilot
Mr. Kwiatkowski	Civilian Maintenance Technician

L

Larry Lackey	Pilot
Fred H. Lackner	
Donald F. Lacy	Gunner
James R. Lampp	
Paul E. Lancaster	Communications
James M. Lange	Engineering
George J. Lauer	Communications
Keith L. Lawrence	R/O
Burl L. Leavell	Tech. Supply
Robert A. LeBeuf	R/O
John G. Leckie	Pilot
Edwin J. Lee	
William Lee	Mess
Emanuel J. Leestuki	Aircraft Maintenance
Bruce K. Leford	
Adolph A. LeGrand	Engineering
Albert J. LePage	Aircraft Maintenance
Harold V. Leslie	1st Sgt.
Emanuel J. Lesovsky	Aircraft Maintenance
Norman H. Levesque	Engineering
Warren D. Lewis	Pilot
Melvin H. Limberman	R/O
Albert W. Lockhard	Pilot
Lavern E. Lockman	Communications
Fred H. Lockner	
Efraim L. Lopez	Armaments
Jacob T. Loran	Headquarters Staff
Joseph B. Lugara	Communications
Goerge Luggens	
Erich R. Lundstrom	Gunner
George W. Lutgens	Engineering
Mathew J. Lux	

M

Robert A. MacDonald	
Donald C. Macleod	
Earl Madsen	Pilot
Nick J. Magdic	Communications
Francis J. Maguire	Aircraft Maintenance
Fred R. Mahoney	Aircraft Maintenance
Loyal F. Males	Aircraft Maintenance
Thomas E. Malone	Pilot
Joseph J. Manelli	
Calvin S. McGuire	Pilot
James F. Maquire	Aircraft Maintenance
Nasario Martinez	Mess
John D. Mash	Pilot
Gerald A. Mathews	Pilot
Raymond G. Mazalan	R/O

Joseph Mazur	Gunner
Henry L. McCarley	Communications
Raymond M. McComb	
Robert McCormick	Mess
Robert McCullough	R/O
Ralph H. McDaniel	Gunner
Carl W. McDowell	Gunner
Daniel L. McGuire	R/O
Paul McKenzie	Radar
William B. McLaughlin	Communications
Robert A. McMaster	Pilot
Robert M. McNulty	
James T. McQuire	
Luther E. Meadors	Transportation
James J. Meeks	R/O
Glen R. Meeks	Engineering
James A. Meeks	Armament
Herbert G. Mende	Ordinance
William C. Mercer	Radar
Morris Messinger	
Wayne A. Miles	
Larry B. Miller	
William S. Miller	Engineering Officer
Wade W. Mitchem	Armaments
Virgil C. Moe	Pilot
Bernard R. Moehn	
Thomas J. Montgomery	Armaments
Burl W. Moore	
Charles E. Moore	R/O
Myler K. Moore	Pilot
Ralph B. Moore	R/O
Samuel N. Moore	Ordinance
William C. More	
Jose V. Morlet	
Charles W. Moss	R/O
Ray D. Moss	Ordinance
Arthur C. Mott	Pilot
Frank G. Mott	Gunner
Willis K. Moyes	
Harold E. Mrotzok	Communications
John A. Mull	Pilot
Richard J. Mulligan	Engineering/ Line Chief
Alto R. Munn	Radar
William D. Murphy	
Donald H. Musser	Radar

N

Michael M. Nabasny	Communications
Isadore Nachman	Intelligence Officer
Nicholas Natiello	Gunner
Walter F. Nernsing	Ordinance
Clifford J. Nelson	Armaments
Lawrence J. Neville	Armaments
Ward R. Niver	
Borgeron J. Norris	Armament
Edward K. Noyes	Supply

O

Bernard R. O'Conner	
Herman W. Ohmstad	Armament
Norman W. Olmstad	Armaments
Robert O'Lone	R/O
John J. Olley	Engineering Officer
Marion R. Olsen	
Raymond Olson	
Charles J. O'Neil	
Dwight C. Orcutt	
Sidney M. Orloff	Supply
Jack R. Owen	R/O
James M. Oxley	Armament

P

William T. Page	Executive Officer
David J. Pahlka	Pilot
Gerald C. Parker	Pilot
Lloyd Partridge	Pilot
Raymond A. Passler	
John M. Patrija	Mess
Hurshell F. Pattison	Armament
Louis Paulo	Aircraft Maintenance
Tito Pellicone	Armament
James A. Peoples	
Michael A. Petretta	Communications
Nicolus Petric	Mess
Robert C. Pew	Pilot
Walter S. Pharr	Pilot/Commander
Leroy T. Phillips	
Archie H. Picard	Aircraft Maintenance
James W. Pilling	Gunner
Theron R. Pitzer	Supply Officer
Stephen P. Podibinski	Engineering
Aurther E. Poggensee	Aircraft Maintenance
Edwin Pokorski	Communications
Rodney Polter	Radar
Douglas C. Ponsford	Aircraft Maintenance
Harry Popovich	Armament
Lacy Potter	Gunner
Robert C. Pough	Pilot
Charles F. Powell	Engineering
Frank Powell	Radio
Beverly S. Powers	Pilot / Engineering Officer
Lewis Powers	Radar
William J. Powers	Aircraft Maintenance
Robert C. Pough	
Nile D. Poyner	Technical Supply
Noah E. Pratt	Aircraft Maintenance
Winston Puttick	R/O

R

Anthony J. Radisich	Technical Supply
Jacob J. Rantz	Communications
Oliver V. Recos	
Russell F. Rector	
Harry Redlinger	Engineering
Oliver V. Reece	Medical
George L. Reese	Communications
John Reid	
Neal E. Reinerd	Pilot
Carl R. Remington	Pilot
Charles R. Renker	Comminations
Robert H. Reynolds	Pilot
William Rife	
Martin E. Riley	Pilot
Allen E. Rishal	Medical
William B. Robbins	Pilot
Earl C. Roberts	
James F. Robinson	
Harry E. Rodlinger	
Elston E. Roady	Radar Officer
Loda A. Rogers	Engineering
Ray Romens	
William F. Rossell	R/O
Albert A. Routtu	Pilot
Robert Rothen	Flight Surgeon
Bowman W. Rowland	1st Sgt.
Victor W. Rudinski	Tech. Supply
John L. Russo	Engineering

S

Peter L. Sabella	Communications
Joseph F. Samudio	Mess
Eric C. Sandstrom	Communications
William K. Sansing	Aircraft Maintenance
Robert E. Savaria	Pilot
Julius Schiff	
Frank L. Schleichor	Engineering
Victor S. Schmidt	Communications
Robert M. Schoonover	R/O
Lyle A. Schutt	
George E. Schwedler	Aircraft Maintenance
Richard E. Scoles	Engineering
Delbert W. Searles	R/O
Donald G. Seifferman	
Michael Severino	
Oscar F. Shaver	Radar
Donald G. Shepard	
Richard L. Shepard	Intelligence
Maurice Sherrill	Aircraft Maintenance
Gilbert M. Shook	
Walter J. Sikersky	Mess
Henry Simacek	Communications
Stephen M. Simak	
Elmer A. Simpson	
John W. Slocum	Gunner
James K. Smallwood	Armament
Emile C. Smith	
Frank L. Smith	Communications
Hoke Smith	Pilot
Robert L. Smith	Armament
Wilfred M. Smith	Mess
William Smith	
Sidney Smolowitz	Headquarters Staff
James A. Snyder	Armament
Clinton E. Sosnell	
Lee Roy Stancik	Medical
Franklin E. Starr	Aircraft Maintenance
Ray E. St. Clair	
Lorenzo E. Stephenson	Communications
Bernard Stewart	R/O
Warren L. Stevens	Intelligence
Paul L. Stickley	
Isadore Stien	Mess
Louis Stisowain	Aircraft Maintenance
Frederick C. Stout	Technical Supply
Albert Summerville	
Willard P. Surgin	
Edsell H. Swauger	
Sheldon R. Sweet	Aircraft Maintenance
Brady W. Swinney	Gunner

T

Alexander Tainsch	
Harold D. Talbot	Communications Officer
Fredrick H. Taylor	
Morris Thebner	Communications
Louis H. Thiede	Aircraft Maintenance
Stuart A. Thornton	R/O
Gordon D. Timmons	Pilot/Commander
Edward L. Tingen	pilot
Theodore L. Tollefson	
Ernst R. Torres	Communication
Joseph E. Tosh	Armament
Ralph P. Tourso	
Charles M. Townsend	Executive Officer
Donald H. Trabing	Gunner
Claude S. Trull	Aircraft Maintenance
Raymond M. Tucker	

U

Robert S. Umfreville	Communications

V

Robert L. Vance	Aircraft Maintenance
James J. Vanderbeck	Gunner

Carmen A. Vando Linde	Communications
Robert E. Van Sant	R/O
Herbert L. Vermillion	Engineering
Howard L. Voland	Armament
George Vrgevich	

W

George O. Wagner	R/O
Harry Wagner	
Claude W. Waite	Aircraft Maintenance
Frederick J. Waldron	Pilot
Leon T. Ward	
William C. Warfield	
Mason Webb	Aircraft Maintenance
Emil K. Weisher	Gunner
David B. Weisman	Pilot
Donald Welch	R/O
Hubert Welder	Draftsman / Intelligence
Donald H. Welsh	R/O
Walter F. Wernsing	Armaments
George West	R/O
Harry G. Weston	Aircraft Maintenance
Arthur Wheaton	Communications
Edwin W. Wheeler	
Johnnie White	Medical
Philip B. Whitford	R/O
Gordon L. Wigley	
George W. Williams	Supply
Robert C. Williams	R/O
Julius Willinger	Headquarters Staff
Preston C. Wilson	Ordinance Officer
Robert D. Wimberley	
Andrew M. Winter	
Hubert W. Wolder	Intelligence
Owen H. Wolf	Pilot
George H. Wolfe	R/O
William H. Wolfrom	Communications
John L. Wood	
Alton C. Woodring	R/O
Robert C. Wressig	Transportation
Henry W. Wright	

Y

Frank P. Yando	Medical
Robert L. Yoder	Pilot
Laurel B. Youker	Pilot
Robert S. Young	Gunner
Wade Young	Technical Supply
William L. Young	Gunner

Z

Frank J. Zabilski	Aircraft Maintenance
John C. Zane	Mess
Paul R. Zimmer	Pilot/ Commander
David L. Zimmerman	Pilot
Hyman Zimmerman	Mess
Stanislous Zylonis	Armament

Appendix B: 421st Mission List

DATE	AIRCRAFT	T.O./ LANDING	COMMENTS
6/8/44	P-61	0845 / 1200	Courier from Nadzab to Wakde.
6/8/44	P-61	2025 / 2245	Patrol Wakde to Sarmi Point.
6/8/44	P-61	2215 / 0115	Patrol Wakde to Sarmi Point.
6/9/44	P-61	0130 / 0350	Patrol Wakde to Sarmi Point. Fighter Sector gave vector on bogie at 10,000 feet. At 15,000 feet radar transmitter burned out. Gasoline gauges did not function properly, and the cockpit was filled with smoke, plane was forced to land.
6/9/44	P-61	1155 / 1500	Courier Wakde to Nadzab.
6/10/44	P-61	1400 / 1515	Radar calibration mission for Sector Controller.
6/10/44	P-61	1030 / 1230	Courier Nadzab to Tadji and on to Wakde. 1445 / 1600
6/11/44	P-61	0010 / 0110	Patrol Wakde area. Possible burst of medium A/A observed near Sarmi Point . Observed at 5,000 feet. Altitude unknown. Force to land before patrol was completed because radar set did not function properly.
6/11/44	P-61	0130 / 0235	Patrol Wakde area. As soon as pilot landed Sector Controller called a Red Alert.
6/11/44	P-61	0145 / 0400	Patrol Wakde area. Pilot was given a vector at 0205. Vectored in 11 miles from enemy aircraft. Given a heading of 160°, which took the pilot 20 miles inland. Sector then vectored pilot to a point west of Wakde, out of A/A range. After enemy aircraft made his pass Sector vectored pilot 180°, he flew 35 minutes and then a heading of 260° was given. Pilot closed in from 6 miles to 3 miles at which time he was going out of Sector's scope. Due to failure of ship's radar equipment the pilot could not get enemy aircraft in his scope. At approximately 50 miles west, the pilot turned to return to home base.
6/11/44	P-61	1245 / 1400	Courier Wakde to Tadji and on to Nadzab.
6/11/44	(2) P-61	1550 / 1700	Night Fighter Test Wakde area.
6/11/44	P-61	1430 / 1700	Courier from Nadzab to Wakde.
6/12/44	P-61	2400 / 0200	Patrol area Wakde.
6/12/44	P-61	0145 / 0245	Patrol Wakde area.
6/12/44	P-61	0255 / 0525	Patrol Wakde area.
6/12/44	P-61	0450 / 0550	Patrol Wakde area.
6/12/44	P-61	0600 / 0645	Patrol Wakde area.
6/13/44	P-61	0055 / 0300	Patrol Wakde area.
6/13/44	P-61	0245 / 0550	Patrol of Wakde area with stopover at 0715 / 0800 Hollandia and back. P-61 contacted seven bogies with radar. Intercepted two bogies twelve minutes after take-off. Gained altitude to a height of 21,000 feet. Bogie peeled off his target at target and last contact was made 15 degrees above 10,000 feet range. Contact was lost east of Wakde. Continued patrol west end of island in an attempt to make contact after raid, but no contact was made. Patrolled south of island and made contact with five bogies. Passed under them head on. The formation Broke up as the P-61 passed by. Two peeled to the left and three to the right. P-61 followed the three into the Ack-Ack ring, but had to cut off contact. Was

			advised to proceed to Hollandia to land because of damage to Wakde strip. Left Hollandia a few hours later to Wakde.
6/13/44	P-61	0930 / 1130	Courier Nadzab to Tadji and on to Wakde. 1330 / 1500
6/13/44	P-61	1650 / 1700	Night Fighter Test Wakde area.
6/13/44	P-61	1730 / 1800	Night Fighter Test Wakde area.
6/14/44	P-61	0200 / 0245	Patrol Wakde area.
6/14/44	P-61	0330 / 0545	Patrol Wakde area.
6/14/44	P-61	1430 / 1530	Night Fighter Test Wakde area. Test not completed because radar set malfunctioned.
6/14/44	P-61	2205 / 2400	Patrol Wakde area.
6/14/44	P-61	2330 / 0030	Patrol Wakde area. Not completed because radar set malfunctioned.
6/15/44	P-61	0005 / 0020	Patrol Wakde area. Ship was forced to return immediately because of mechanical malfunction.
6/15/44	P-61	0240 / 0310	Patrol Wakde area. Not completed because radar was out. Aircraft encountered slight A/A fire at 6,000 feet, medium caliber, inaccurate. Apparently 2 or 3 medium A/A guns between Maffin Drome and Sarmi Point. Pilot noticed four bursts.
6/15/44	P-61	0315 / 0515	Patrol Wakde area. Encountered slight medium and inaccurate A/A at unobserved altitude. Pilot observed 2 bursts of A/A just SE of Sarmi Point.
6/15/44	P-61	1005 / 1035	Night Fighter Test Wakde area.
6/15/44	P-61	1045 / 1145	Night Fighter Test Wakde area.
6/15/44	P-61	1045 / 1300	Night Fighter Test Wakde area.
6/15/44	P-61	1645 / 1745	Night Fighter Test Wakde area. Mission not complete because radar set malfunctioned.
6/15/44	P-61	1655 / 1725	Night Fighter Radar Test.
6/15/44	P-61	1850 / 1920	Night Fighter Radar Test.
6/15/44	P-61	2115 / 2230	GCI ordered ship off ground to intercept possible bogie on tail of B-24. Patrol discontinued after bogie was found to be a ghost target.
6/16/44	P-61	1315 / 1600	Courier Wakde to Nadzab.
6/16/44	P-61	0200 / 0345	Patrol Wakde area.
6/16/44	P-61	0415 / 0445	Patrol Wakde area. Patrol not finished because radar set malfunction.
6/16/44	P-61	0500 / 0600	Patrol Wakde area. Patrol not finished because radar went out near end of flight.
6/16/44	(2) P-61	1845 / 1930	Night Fighter Radar Test. One ship landed at 1915 because radar checked OK and mission was completed.
6/17/44	P-61	0445 / 0630	Patrol Wakde area.
6/17/44	P-61	0740 / 1100	Courier Wakde to Nadzab.
6/17/44	P-61	1030 / 1330	Courier from Nadzab to Wakde.
6/17/44	P-61	1515 / 1645	Night Fighter Radar Test.
6/17/44	P-61	1500 / 1745	Courier from Nadzab to Wakde.
6/17/44	P-61	2100 / 2130	Patrol Wakde area. Pilot forced to return because of bad weather.
6/18/44	P-61	0945 / 1030	Courier from Wakde to Hollandia and return. 1100 / 1200
6/18/44	(2) P-61	1430 / 1630	Night Fighter Radar Test.
6/19/44	P-61	1500 / 1600	Night Fighter Radar Test. Test not completed because radar set malfunctioned.
6/19/44	P-61	1445 / 1645	Homing Calibration Mission.
6/20/44	P-61	0001 / 0215	Patrol Wakde area.
6/20/44	P-61	1300 / 1430	Night Fighter Radar Test.
6/20/44	P-61	1315 / 1530	Night Fighter Radar Test.
6/20/44	P-61	1400 / 1530	Night Fighter Radar Test.
6/20/44	P-61	1545 / 1730	Night Fighter Radar Test.
6/21/44	P-61	1115 / 1145	Night Fighter Radar Test. Ship forced to land because radar set malfunctioned.
6/21/44	P-61	0900 / 1215	Courier from Nadzab to Wakde.
6/21/44	P-61	1515 /1545	Night Fighter Radar Test. Mission not completed because radar set malfunctioned.
6/21/44	P-61	1500 / 1640	GCI Calibration Mission.
6/21/44	P-61	0930 / 1100	Courier Wakde to Tadji, on to Nadzab. Mission 1130 / 1430 incomplete due to weather. Plane force back to land at Tadji.
6/22/44	P-61	0215 / 0345	Patrol Wakde area.
6/22/44	P-61	0300 / 0415	Patrol Wakde area.

6/22/44	P-61	0430 / 0530	Patrol Wakde area.
6/22/44	(2) P-61	1430 / 1530	Night Fighter Radar Test.
6/22/44	P-61	0915 / 1100	Courier Tadji, Gusap and Nadzab. 1115 / 1145
6/23/44	P-61	1440 / 1640	GCI Calibration Test.
6/23/44	P-61	1445 / 1645	Night Fighter Radar & Radio Test.
6/24/44	P-61	0900 / 1245	Courier from Nadzab to Wakde.
6/24/44	(2) P-61	1445 / 1615	Night Fighter Radar Test.
6/24/44	P-61	1900 / 1950	Patrol Wakde area. Mission was not completed because of radio and radar malfunction.
6/24/44	P-61	2030 / 2215	Patrol Wakde area.
6/25/44	P-61	1850 / 1905	Patrol Wakde area. Ship forced to return because radar as inoperative.
6/25/44	P-61	2000 / 2130	Patrol Wakde area.
6/25/44	P-61	2115 / 2250	Patrol Wakde area.
6/26/44	P-61	0930 / 1245	Courier from Nadzab to Wakde.
6/26/44	P-61	1445 / 1545	Night Fighter Test.
6/26/44	P-61	1450 / 1635	Night Fighter Radar Test.
6/26/44	P-61	1845 / 1930	Patrol Wakde area. Mission was not completed because of bad weather and radar inoperative.
6/27/44	(2) P-61	1345 / 1515	Night Fighter Test.
6/27/44	P-61	1900 / 2100	Patrol Wakde area.
6/27/44	P-61	2025 / 2215	Patrol Wakde area.
6/27/44	P-61	1445 / 1800	Courier Wakde to Nadzab.
6/28/44	(2) P-61	1015 / 1215	Night Fighter Test.
6/28/44	P-61	1005 / 1150	Night Fighter Radar Test.
6/28/44	(2) P-61	0830 / 1130	Courier Nadzab to Wakde.
6/28/44	P-61	1500 / 1530	Night Fighter Test.
6/28/44	P-61	1600 / 1630	Night Fighter Test.
6/28/44	P-61	1430 / 1725	Courier from Wakde to Hollandia and return.
6/28/44	P-61	1900 / 2030	Patrol Wakde area.
6/28/44	P-61	1830 / 1900	Night Fighter Test.
6/28/44	P-61	2015 / 2200	Patrol Wakde area.
6/28/44	P-61	2130 / 2230	Patrol Wakde area. Mission incomplete due to radar failure.
6/28/44	P-61	2200 / 2215	Patrol Wakde area. Mission not completed due to part of canopy blowing off.
6/28/44	P-61	2245 / 0015	Patrol Wakde area.
6/28/44	(2) P-61	0830 / 1135	Courier from Nadzab to Wakde to Owi Island. 1400 / 1515
6/28/44	(2) P-61	0840 / 1140	Courier from Nadzab to Wakde to Owi Island. 1430 / 1545
6/28/44	P-61	0740 /1130	Courier from Nadzab to Wakde to Owi Island. 1515 / 1615
6/29/44	P-61	1000 / 1100	Courier from Wakde to Owi and return. 1600 / 1715
6/29/44	P-61	0945 / 1030	Night Fighter Test.
6/29/44	P-61	1100 / 1315	Night Fighter Test.
6/29/44	(2) P-61	1545 / 1645	Night Fighter Test.
6/29/44	P-61	1910 / 2045	Patrol Wakde area.
6/29/44	P-61	2020 / 2140	Patrol Wakde area.
6/29/44	P-61	2150 / 2315	Patrol Wakde area.
6/29/44	P-61	1045 / 1245	Patrol Wakde area.
6/29/44	P-61	0830 / 1130	Courier Nadzab to Wakde to Owi. Plane left 1130 / 1245 Nadzab on 28th and stayed at Wakde overnight. It went on to Owi on the 29th.
6/30/44	P-61	0950 / 1020	Night Fighter Test.
6/30/44	P-61	1045 / 1200	Night Fighter Test.
6/30/44	P-61	1115 / 1145	Night Fighter Test.
6/30/44	P-61	1550 / 1635	Night Fighter Test.
6/30/44	P-61	1200 / 1530	Courier mission from Nadzab to Wakde.
6/30/44	P-61	1900 / 1945	Patrol Wakde area. Mission incomplete due to radar inoperative.
6/30/44	P-61	1600 / 1715	Courier mission from Owi to Wakde.
6/30/44	P-61	1950 / 2125	Patrol Wakde area.
6/30/44	P-61	2330 / 0015	Patrol Wakde area.

6/30/44	P-61	1250 / 1330	Courier mission to Hollandia.
6/30/44	P-61	2100 / 2400	Patrol Wakde area. Mission incomplete due to radar inoperative and engine cutting out. GCI gave pilot 3 vectors in a period of 2 minutes. Radar went out due to lack of pressure in tank. GCI was taking pilot to target when right engine cut out. Target was then 10 miles away. GCI called pilot off, circled north of strip and vectored to Hollandia.
6/30/44	P-61	1050 / 1120	Night Fighter Radar Test.
6/30/44	P-61	1030 / 1115	Courier from Owi to Wakde and return. 1650 / 1740
7/7/44	P-61	0045/ 0125	Scrambled to investigate bogie southwest of Owi Island. Lt. Owen Wolf (pilot), Lt. Byron Byron Allain (R/O), and S/Sgt. Emil Weishar (gunner) intercept and shoot down Japanese "Sally" type bomber near Japen Island. It was observed to explode when it hit the water.
7/21/44	P-61	0845 / 1015	Courier from Wakde to Owi and return. 1625 / 1725
7/21/44	P-61	1315 / 1450	Engineering test hop.
9/1/44	P-61	2400 / 0145	Patrol Owi Island, Biak area.
9/1/44	P-61	0130 / 0215	Patrol Owi island, Biak area.
9/1/44	P-61	2330 / 0145	Courier to Middleburg Island and return. 0155 / 0240
9/1/44	(2) P-61	1020 / 1140	Calibration Test.
9/1/44	P-61	1835 / 1935	Patrol Owi Island, Biak area. Aircraft returned early due to radio malfunction.
9/1/44	P-61	1925 / 2115	Patrol Owi, Biak area.
9/1/44	P-61	2100 / 2245	Patrol Owi, Biak area. At 2120 GCI informed the Queen, which was on regular patrol course, that a bogie was approaching head on. The Queen was turned by GCI and at 250 MPH and at 9,000 feet tracked bogie which changed altitude often and headed over Biak strips. GCI vectored Queen back to patrol area and P-61 let down to intercept bogie on return from target. Bogie turned west and out approaching the area. The P-61 climbed from 4,000 to 12,000 feet and was sent to lower altitudes. The bogie was picked up on the airborne scope as GCI lost the enemy plane in the ground echo over Biak. When the radio observer switched to near range, he could not pick up the bogie and had to return to 10 mile range. At this time he could not find the bogie and GCI could not tell Queen's exact position so sent the P-61 on a south vector. The queen was over the on Biak and was fired upon by A/A and at one time was caught in a searchlight at 14,000 feet. Leaving the A/A ring, the Queen was vectored to the NW but did not regain contact with the bogie.
9/1/44	P-61	2230 / 2300	Patrol Owi, Biak area. Aircraft returned early due to radio failure.
9/1/44	(2) P-61	1020 / 1140	Calibration Test order by GCI.
9/1/44	P-61	2255 / 0055	Patrol Owi, Biak area.
9/2/44	P-61	0025 / 0140	Patrol Owi, Biak area. Plane returned early due to weather.
9/2/44	P-61	0940 / 1135	Patrol Owi, Biak area.
9/2/44	P-61	1645 / 1750	Patrol Owi, Biak Area.
9/2/44	P-61	1840 /1905	Patrol Owi, Biak area.
9/2/44	P-61	1900 / 2045	Patrol Owi, Biak area.
9/2/44	P-61	2030 / 2215	Patrol Owi, Biak area.
9/2/44	P-61	2200 / 2300	Patrol Owi, Biak area. Aircraft returned early due to radar failure.
9/2/44	P-61	2230 / 0025	Patrol Owi, Biak area.
9/3/44	P-61	0130 / 0240	Patrol Owi, Biak area.
9/3/44	P-61	0230 / 0330	Patrol Owi, Biak area.
9/3/44	P-61	2400 / 0145	Patrol Owi, Biak area.
9/3/44	(2) P-61	1830 / 1930	Patrol Owi, Biak area. 2015
9/3/44	P-61	2000 / 2200	Patrol Owi, Biak area.
9/3/44	P-61	2130 / 2215	Patrol Owi, Biak area. Plane returned early due to bad weather.
9/4/44	P-61		Patrol Owi, Biak area.
9/4/44	P-61	1100 / 1130	Courier to Noemfoor and return. 1400 / 1430
9/4/44	(2) P-61	1715 / 1815	Weather Recon and patrol, local.
9/4/44	P-61	2000 / 2145	Patrol Owi, Biak area.
9/4/44	P-61	2130 / 2315	Patrol Owi, Biak area.
9/4/44	P-61	2300 / 0045	Patrol Owi, Biak area.
9/5/44	P-61		Patrol Owi, Biak area.
9/5/44	P-61	0025 / 0225	Patrol Owi, Biak area.

9/5/44	P-61	0200 / 0355	Patrol Owi, Biak area.
9/5/44	P-61	0330 / 0530	Patrol Owi, Biak area.
9/5/44	P-61	2345 / 0145	Patrol Owi, Biak area.
9/5/44	P-61	2230 / 0015	Patrol Owi, Biak area.
9/5/44	P-61	2200 / 2230	Patrol Owi, Biak area.
9/5/44	P-61	1800 / 1830	Weather Recon and patrol, Owi, Biak area.
9/5/44	P-61	2030 / 2220	Patrol Owi, Biak area. At 2110 Sector gave Night Fighter unidentified plot due north of Owi. Night Fighter at west end of Japen closed in to 5 miles When plane was identified as a Black Cat.
9/6/44	P-61	0115 / 0300	Patrol Owi, Biak area.
9/6/44	P-61	0245 / 0430	Patrol Owi, Biak area.
9/6/44	P-61	0400 / 0545	Patrol Owi, Biak area.
9/6/44	P-61	2200 / 2345	Patrol Owi, Biak area.
9/6/44	P-61	2330 / 0120	Patrol Owi, Biak area.
9/7/44	P-61	0100 / 0245	Patrol Owi, Biak area. Pilot heard "Cluckie" call 2 bogies 75 miles south of "Cluckie" base (Noemfoor). Plane was at the end of his patrol and ordered to land by GCI.
9/7/44	P-61	0125 / 0155	Scramble to intercept bogie. Night Fighter was sent to 5,000 feet. Plane #1 was airborne, vectored heading of 300°. Bogie was definitely identified as a "Cat", and Night Fighter returned to base.
9/7/44	P-61	0430 / 0545	Patrol Owi-Biak area.
9/7/44	P-61	0250 / 0345	Patrol Owi-Biak area. Lt. Carl Bjorum (pilot), Lt. Robert Williams (R/O), and S/Sgt. Henry Bobo shot down a Japanese "Betty" bomber south of Japen Island.
9/7/44	(2) P-61	1815 / 1845	Weather Recon and local patrol.
9/7/44	P-61	2230 / 2315	Patrol Owi, Biak area. Plane returned early due to weather.
9/7/44	P-61	1640 / 1810	Courier Owi to Hollandia and back.
9/8/44	P-61		Courier Owi to Wakde.
9/8/44	P-61		Courier Wakde to Owi.
9/8/44	P-61		Patrol Owi area.
9/8/44	P-61	0900 /1030	Courier Hollandia to Owi.
9/8/44	P-61	1730 / 1900	Patrol Owi, Biak area.
9/8/44	P-61	2330 / 0115	Patrol Owi, Biak area.
9/9/44	(2) P-61	1710 / 1840	Patrol Owi, Biak area. No strip lights for landings at Owi.
9/9/44	P-61	0400 / 0615	Patrol Owi- Biak area. Lt. Bjorum (pilot), Lt. Robert Williams (R/O), and S/Sgt. Henry Bobo intercepted a Japanese "Dinah" bomber and shot it down on the northern part of Japen Island.
9/9/44	P-61		Courier Owi to Wakde.
9/10/44	P-61	0200 / 0350	Patrol Owi, Biak area.
9/10/44	P-61	0330 / 0500	Patrol Owi, Biak area.
9/10/44	P-61	0430 / 0545	Patrol Owi, Biak area. Plane returned early due to radio failure.
9/10/44	(2) P-61	1715 / 1845	Patrol Owi, Biak area.
9/10/44	P-61		Courier Wakde to Owi.
9/11/44	P-61	0130 / 0315	Patrol Owi, Biak area.
9/11/44	P-61		Patrol Owi, Biak area.
9/11/44	P-61	0300 / 0400	Patrol Owi, Biak area. Patrol incomplete due to weather.
9/11/44	(2)P-61	1705 / 1905	Patrol Owi, Biak area.
9/12/44	P-61	0200 / 0350	Patrol Owi, Biak area.
9/12/44	P-61		Patrol Owi, Biak area.
9/12/44	P-61		Owi area.
9/12/44	P-61	1100 / 1140	Owi area.
9/12/44	P-61	0330 / 0415	Patrol Owi, Biak area. Plane returned early due to generator failure.
9/12/44	P-61	0350 / 0550	Patrol Owi, Biak area.
9/12/44	(2) P-61	1715 / 1830	Patrol Owi, Biak area. One plane returned early due 1900 to radio failure.
9/13/44	P-61	0300 / 0430	Patrol Owi, Biak area. Plane returned early due to weather.
9/13/44	(3) P-61	1715 / 1900	Patrol Owi, Biak area. One plane returned early 1715 / 1730 because of smoke in cockpit; another plane 1800 / 1900 resumed patrol.

9/14/44	(2) P-61	1710 /1855	Patrol Owi, Biak area.
9/15/44	(2) P-61	1715/ 1830	Patrol Owi, Biak area. 1845
9/15/44	P-61	1850/ 1925	Owi area.
9/16/44	P-61	0500 / 0545	Owi area.
9/16/44	P-61	0800 / 0845	Courier Owi to Noemfoor and back. 1315 / 1400
9/16/44	(2) P-61	1715 / 1845	Patrol Owi, Biak area. 1900
9/17/44	(2) P-61	1700 /1835	Patrol Owi, Biak area.
9/18/44	P-61	1300 / 1345	Courier Owi to Noemfoor and back. 1600 / 1645
9/18/44	(2) P-61	1730 / 1745	Patrol Owi, Biak area. Both planes returned due 1720 / 1800 to engine trouble.
9/18/44	P-61	1815 / 1905	Patrol Owi, Biak area.
9/19/44	(2) P-61	1715 / 1830	Dusk patrol of Owi-Biak area. Search mission for for two men lost in a P-47 belly tank, modified to a sail boat. Lt. Byron Allain (R/O) picked up a blip on the radar set. Upon circling Captain William Bradley sighted a small object with a sail. Air-Sea Rescue was called to pick up the men.
9/20/44	P-61	1415 / 1545	Calibration mission with GCI, Japen to Aoeri Islands
9/20/44	(2) P-61	0530 / 0700	Search for sailboat. Lt. Owen Wolf again located two in P-47 tank. They had been spotted the day before, but Air-Sea Rescue was not able to recover them. Both were picked up at 0645.
9/20/44	(2) P-61	1740 / 1900	Patrol Owi, Biak area.
9/21/44	P-61	1300 / 1420	Patrol Owi, Biak area.
9/21/44	P-61	1715 / 1830	Patrol Owi, Biak area.
9/21/44	(2) P-61	1835 /2035	Patrol Owi, Biak area.
9/20/44	P-61	1900 / 2015	Patrol Owi, Biak area.
9/22/44	P-61	1725 / 1825	Patrol Owi, Biak area.
9/22/44	(2) P-61	1715 /1845	Patrol Owi, Biak area. 1915
9/22/44	P-61	1830 / 2030	Patrol Owi, Biak area.
9/22/44	P-61	2000 / 2130	Patrol Owi, Biak area.
9/23/44	(3) P-61	1700 / 1845	Patrol Owi, Biak area. 1715 / 1840
9/24/44	(2) P-61	1715 / 1845	Patrol Owi, Biak area.
9/24/44	P-61	2030 / 2230	Patrol Owi, Biak area.
9/25/44	(2) P-61	1715 / 1845	Patrol Owi, Biak Area.
9/25/44	P-61	1830 /1915	Patrol Owi, Biak area. Plane returned early due to radar failure.
9/25/44	P-61	1900 / 2045	Patrol Wakde, Biak area.
9/25/44	P-61	2030 / 2230	Patrol Owi, Biak area.
9/25/44	P-61	2245 / 2345	Patrol Owi, Biak area. Courier of Bomber Command to Biak.
9/26/44	(2) P-61	1705 / 1850	Patrol Owi, Biak area. 1715 / 1900
9/26/44	P-61	1830 / 2015	Patrol Owi, Biak area.
9/26/44	P-61	2000 / 2150	Patrol Owi, Biak area.
9/26/44	P-61	2130 / 2245	Patrol Owi, Biak area. Patrol incomplete due to radar failure.
9/26/44	P-61	2240 / 0040	Patrol Owi, Biak area.
9/27/44	(2)P-61	1715 / 1845	Patrol Owi, Biak area. 1900
9/27/44	P-61	1815 / 2030	Patrol Owi, Biak area.
9/27/44	P-61	2000 / 2030	Patrol Owi, Biak area. Patrol incomplete due to radar failure.
9/27/44	P-61	2010 / 2210	Patrol Owi, Biak area.
9/27/44	P-61	2145 / 2355	Patrol Owi, Biak area.
9/27/44	P-61	2330 / 0030	Patrol Owi, Biak area. Patrol incomplete due to radar failure.
9/28/44	P-61	0015 / 0215	Patrol Owi, Biak area.
9/28/44	(2) P-61	1715 /1845	Patrol Owi, Biak area.
9/28/44	P-61	2000 / 2035	Patrol Owi, Biak area. Returned early because of mechanical malfunction.
9/28/44	P-61	2015 / 2145	Patrol Owi, Biak area.
9/28/44	P-61	2130 / 2315	Patrol Owi, Biak area.
9/28/44	P-61	2300 / 0100	Patrol Owi, Biak area.
9/28/44	P-61	2300 / 2335	Owi area.
9/29/44	P-61	0030 / 0230	Patrol Owi, Biak area.
9/29/44	P-61	0535 / 0630	Patrol Owi, Biak area.

9/30/44	(2)P-61	1715 / 1745	Patrol Owi, Biak area. One plane returned early 1845 due to radio failure.
9/30/44	P-61	1830 / 2030	Patrol Owi, Biak area.
9/30/44	P-61	2030 / 2100	VFC courier to Biak.
9/30/44	P-61	2000 / 2205	Patrol Owi, Biak area.
9/30/44	P-61	2130 / 2315	Patrol Owi, Biak area.
9/30/44	P-61	2300 / 0055	Patrol Owi, Biak area.
9/30/44	P-61	1300 / 1410	Patrol Owi area.
10/1/44	P-61	0030 / 0230	Patrol Owi, Biak area.
10/1/44	P-61	0200 / 0400	Patrol Owi, Biak area.
10/2/44	P-61	1715 / 1845	Patrol Owi, Biak area.
10/2/44	P-61	1830 / 2015	Patrol Owi, Biak area.
10/2/44	P-61	1950 / 2150	Patrol Owi, Biak area.
10/2/44	P-61	2130 / 2300	Patrol Owi, Biak area. Plane returned early due to radar failure.
10/2/44	P-61	2250 / 0050	Patrol Owi, Biak area.
10/3/44	P-61	0025 / 0040	Patrol Owi, Biak area.
10/3/44	P-61	0045 / 0115	Patrol Owi, Biak area.
10/3/44	P-61	0100 / 0250	Patrol Owi, Biak area.
10/3/44	P-61	0230 / 0350	Patrol Owi, Biak area.
10/27/44	(3) P-61	1215 / 1515	Cross-country to Morotai.
10/28/44	(3) P-61	0845 / 1045	Morotai.
10/31/44	(3) P-61	1030 / 1400	Cross-country from Morotai to Tacloban.
10/31/44	(3) P-61	0525 / 0755	Cross-country to Morotai, on to Tacloban. 1055 / 1425
10/31/44	P-61	2200 / 2345	Patrol Tacloban area.
10/31/44	P-61	2315 / 0200	Patrol Tacloban. With recognition lights on and on final approach during red alert due to low fuel, the aircraft was fired on by friendly anti-aircraft. The fuselage was holed and one rudder was shot up.
11/10/44	(4) P-61	1700 / 1900 (blue flight)	Fighter sweep to Camotes Island (blue) and Recce. 1630 / 1900 (red flight) shipping Ormoc Bay (red).
11/18/44	(2) P-61	0705 / 1020	Cover PT Boats from Panaon Island to Taytay Point. P-61s were flying at 7,000 feet and met up with four P-38s flying at about 14,000 feet. Four Japanese "Zeke" fighters made a diving pass at the P-38s shooting one down. Three of the Zekes continued on down to the P-61s. One P-61 hit a Japanese plane with the .50 caliber turret and it went down. P-61s escaped unharmed and returned to base.

421st Night Fighter Squadron (P-61 Missions 1945)

DATE	AIRCRAFT	T.O./LAND	COMMENTS
1/21/45	(2) P-61	1815 / 1930	Patrol Palompon. One plane returned early due to weather.
1/21/45	P-61	1945 / 2115	Patrol Palompon. Ship returned early because of gas fumes in Radio Observer's compartment.
1/21/45	P-61	2115 / 2300	Patrol Polompon. Plane returned early due to pilot having trouble with his ears.
1/21/45	P-61	2145 / 0045	Patrol Negros area.
1/21/45	P-61	2215 / 0210	Patrol Negros with stop at Tanuan. Plane landed at 0225 / 0300 at Tanuan during red alert because gas supply was nearly exhausted. Friendly A/A fired at night fighter trailing to port side.
1/21/45	P-61	2200/ 2315	Patrol Negros. Mission incomplete. Plane recalled by Base Operations; strip closed for repair.
1/22/45	P-61	2230 / 2300	Patrol Negros. Mission incomplete. Planes recalled by Base Operations; strip closed for repairs.
1/22/45	P-61	0500 / 0733	Patrol Palompon area.
1/22/45	P-61	0515 / 0700	Patrol Garigara Bay. Vectored by GCI to three friendly aircraft.
1/22/45	(2) P-61	0500 / 0545	Patrol Palompon area. Plane #1 returned early due to prop trouble. / 0700
1/22/45	P-61	0500 / 0745	Patrol Carigara area.
1/22/45	P-61	0645 / 0715	Scrambled to relieve pilot patrolling Carigara area forced back because of prop trouble.
1/23/45	P-61	0500 / 0715	Patrol Carigara area.

1/23/45	P-61	1840 / 2010	Patrol Carigara. Plane returned early due to radar failure.
1/24/45	P-61	1845 / 2200	Patrol Palompon area. While on patrol in the Ormoc Bay area in the vicinity of MATAG-OB the night fighter was given vectors on a bogie heading west of Ormoc toward Burauen. The night fighter was flying west at 10,000 feet and did a 150 degree turn when the ground controller told the pilot to fly a heading of 90 degrees. The R/O broke in to report a blip on his scope and took over the interception, only to have the bogie disappear. The pilot was given a starboard turn by the ground controller and again the R/O made contact on his airborne equipment. The night fighter was doing approx. 250 MPH, having climbed to 12,000 feet, and was closing on the bogie with approx. 20 MPH advantage. At about 1,500 feet the gunner sighted the bogie off the port side of the night fighter. The pilot throttled back and made a general port turn, closing to approx. 1,000 feet, where both the pilot and gunner opened fire simultaneously with the 20mm cannons and .50 cal machine guns. Tracers and high explosive ammunition were seen to hit the fuselage, wings, and engine cowling of the bandit, parts of which flew from the plane. The bogie then did a split s into the overcast, bursting into flames and crashing on the east side of the hills near Burauen. The plane was a Zeke 32, camouflaged brown. The Nip pilot had no idea of a night fighter in the area as no evasive action was taken. Pilot of the P-61 Lt. Owen M. Wolf, R/O Lt. Byron N. Allain, and Gunner S/Sgt. Donald H. Trabing. Duration of combat 30 seconds.
1/24/45	P-61	1930 / 2200	Patrol Carigara area. After crossing the south tip of Biliran Island pilot took up a direct heading south when GCI station reported a bogie in the area 7 miles from the night fighter at 2 O'clock. Bogie was approaching from the south. Request for altitude was not an swered, the station reported that they could not read the bogie's altitude. At this time the night fighter was at 10,000 feet and dropped to 5,000 feet, indicating approx. 300 MPH airspeed, when R/O reported blip on his scope. Bogie at that time was 5 miles out, 10 degrees to the starboard. The night fighter was still flying a southern course and the bogie approached on a straight north heading. The blip was lost by the R/O and at that time the GCI reported their ground equipment had gone out and there was no further radar contact with bogie.
1/24/45	(2) P-61	2045 / 2220	One plane patrolled Carigara and one Palompon area. / 2305 The second plane returned due to a radar snafu. This plane was also twice given vectors to the north to a bogie coming south. No contact was made. The first aircraft was contacted by GCI (Blue-eyes) and was told they thought there was bogie in his area. The ground radio was not readable and the pilot asked for a repeat on the transmission and fighter sector (Austere) relayed information pertaining to a bogie flying a course of 230 degrees. The time lag brought about by this shuttling of information caused the night fighter to lose what little chance he might have had for aerial contact. Another vector was given, but not readable and the pilot left Blue Eyes control to work with "Brogade." This station had no Contact with the bogie.
1/24/45	(2) P-61	2345 / 0030	Courier Tacloban to Dulag.
1/24/45	P-61	2345 / 0200	Patrol Palompon area.
1/25/45	P-61	0515 / 0745	Patrol Palompon area.
1/25/45	P-61	0530 / 0700	Patrol Carigara area.
1/25/45	(2) P-61	1825 /1925	One plane patrol Palompon and the other Carigara. 1835 / 2130 The latter patrol returned early due to instrument lights out.
1/25/45	P-61	1930 / 2130	Relief for Carigara patrol.
1/25/45	P-61	2200 / 2400	Patrol Palompon area.
1/25/45	(2) P-61	2330 / 0230	One plane patrol Palompon and the other Carigara.
1/26/45	(3) P-61	2100 / 2130	(plane 1&2) XC Tacloban to Tanauan. 2210 / 2230 (plane 3)
1/26/45	(2) P-61	2050 / 2150	One plane patrol Palompon and the other Carigara. 2100 / 2400 Palompon aircraft re turned early due to radar and armament out.
1/26/45	(2) P-61	0200 / 0245	One plane patrol to Palompon, but returned early due / 0500 to prop trouble. The other plane patrolled Carigara.
1/26/45	P-61	0300 / 0500	Sent to relieve Palompon patrol, who returned with prop trouble.
1/26/45	(2) P-61	0530 / 0730	One plane patrol Palompon and the other Carigara. 0545 / 0730

1/26/45	(3) P-61	0545 / 0700 (plane 1&2) XC Tanauan to Tacloban. 0630 / 0715 (plane 3)	
1/26/45	(2) P-61	1630 / 2030	One plane patrol Palompon and the other Carigara. First plane returned early due to radar out.
1/26/45	P-61	1950 / 2215	Sent to relieve Polompon patrol, who returned with radar trouble.
1/26/45	P-61	2100 / 2345	Patrol Carigara area.
1/26/45	P-61	2200 / 0300	Patrol Polompon area.
1/26/45	P-61	2330 / 0245	Patrol Carigara area.
1/27/45	(2) P-61	0200 / 0145	One plane patrol Palompon and the other Carigara. Second plane returned early due to radio out.
1/27/45	P-61	0315 / 0500	Sent to relieve Carigara patrol, who returned with radio out.
1/27/45	P-61	0600 / 0740	Patrol Carigara area.
1/27/45	P-61	1900 / 2030	Patrol Palompon area, returned early due to radar failure.
1/27/45	P-61	2000 / 2315	Patrol Carigara area.
1/27/45	P-61	2015 / 2325	Patrol Palompon area.
1/27/45	(2) P-61	2250 / 0200	One plane patrol Palompon and the other Carigara. 2315 / 0115 First aircraft returned due to radar out.
1/27/45	P-61	1900 / 2100	Sent to relieve Palompon patrol, who returned with radar out.
1/28/45	P-61	2035 / 0015	Patrol Palompon. Plane returned early due to turret out.
1/28/45	P-61	2145 / 0045	Sent to relieve Palompon patrol, who returned early due to turret out.
1/28/45	P-61	2125 / 2225	Patrol Palompon area.
1/28/45	P-61	2000 / 2235	Patrol Carigara area.
1/28/45	(2) P-61	1820 / 1915	One plane patrol Palompon and the other Carigara. First aircraft returned due to engine problem.
1/28/45	P-61	0300 / 0515	Patrol Palompon area. Pilot returned early due to sickness.
1/28/45	P-61	0100 / 0400	Patrol Carigara area.
1/28/45	P-61	0345 / 0645	Patrol Carigara area.
1/28/45	P-61	0500 / 0700	Patrol Palompon area.
1/29/45	P-61	1830 / 1915	Patrol Carigara area. Returned early due to weather.
1/29/45	P-61	0330 / 0700	Patrol Palompon area.
1/29/45	P-61	0240 / 0335	Patrol Carigara area.
1/29/45	(2) P-61	0015 / 0200	One plane patrol Palompon and the other Carigara. 0001 / 0300 First plane returned early due to radar out.
1/30/45	P-61	1900 / 1930	Weather check and patrol.
1/30/45	P-61	2030 / 2130	Patrol Carigara area.
1/30/45	P-61	2130 / 0015	Patrol Carigara area.
1/30/45	P-61	2350 / 0130	Patrol Ormoc area.
1/31/45	P-61	0230 / 0335	Scrambled by fighter sector for bogie north of Leyte Island.
2/1/45	P-61	0045 / 0230	Patrol Carigara area.
2/1/45	(2)P-61	0530 / 0700	One plane patrol Palompon and the other Carigara.
3/26/45	P-61	2330 / 0235	Patrol Tarlac area.
3/26/45	P-61	2140 / 2340	Patrol Tarlac area. Plane returned early due to radar out.
3/26/45	P-61	1930 / 2200	Patrol Tarlac area.
3/27/45	P-61	0400 / 0645	Patrol Tarlac area.
3/27/45	P-61	0145 / 0425	Patrol Tarlac area.
3/27/45	P-61	2330 / 2400	Patrol Tarlac area. Returned early due to radar out.
3/27/45	P-61	2115 / 2400	Patrol Tarlac area.
3/27/45	P-61	1900 / 2150	Patrol Tarlac area.
3/28/45	P-61	0400 / 0645	Patrol Tarlac area.
3/28/45	P-61	2045 / 2100	Patrol Tarlac area. Returned early due to engine trouble.
3/30/45	P-61	0345 / 0645	Patrol Tarlac area.
3/31/45	P-61	0010 / 0110	Scrambled to investigate bogie. Bogie identified as Navy B-24.
4/8/45	P-61	0430 / 0700	Patrol Tarlac area.
4/10/45	(2) P-61	1830 / 1915	Patrol Tarlac area. Both planes returned due to bad 1945 / 2015 weather.
4/11/45	(2)P-61	0430 / 0700	Patrol Tarlac area.
4/30/45	P-61	1900 / 2200	Patrol San Marcelino area.

4/30/45	P-61	1905 / 2250	Patrol Tarlac area.
4/30/45	P-61	2215 / 0115	Patrol Tarlac area.
6/14/45	P-61	0145 / 0415	Snooper mission to Cagayah Valley. At an altitude of 5,000 feet, while investigating some flashing white lights in the water about 20 miles off coast of Luzon, which pilot believed to be coming from a group of boats, pilot sighted an aircraft flying with his lights on. Bogey cut lights off and on intermittently as if to signal night fighter. Night fighter chased bogie down to deck but overshot him, night fighter pilot to believe that the boogie pulled flaps. Bogie's lights went out at this time and this was the last the night fighter saw of him.
8/20/45	(8) P-61	0230 / 0400 (#1)	Patrol Okinawa area. One ship per GCI stations. One ship / 0600 (#2,3,4,5) returned early due to communications trouble. Three ships unable to get airborne due to mechanical failure.
8/21/45	(4) P-61	1840 / 2010 (spares)	Escort Japanese envoy plane. Ie Shima to Kyushu. 2210 Completed escort to Jap envoy plane and B-25's as ordered. Left Jap at 2040 approx. 15 miles off southern tip of Kyushu. Radio contact maintained with B-25's. Two spare planes began flight with escort and turned back 100 miles north of base. At order of flight leader.
8/22/45	(5) P-61	2130 / 2300	Patrol Okinawa area. One ship returned early due to 2130 / 0020 engine trouble. 2145 / 0115 2150 / 0050 2150 / 0105
8/23/45	(4) P-61	0230 / 0545 (#1,2)	Patrol Okinawa area. Three aircraft for mission and one 0230 / 0600 (#3) plane was scrambles after the first take-off. 0430 / 0610 (#4)
8/26/45	(4) P-61	1850 / 0010	Surveillance sweep Kyushu. 2100 / 0120 2345 / 0350 0100 / 0550
8/27/45	(5) P-61	1900 / 1935	Surveillance sweep of Kyushu, Shikoku, and Honshu. 2025 / 2125 (spare) Plane #1 returned early because of communication 2200 / 0415 trouble and spare returned early because he was unable 2300 / 0645 to switch to external tanks.
8/28/45	(4) P-61	1850 / 2005	Surveillance sweep of Kyushu, Shikoku, and Honshu. Mission incomplete. Plane #1 returned early due to weather and operations were cancelled for remainder of period.
8/29/45	(4) P-61	2000 / 0430	Surveillance sweep of Kyushu, Shikoku, and Honshu. 2200 / 0550 Plane #3 returned early due to weather. 2400 / 0410 0100 / 0800
8/30/45	(4) P-61	1845 / 1930	Surveillance sweep of Kyushu, Shikoku, and Honshu. 1915 / 0315 (spare) Plane #1 returned early with a bent weapon. Spare 2300 / 0640 took it's place. 0100 / 0700

421st Night Fighter Squadron (P-70 Missions)

DATE	AIRCRAFT	T.O/Landing	Comments
3/25/44	P-70A	1030 / 1110	Courier to Saidor and return 1630 / 1745
3/26/44	P-70A	0830 / 0910	Courier to Saidor and return. 1135 / 1215
3/27/44	P-70A	1025 / 1110	Courier to Finschafen, Saidor, and return. 1450 / 1530 1645 / 1755
3/28/44	P-70A	1530 / 1730	Orientation flight to Dumpu area.
3/29/44	P-70A	1530 / 1615	Courier to Lae and return. 1650 / 1800
3/30/44	P-70A	1025 / 1125	Courier to Finschafen, Saidor, and return. 1520 / 1605 1735 / 1840
4/1/44	P-70A	1245 / 1415	Courier to Saidor and return. 1545 / 1745
4/2/44	P-70A	1005 / 1045	Courier to Saidor and return. 1320 / 1425
4/2/44	P-70A	1330 / 1430	Courier to Finschafen and return. 1520 / 1630
4/3/44	P-70A	1620 / 1730	Courier to Saidor. Plane failed to reach Saidor because of a vapor lock in right engine over the mountains. Returned to base.
4/5/44	P-70A	1430 / 1545	Courier Saidor to Nadzab and back. 1710 / 1810
4/5/44	(2) P-70A	1115 / 1200	Courier Nadzab to Saidor.
4/5/44	P-70A	1600 / 1730	Courier Nadzab to Saidor.
4/5/44	P-70A	1200 / 1330	Courier Nadzab to Saidor.
4/5/44	P-70A	1400 / 1530	Courier Saidor to Nadzab.
4/5/44	P-70A	1615 / 1745	Courier Saidor to Nadzab.
4/7/44	(2) P-70A	1630 / 1730	Patrol Saidor, Long Island, and Bagabag Island. 1730 / 1830
4/7/44	P-70A	2130 / 2350	Patrol Saidor, Long Island, and Bagabag Island.
4/7/44	P-70A	2130 / 2350	Patrol Saidor and Long Island.
4/8/44	P-70A	0830 / 1000	Courier Saidor to Nadzab and on to Port Moresby. 1400 / 1535

4/8/44	P-70A	2230 / 0030	Patrol Long Island.
4/8/44	P-70A	0015 / 0220	Patrol Saidor, Long Island, and Bagabag Island.
4/8/44	P-70A	0730 /0820	Courier Saidor to Nadzab.
4/9/44	P-70A	0820 / 0945	Courier Port Moresby to Nadzab on to Saidor. 1345 / 1500
4/9/44	P-70A	1625 / 1725	Courier Saidor to Nadzab and return. 1800 / 1930
4/10/44	P-70A	0530 / 0600	Patrol Saidor, Long Island, Bagabag Island. Mission incomplete due to mechanical failure. Aircraft returned to base.
4/10/44	P-70A	0730 / 0800	Courier Saidor to Nadzab.
4/10/44	P-70A	1330 / 1515	Courier Nadzab to Saidor.
4/10/44	(2) P-70A	1600 / 1730	Recon. flight from Bunabun Harbor to Alexishafen.
4/10/44	(2) P-70A	1645 / 1745	Test in the Saidor area.
4/10/44	P-70A	2020 / 2040	Bomb and strafing mission from Palas Point to Walog; not completed because of heavy wing vibration in aircraft.
4/10/44	P-70A	2115 / 2245	Bomb and strafing mission Karkar Island, possible bivouac area. Used 400 .50 cal. rounds and twenty-four 20lb. fragmentation bombs on target.
4/11/44	P-70A	0100 / 0310	Patrol Saidor, Long Island, Bagabag Island. The plane was given a vector toward bogie in vicinity of Karkar Island. One amber light, thought to be a plane running light was sighted at 8,000 feet and a visual obtained. The P-70 climbed to 15,000 in pursuit, but the bogie pulled out of range at high altitude.
4/11/44	P-70A	0400 / 0600	Patrol Saidor, Long Island, and Karkar Island.
4/11/44	P-70A	1335 / 1350	Test flight near Saidor area.
4/11/44	P-70A	1630 / 1640	Recon. flight Alexischafen to Sarang Harbor.
4/11/44	P-70A	1610 / 1645	Weather Recon. to Astrolabe Bay.
4/11/44	P-70A	1640 / 1740	Test flight near Saidor area.
4/12/44	P-70A	0840 / 0925	Courier Saidor to Nadzab and return. 1430 / 1600
4/12/44	(3) P-70A	1615 / 1730	Recon. to Bagabag Island, Karkar Island, Bunabun Harbor, Cape Croisselles, Alexischafen, and Madang. One rowboat destroyed by Lt. Lockhart.
4/13/44	(2) P-70A	1545 / 1715	Recon. to Bagabag Island, Karkar Island, Bunabun Harbor, Cape Croiselles, Alexischafen, and Madang.
4/14/44	P-70A	0645 / 0730	Courier Saidor to Nadzab and return. 1515 / 1645
4/14/44	P-70A	0830 / 0915	Courier Saidor to Nadzab and return. 1300 / 1430
4/14/44	P-70A	1540 / 1610	G.C.I. calibration flight. Plane returned early when one engine failed.
4/14/44	P-70A	1710 / 1825	Weather Recon. to Karkar Island.
4/15/44	(2) P-70A		Armed Recon. to Bunabun Harbor. Planes bombed bridge with two 300 lb. bombs, one missed the other did not go off. Coming down the coast of Mandang, two barges and one building were strafed. Light machine gun A/A noted.
4/16/44	(2) P-70A	0600 / 0730	Armed Recon. to Bunabun Harbor, Mandang. One puff of black smoke, 100 yards behind aircraft and small arms fire. Eight 250lb. bombs dropped from 50 feet over bridge, across Umai River. Huts at Yadikum Village, huts at Cape Mossemberg, and buildings at Sair Island strafed with 650 rounds of .50 cal ammunition.
4/19/44	P-70A	1410 / 1540	Test flight from Saidor to Karkar Island.
4/19/44	P-70A	0550 / 0710	Armed Recon. Karkar Island, Bunabun Harbor, Madang. One plane dropped four 250lb. bombs at bridge at Harinap from 50 feet over bridge. Bombs went into river. One plane dropped four 250lb. bombs on village huts at Badilu Village on Bagabag Island. Plane also strafed using 1,550 rounds of .50 cal. ammunition.
4/19/44	P-70A	1415 / 1500	Test flight from Saidor to Karkar Island.
4/20/44	P-70A	0530 / 0800	Armed Recon. to Palas Point. Strafed some machine gun positions along the coast. Also dropped six 250-lb. bombs.
4/20/44	P-70A	1730 / 2010	Armed Recon. to Sarang Harbor. Dropped six 250 lb. bombs and strafed a couple villages one the way back to base. Aircrew noted a number of fires breaking out.
4/22/44	(2) P-70A	0530 / 0815	Armed Recon. to Hansa Bay. Attacked two barges that were heading for the beach. One plane dropped four 250 lb. bombs on the beach ahead of them. Both aircraft made three strafing passes also.
4/24/44	P-70A	1330 / 1500	Courier to Saidor and return. Upon approach to Saidor, 1630 / 1745 pilot was contacted by fighter sector and requested to lead in four P-47's which were unable to reach

			Saidor from Cape Croiselles area because of weather. The mission was accomplished and all planes landed safely at Saidor
5/2/44	P-70A	0515 / 0810	Weather Recon. to Wewak. Strafed and hit two shacks at Manham Island. Dropped two 250lb. bombs on barge scoring a near miss.
5/2/44	P-70A	0515 / 0815	Weather Recon. and harassing mission from Saidor to 20 miles north of Sepik River. Dropped three 250lb. bombs near a hut at Uligan Harbor. One bomb failed to go off over Harbor. One bomb failed to go off. Over Manham Island aircraft strafed 2 metal covered huts approximately 30 feet long and 20 feet wide.
5/3/44	P-70A	0530 / 0840	Armed Recon. to Wewak. Two 250lb. bombs were dropped from minimum altitude on small bridge between Kumil River and Umbarum River, both scored near misses. Two 250lb. bombs were dropped on small bridge south of Taviltae village at minimum altitude, both scored near misses.
5/4/44	(3) P-70A	0915 / 1145	Twelve 250lb. bombs were dropped from an altitude of 50 feet; four made a direct hit on a kunai hut near an old mission on Manam Island; four were near misses, four overshot the target by 100 feet. Targets strafed using 5,765-.50 cal. rounds.
5/5/44	P-70A	1015 / 1315	Armed Recon. to Cape Girgir. Four 250lb. bombs were dropped on a building on the SW end of Aris Island from an altitude of 300 feet. The building was entirely destroyed. Several huts were strafed with 950 rounds of .50 cal. ammunition and entirely destroyed.
5/5/44	P-70A	1015 / 1330	Armed Recon. to Manam Island. The aircraft dropped two 250lb. bombs from a 300-foot altitude on a 30 x 60 foot hut, which looked like a barracks on Kairiru Island. The Hut was destroyed. The bombs dropped from a 300-foot altitude. Dropped two 250lb. bombs on a 20 x 40 wooden hut on Kairiru Island also from a 300 foot altitude. Area was strafed with 1,750 rounds of .50 cal. ammunition.
5/6/44	P-70A	0500 / 0620	Three 300lb. bombs dropped on two bridges about 30 yards apart, north of Nubia Strip. One 300lb. bomb dropped on what looked like a camouflaged gun position east of Nubia Strip about 400 yards inland. Targets strafed with 750 rounds of .50 cal. ammunition.
5/6/44	P-70A	1300 / 1605	Armed Recon. to Hansa Bay area. Two 300lb. bombs skipped over dual-purpose gun position east of Nubia Strip 10 yards inland. One 300lb. bomb dropped on west side of Liang Island, no results. Twenty 20lb. bombs Dropped one half mile north of Awar Point on coastal gun. Targets also strafed with 1,550 rounds of .50 cal. ammunition.
5/9/44	P-70A	2300 / 0130	Armed Recon. in conjunction with PT Boats to Uligan Harbor. One cluster of incendiaries were dropped, starting 2 fires on north side of Uligan Harbor at Uligan Village, supposedly a stores dump. Three 300lb. bombs were also dropped. Target was strafed with 1,100 rounds of .50 cal. ammunition.
5/10/44	P-70A	0440 / 0740	Armed Recon. to Hansa Bay and Sepik River. Four 250lb. bombs were dropped over A/A position from minimum altitude. Huts were strafed with 1,600 rounds of .50 ammunition on Manam Island with. Native boat off Laing Island strafed.
5/11/44	P-70A	1600 / 1715	Weather Recon to Cape Croiselles.
5/11/44	P-70A	1700 / 2000	Armed Recon. to Hansa Bay and Sepik River. Strafed approximately a dozen huts at Marienberg and a truck a mile north of Condor Point with 900 rounds of .50 cal. ammunition. Four 250lb. bombs were dropped on Awar Point.
5/11/44	P-70A	2200 / 0100	Armed Recon. to Manam Island. No bombs were dropped or ammunition expended due to low cloud cover in the target area.
5/12/44	P-70A	0515 / 0745	Armed Recon. to Manam Island. Dropped four 300lb. bombs and one cluster of incendiaries on shack NW side of Manam Island. Target was also strafed with 500-.50 cal. ammunition.
5/12/44	P-70A	0600 / 0830	Armed Recon. to Hansa Bay. Dropped three 300lb. bombs shacks east of south end of Awar Strip. A gun position, appearing to be dummy and a truck _ mile north of Awar Point were strafed with 1,300 rounds of .50 cal. ammunition.
5/12/44	P-70A	0920 / 1000	Weather Recon to Karkar Island.
5/12/44	(3) P-70A	1630 / 1915	Armed Recon to Awar Point to Cape Girgir. Four 250lb. bombs dropped on stores dump midway between Awar Point and Boroi River. Two were direct hits and two near misses. Four 250lb. bombs dropped on shacks at Boroi. Two shacks were destroyed and a fire started in another. Three 250lb. bombs were dropped on an A/A position. Two fell short and one skipped over. Targets were strafed with 4,400 rounds of .50 cal. ammunition.

5/12/44	P-70A	2100 / 2400	Harassing raid on Hansa Bay. Four 250lb. bombs dropped on four runs on Awar Point at minimum altitude. Target was also strafed with 2,400 rounds of .50 cal. ammunition.
5/13/44	P-70A	0430 / 0800	Armed Recon. to Wewak. Four to six trucks seen going north, 5 miles north of Cape Wom. The 250lb. and one cluster of incendiaries were dropped on the trucks, as well as being strafed with 2,200 rounds of .50 cal. ammunition, with unobserved results.
5/13/44	(2) P-70	0445 / 0715	Armed Recon to Awar Point. Dropped two 250lb. bombs on gun position 10 yards SW of Awar point, both being misses. Dropped two incendiaries on shacks on Awar point, starting fires. Dropped two 250lb. bombs 20 yards from shore on NE of Condor strip shacks. One 250lb. bomb dropped on road north of jetty, with unobserved results. Strafed two trucks with 2,900 rounds of .50 cal. ammunition north of Sukula Bridge, with unobserved results.
5/17/44	P-70A	1400 / 1700	Cross-country Nadzab to Hollandia.
5/18/44	P-70A	1515 / 1630	Cross-country Nadzab to Hollandia.
5/18/44	P-70A	0850 / 1200	Cross-country Hollandia to Nadzab. Strafed huts at Marienburg on route with 300 rounds of .50 cal.
5/28/44	(4) P-70A	0945 / 1315	Courier Nadzab to Wakde.
5/28/44	P-70A	1900 / 2145	Patrol Wakde to Sarmi Point.
5/28/44	P-70A	2135 / 2305	Patrol Wakde to Sarmi Point.
5/29/44	P-70A	0500 / 0710	Patrol Wakde to Sarmi Point.
5/29/44	P-70A	2015 / 2300	Patrol Wakde to Sarmi Point.
5/29/44	P-70A	2300 / 0115	Patrol Wakde to Sarmi Point. One burst of friendly fire A/A from point unknown.
5/30/44	P-70A	0400 / 0630	Patrol Wakde to Sarmi Point.
5/30/44	P-70A	2015 / 2245	Patrol Wakde to Sarmi Point. Plane scrambled on yellow alert from sector. Vector given 25 miles NW of Wakde at 2210, apparently single engine. No visual or radar contact.
5/30/44	P-70A	2300 / 0100	Armed Recon. to Sarmi Point.
5/31/44	(3) P-70A	1415 / 1530	Test Flight out of Wakde.
31/5/44	P-70A	0800 / 0830	Patrol Wakde to Sarmi Point. Mission not completed because of bad weather.
6/1/44	P-70A	0900 / 1300	Cross-country Wakde to Nadzab.
6/1/44	(3) P-70A	1415 / 1530	Test flight out of Wakde.
6/1/44	P-70A	2000 / 2200	Patrol Wakde to Sarmi Point.
6/2/44	P-70A	1900 /1945	Weather Recon.
6/2/44	P-70A	2030 / 2245	Patrol Wakde to Sarmi Point.
6/2/44	P-70A	2300 / 0130	Patrol Wakde to Sarmi Point.
6/3/44	(2) P-70A	0515 / 0700	Four 250lb. bombs dropped in stores and dispersal area just west of Woske River 1 mile inland. Two 250lb. bombs were dropped on village east and one on Village west of Sawar Drome. The targets were strafed with 2,250 rounds of .50 cal. ammunition. GCI sent patrol to investigate possible crashed aircraft 10 miles east of Wakde Island. Observed oil slick on water 3 miles directly east of strip. No life rafts or wreckage seen in patrol 20 miles east Wakde Island.
6/3/44	P-70A	0830 / 1220	Courier Nadzab to Wakde.
6/3/44	P-70A	1400 / 1500	Test flight at Sawar Point .
6/3/44	P-70A	1400 / 1500	Test flight at Sawar Point.
6/3/44	P-70A	1900 / 2030	Armed Recon. to Sawar Drome. One 250lb. demo. Bomb dropped on tip of Sarmi Point in area with half a Dozen small fires. Two 250lb. bombs dropped Sawar stores and personnel area. One bomb 250lb. bomb dropped on bridge. Targets also strafed with 1,250 rounds of .50 cal. ammunition.
6/3/44	P-70	1900 / 2100	Armed Recon. patrol to Sawar Point. Four 250lb. demo. bombs dropped on plantation on Sarmi Point. One bomb started fire. Target was strafed with 1,500 rounds of .50 cal. ammunition.
6/3/44	P-70A	2145 / 0015	Patrol Wakde to Sarmi Point.
6/4/44	P-70A	2400 / 0300	Armed patrol Wakde to Sarmi Point. Strafed Sarmi point with 1,400 rounds of .50 cal. ammunition. Also strafed road running along Sarmi Point and Woske River. Strafed target on shore in conjunction with PT Boats.

6/4/44	(2) P-70A	0600 / 0700	Armed Recon. to Sawar Point. Area was bombed with 0625 / 0800 Frag bombs (120lbs. per cluster). Also used one cluster incendiaries on target. Area was strafed with 2,200 rounds of .50 cal. ammunition.
6/4/44	P-70A	1045 / 1415	Cross-country Wakde to Nadzab.
6/4/44	P-70A	1900 / 2030	Armed Recon. to Woske River and Sawar Drome. Dropped four clusters of frags _ mile east of Sawar Point. A fire was seen burning in this area 2 hours later, believed to be a gasoline truck. Area was also strafed with 2,250 rounds of .50 cal. ammunition.
6/5/44	P-70A	1900 / 2010	Armed Recon. Sawar Drome. Four clusters of Frag bombs dropped on huts near north end Sawar strip; area was strafed with 1,250 rounds of .50 cal. ammunition.
6/5/44	P-70A	1900 / 2230	Armed Recon. patrol Sawar Drome. Eight cluster of frag bombs dropped on Huts near north end Sawar strip; area strafed with 2,500 rounds of .50 cal. ammunition.
6/8/44	P-70A	1330 / 1500	Radar calibration mission in Wakde area.
6/8/44	P-70A	1330 / 1715	Courier from Nadzab to Wakde.
6/9/44	P-70A	1015 / 1115	Courier to Wakde to Hollandia on to Nadzab. 1500 / 1800
6/10/44	P-70A	1015 / 1315	Courier to Nadzab to Hollandia on to Wakde 1330 / 1430
6/11/44	P-70A	0130 / 0235	Patrol Wakde area.
6/11/44	P-70A	1230 / 1409	Courier Wakde to Tadji on to Nadzab. 1445 / 1645
6/18/44	P-70A	1115 / 1200	Courier Hollandia, Wakde, to Nadzab. 1335 / 1605
6/19/44	P-70A	1150 / 1510	Courier from Nadzab to Wakde
6/20/44	P-70A	0900 /1230	Courier from Wakde to Nadzab.
6/21/44	P-70A	0900 / 1215	Courier from Nadzab to Wakde.
6/22/44	P-70A	1000 / 1120	Courier Wakde, Hollandia to Nadzab. 1345 / 1600
6/24/44	P-70A	0930 / 1245	Courier Wakde to Nadzab.
6/25/44	P-70A	0945 / 1300	Courier Wakde to Nadzab.

Appendix C:
Aircraft Log 1943-1947

P-61 "Black Widow"	**(54 Total A's & B's used by Unit)**		
42-5494 (P-61A-1-NO)	Gained 5/3/44	Lost 7/5/44	Accident
42-5498 (P-61A-1-NO)	Gained 4/7/44	Lost 7/24/45	Accident
42-5499 (P-61A-1-NO)	Gained 5/7/44	Lost 1/20/45	Accident
42-5500 (P-61A-1-NO)	Gained 5/7/44	Lost 1/16/45	Accident
42-5501 (P-61A-1-NO)	Gained 5/10/44	Lost 5/2/45	Accident
42-5502 (P-61A-1-NO)	Gained 4/7/44	Lost 11/15/44	Bombed "Skippy / Nocturnal Nuisance"
42-5503 (P-61A-1-NO)	Gained 4/7/44	Lost 8/12/44	Accident
42-5504 (P-61A-1-NO)	Gained 4/7/44	Lost 2/2/45	Accident "Bright Eyes"
42-5509 (P-61A-1-NO)	Gained 4/20/44	Lost 6/12/45	Salvaged after war.
42-5510 (P-61A-1-NO)	Gained 4/26/44	Lost 7/26/44	Accident
42-5511 (P-61A-1-NO)	Gained 4/26/44	Lost 11/1/44	Flak
42-5512 (P-61A-1-NO)	Gained 5/6/44	Lost 12/6/44	Accident
42-5516 (P-61A-1-NO)	unknown		"Dame de la Nuit"
42-5518 (P-61A-1-NO)	Gained 4/16/44	Lost 8/25/44	Accident
42-5519 (P-61A-1-NO)	Gained 5/6/44	Lost 5/3/45	Accident
42-5520 (P-61A-1-NO)	Gained 5/10/44	Lost 2/21/45	Accident "Janie"
42-5521 (P-61A-1-NO)	Gained 5/6/44	Lost 1/14/45	Salvaged after war.
42-5555 (P-61A-5-NO)	Gained 12/18/44	Lost 6/12/45	Salvaged after war.
42-5562 (P-61A-5-NO)	Gained 5/22/44	Lost 2/3/45	Accident
42-5602 (P-61A-10-NO)	Unknown		
42-5622 (P-61A-10-NO)	Unknown		
42-39370 (P-61A-10-NO)	Unknown		
42-39380 (P-61A-11-NO)	Gained 12/18/44	Lost 3/20/45	Accident
42-39381 (P-61A-11-NO)	Unknown		
42-39382 (P-61A-11-NO)	Unknown		
42-39410 (P-61B-1-NO)	Unknown		
42-39439 (P-61B-1-NO)	Unknown		
42-39443 (P-61B-1-NO)	Gained 12/18/44	Lost unknown.	
42-39448 (P-61B-1-NO)	Gained 3/13/45	Lost unknown.	Salvaged after war.
42-39450 (P-61B-1-NO)	Unknown		
42-39452 (P-61B-2-NO)	Gained 3/13/45	Lost unknown.	Salvaged after war.
42-39465 (P-61B-1-NO)	Gained 3/13/45	Lost 7/10/45.	Accident
42-39466 (P-61B-2-NO)	Gained 3/13/45	Lost unknown.	Salvaged after war
42-39546 (P-61B-6-NO)	Unknown		
42-39560 (P-61B-10-NO)	Unknown		
42-39567 (P-61B-10-NO)	Unknown		
42-39574 (P-61B-15-NO)	Unknown	"Dirty Delmar"	

42-39575 (P-61B-15-NO)	Unknown
42-39581 (P-61B-15-NO)	Unknown
42-39585 (P-61B-15-NO)	Unknown
42-39592 (P-61B-15-NO)	Unknown
42-39638 (P-61B-15-NO)	Unknown
42-39660 (P-61B-15-NO)	Unknown
42-39682 (P-61B-15-NO)	Unknown
42-39688 (P-61B-15-NO)	Unknown
42-39730 (P-61B15-NO)	Unknown
42-39752 (P-61B-15-NO)	Unknown
43-8239 (P-61B-20-NO)	Unknown
43-8250 (P-61B-20-NO)	Unknown
43-8261 (P-61B-20-NO)	Unknown

Note-One of the original P-61As that came to Brisbane was taken by John Myers. Serial Number is unknown.
-five of the serial numbers are unknown.

Appendix D: Nose Art & Names

"Nocturnal Nuisance" Lt. Tom Malone pilot.
"Sleepy Time Gal" Lt. Fred Kohl pilot.
"Midnight Mama"
"Old Forrester" Lt. Roland Forrester pilot.
"Chris Couldn't Wait" Captain Paul Zimmer pilot.
"Which Way'd They go George" Lt. Robert Savaria pilot.

P-70
(13 total P-70s used by unit, 7 in Florida & 6 at Nadzab & Wakde)
(Aircraft listed were used at Kissimmee AAF, Florida)
39-791
39-792
39-793
39-794
39-795
39-796
39-797

P-40
44-7788 Lost 5/5/45.

P-38J
(5 total P-38s used by unit at Nadzab)
Serial numbers are unknown.

P-38M
(3 flown at Ashiva and Itazuke, Japan)
42-7234
42-27245
42-6865

B-25
Unknown serial number "Two Bits"

Appendix E: Chronology of 421st Aircraft

1943

Seven P-70s furnished to the squadron for training by the 481st NFOTG.

1944

January:

(31st) Two P-38F aircraft assigned to the squadron.

February:

(13th) One P-70 aircraft transferred from the 418th NFS.
(16th) Two P-38Fs and one P-70A aircraft assigned to squadron.
(19th) One P-38F aircraft assigned to squadron.
(28th) First combat mission flown by 421st. (Lt.'s Jones, Zimmer, Robbins.)
(28th) One P-38F lost when 1st. Lt. Zimmer bailed out due to mechanical failure.
(28th) Two P-70 and four P-38F aircraft in squadron.

March:

(10th) Three P-70 aircraft received from 418th NFS.
(11th) One P-70 aircraft received from Brisbane, Australia.
(24th) One P-38 lost. Lt. Malone bailed out of Richard Bong's P-38 "Marge." #42-103993.
(31st) Five P-70 and 3 P-38F aircraft in squadron.

April:

(8th) One P-38F aircraft lost. Lt. Alexander A. Kuzmick killed in landing accident.
(19th) Three remaining P-38F aircraft were transferred out of the squadron.
(19th) Five P-61A aircraft arrived at Brisbane to assembled.
(23rd) Two P-61A aircraft arrived at Brisbane to be assembled.
(30th) Five P-70A aircraft in squadron.

May:

(31st) Five P-70A aircraft in squadron.

June:

(1st) Three P-61A aircraft recieved from Brisbane.
(5th) Two P-70A aircraft damaged in bombing.
(8th) Two P-61A aircraft recieved from Brisbane.
(8th) First combat mission flown by 421st P-61A.
(9th) Two P-61A aircraft recieved Brisbane.
(19th) Five P-61A aircraft recieved from Brisbane.
(23rd) Two P-61A aircraft recieved from Brisbane.
(24th) Three P-70A aircraft dropped from squadron.
(30th) Fourteen P-61 aircraft in squadron.

July:

(1st) One P-61 recieved from Brisbane.
(5th) One P-61 lost. P-61A #5494 crash landed by Lt. Malone after gear failure. Salvaged 7/27/44.
(7th) First 421st P-61 victory. Wolf, Allain, and Weishar. (Dinah)
(26th) One P-61 lost. P-61A #42-5510 crashed at 10th Serv. Sqdn. B-24 T.O. accident.
(31st) Thirteen P-61 aircraft in squadron.

August:

(12th) One P-61A lost. Lt. Pritchard flying P-61A #42-5503 lost one engine and crashed in ocean.
(25th) One P-61A lost. Lt. Tingen flying P-61A #42-5518 crashes into a B-25 in landing pattern.
(31st) Eleven P-61 aircraft in squadron.

September:

(30st) Eleven P-61 aircraft in squadron.

October:

(31st) Eleven P-61 aircraft in squadron.

November:

(1st) One P-61 was hit by friendly AA. P-61A #42-5511 salvaged.
(8th) One P-61 recieved by unit.

(15th) One P-61 lost. P-61A #42-5502 was hit during a bombing raid. Salvaged 11/15/44.
(30th) Ten P-61 aircraft in squadron.

December:
(6th) One P-61 lost when Japanese transport was shot down at Tacloban, Leyte. P-61A #42-5512.
(10th) One P-61 recieved by unit.
(18th) Three P-61's recieved by unit. P-61A #42-5555, P-61A #42-39380, and P-61B #42-39443.
(31st) Thirteen P-61 aircraft in squadron.

1945
January:
(16th) One P-61 lost. P-61A #42-5500 was lost when a B-24 blew a tire and hit it on landing.
(20th) One P-61 lost. Lt. Robert Reynolds flying P-61A #42-5499 lost an engine and ditched in ocean.
(31st) Eleven P-61 aircraft in squadron.

February:
(2nd) One P-61 lost when Lt. Dorrie Jones landed and the plane caught fire. P-61A #42-5504.
(3rd) One P-61 lost. Lt. Vincent King flying P-61A #42-5562. P-61 ran out of fuel and crashed.
(21st) One P-61 lost. Captain Bowers crashed on landing. P-61A #42-5520 salvaged.
(28th) Eight P-61 aircraft in squadron.

March:
(10th) One P-61 had to be salvaged. P-61A #42-39380. Major Kiick involved in accident at Mindaro.
(13th) Four P-61's recieved by squadron: P-61Bs #42-39448, #42-39452, #42-39465, & #42-39466.
(31st) Eleven P-61 aircraft in squadron.

April:
(8th) One P-61 lost when Lt. John Chew crashed on take-off.
(10th) One P-40N #44-7788 recieved by squadron.
(22nd) One P-61 lost. Sgt. Loyal Males while cleaning P-61 caught fire and destroyed.
(30th) Nine P-61 aircraft in squadron and one P-40N.

May:
(1st) One B-25J recieved.
(2nd) One P-61 lost because of mechanical failure. P-61A #42-5501.
(3rd) One P-61 lost. On landing P-61's gear folded up and aircraft crash landed. P-61A #42-5519.
(5th) One P-40 lost. Lt. Hoke Smith crash landed. Salvaged.
(10th) One B-25J recieved by squadron.
(31st) Seven P-61 aircraft in squadron and one B-25.

June:
(12th) Two P-61's transferred to Service Squadron as "War Weary" P-61A #42-5555 & P-61A #42-5509.
(30th) Five P-61 aircraft in squadron and one B-25.

July:
(2nd) One P-61 lost. Lt. John Leckie flying P-61A #42-5498 crashed into Mt. Arat.
(10th) One P-61 lost. At 10th Service Squadron B-25 crashed and debris hit P-61B #42-39465. Salvaged.
(13th) One P-61 lost. Transferred to 10th Service Squadron as "War Weary."
(15th) Eleven P-61s assigned to squadron.
(31st) Thirteen P-61 aircraft in squadron and one B-25.

August:
(9th) One P-61 lost. Lt. Neil Reinerd's nose gear failed and he had to crash land.
(14th) One P-61 lost. Transferred to 10th Service Squadron as "War Weary" P-61A #42-5521.
(31st) Eleven P-61 aircraft in squadron and one B-25.

September:
(8th) One P-61 lost. Lt. Neil Reinerd's aircraft crashed on T.O. and destroyed.
(15th) Six P-61 lost. Aircraft were destroyed during a typhoon.
(15th) Two P-61s damaged in typhoon sent to Service Squadron for repair.
(30th) Four P-61 aircraft in squadron and one B-25.

October:
(5th) Six P-61s recieved by squadron.
(10th) Five P-61s transferred to Service Squadron "War Weary."
(31st) Two P-61 aircraft in squadron and one B-25.

November:
(30th) Two P-61 aircraft in squadron and one B-25.

December:
(12th) Eight P-61 aircraft were assigned to squadron.
(31st) Ten P-61 aircraft in squadron and one B-25.

1946
January:
(31st) Ten P-61 aircraft in squadron.

February:
(3rd) Three P-38M Night Fighters recieved by squadron. #42-7234, #42-27245, and #42-6865.
(15th) One P-61 transferred to the 45th Service Group in Manila.
(28th) Nine P-61 aircraft, three P-38M, and one B-25 in squadron.

March:
(7th) 3 P-38M transferred to the 45th Service Group in Manila.
(31st) Nine P-61 aircraft in squadron and one B-25.

April:
(30th) Nine P-61 aircraft in squadron and one B-25.

May:
(31st) Nine P-61 aircraft in squadron and one B-25.

June:
(5th) Two P-61 lost. Transferred to the 6th NFS.
(30th) Seven P-61 aircraft in squadron and one B-25.

July:
(31st) Seven P-61 aircraft in sqaudron and one B-25.

August:
(31st) Seven P-61 aircraft in squadron and one B-25.

September:
(30th) Seven P-61 aircraft in squadron and one B-25.

October:
(16th) Two P-61 aircraft received by squadron.
(31st) Nine P-61 aircraft in squadron and one B-25.

November:
(30th) Nine P-61 aircraft in squadron and one B-25.

December:
(31st) Nine P-61 aircraft in squadron and one B-25.

1947
January:
(15th) Three P-61 aircraft received by squadron.
(31st) Twelve P-61 aircraft in squadron and one B-25.

February
(12th) Twelve P-61B aircraft in squadron.
421st Night Fighter Squadron was redesignated on 12th and became the 68th Fighter Squadron (All Weather.

Bibliography

Davis, Larry & Menard, Dave. *P-61 Black Widow in Action*. Carrollton, TX: Squadron/Signal Publications. 1990.

Francillon, Rene. *Japanese Aircraft of the Pacific War*. Annapolis, MD: Naval Institute Press. 1988.

Johnson, Fredrick. *Darkley Dangerous: The Northrop P-61 Black Widow Night Fighter*. Tacoma, WA: Bomber Books. 1981.

Jones, Lloyd. *U.S. Fighters: Army-Air Force 1925 to 1980s*. Fallbrook, CA: Aero Publishers, Inc. 1975.

Green, William & Swanborough. *The Complete Book of Fighters*. London, England: Smithmark Publishers, Inc. 1994.

Maurer, Maurer. *Air Force Combat Units of World War II*. Washington, DC: U.S. Government Printing Office. 1961.

Maurer, Maurer. *Combat Squadrons of the Air Force World War II*. Washington, DC: U.S. Government Printing Office. 1969.

McLaren, David. *Black Widow: The Story of the Northrop P-61*. Colorado Springs, CO: VIP Publishers, Inc. 1993.

Odell, William. *Those Few Who Dared: The History of World War II Night Fighters*. Albuquerque, NM: WWII Night Fighters. 1994.

Olynyk, Frank. *USAAF (Pacific Theater) Credits for the Destruction of Enemy Aircraft in Air-To-Air Combat World War 2*. Aurora, OH: Frank Olynyk. 1985.

Pape, Garry & Campbell, John. *Northrop P-61 Black Widow: The Complete History and Combat Record.* Atglen, PA: Schiffer Publishing LTD. 1995.

Pape, Garry & Harrison, Ronald. *Queen of the Midnight Skies: The Story of America's Air Force Night Fighters*. West Chester, PA: Schiffer Publishing LTD. 1992.

Spector, Ronald. *Eagle Against the Sun: The American War With Japan*. New York, NY: The Free Press. 1985.

Notes

Notes

Notes

Notes

Notes